"Taking a fresh approach, Jillian Turanovic ─── ─── ──── analyze victimization across diverse contexts, ranging from the small confines of the prison to the expansive reach of the internet. This volume is rich in theory and scholarship but masterfully written to be accessible to students at all levels. It also is a work of practical relevance, as readers are encouraged to consider the disquieting consequences of victimization and to evaluate the policies—both effective and foolish—proposed to reduce such harm. Put simply, *Thinking About Victimization* has set the standard for textbooks in this area."

Francis T. Cullen, *Distinguished Research Professor Emeritus,*
University of Cincinnati

THINKING ABOUT VICTIMIZATION

Bringing together cutting-edge theory and research that bridges academic disciplines from criminology and criminal justice, to developmental psychology, sociology, and political science, *Thinking About Victimization* offers an authoritative, comprehensive, and refreshingly accessible overview of scholarship on the nature, sources, and consequences of victimization.

Written in a lively style with sharp storytelling and an appreciation of international research on victimization, this book is rooted in a healthy respect for criminological history and the foundational works in victimization studies. It provides a detailed account of how different data sources can influence our understanding of victimization; of how the sources of victimization—individual, situational, and contextual—are complicated and varied; and of how the consequences of victimization—personal, legal, and political—are just as complex. This book also engages with contemporary issues such as cybervictimization, intimate partner violence and sexual victimization, prison violence and victimization, and terrorism and state-sponsored violence.

Thinking About Victimization is essential reading for advanced courses in victimization offered in criminology, criminal justice, sociology, social work, and public policy departments. With its unapologetic reliance on theory and research combined with its easy readability, undergraduate and graduate students alike will find much to learn in these pages.

Jillian J. Turanovic is an Assistant Professor in the College of Criminology and Criminal Justice at Florida State University. Her research focuses broadly on victimization and its consequences, criminological theory, and correctional policy. She is the author of a number of peer-reviewed articles that have been published in journals such as *Criminology, Journal of Quantitative Criminology, Justice Quarterly, Criminal Justice and Behavior, Journal of Youth and Adolescence*, and *Journal of Pediatrics*. Her most recent work focuses on variability in the effects of adolescent violent victimization on the life course, as well as on the sources of violence and victimization at school.

Travis C. Pratt is a Fellow in the University of Cincinnati Corrections Institute. His research focuses primarily on linking structural theories and individual theories of crime/delinquency and victimization, as well as correctional policy and practice. He is the author of *Addicted to Incarceration: Corrections Policy and the Politics of Misinformation in the United States* (2019) and *Key Ideas in Criminology and Criminal Justice* (2011), and he is the author of over 100 peer-reviewed publications that have appeared in outlets such as *Criminology, Crime and Justice: A Review of Research, Criminal Justice and Behavior, Journal of Quantitative Criminology, Journal of Research in Crime and Delinquency*, and *Justice Quarterly*. His most recent work focuses on the effects (or lack thereof) of formal sanctions on the behavior of offenders under community supervision, as well as how individuals' attitudes concerning the legitimacy of the criminal justice system change over time.

THINKING ABOUT VICTIMIZATION

Context and Consequences

Jillian J. Turanovic and Travis C. Pratt

Routledge
Taylor & Francis Group

LONDON AND NEW YORK

First published 2019
by Routledge
2 Park Square, Milton Park, Abingdon, Oxon OX14 4RN

and by Routledge
52 Vanderbilt Avenue, New York, NY 10017

Routledge is an imprint of the Taylor & Francis Group, an informa business

British Library Cataloguing-in-Publication Data
A catalogue record for this book is available from the British Library

Library of Congress Cataloging-in-Publication Data
Names: Turanovic, Jillian J., 1985- author. | Pratt, Travis C., author.
Title: Thinking about victimization : context and consequences / Jillian J. Turanovic
    and Travis C. Pratt.
Description: 1 Edition. | New York : Routledge, 2019.
Identifiers: LCCN 2018056685 (print) | LCCN 2019006554 (ebook) |
    ISBN 9781315522333 (eBook) | ISBN 9781138697225 (hardback) |
    ISBN 9781138697232 (pbk.) | ISBN 9781315522333 (ebk)
Subjects: LCSH: Victims of crimes. | Victims of crimes—Legal status, laws, etc. |
    Women—Crimes against.
Classification: LCC HV6250.25 (ebook) | LCC HV6250.25 .T867 2019 (print) |
    DDC 362.88—dc23
LC record available at https://lccn.loc.gov/2018056685

ISBN: 978-1-138-69722-5 (hbk)
ISBN: 978-1-138-69723-2 (pbk)
ISBN: 978-1-315-52233-3 (ebk)

Typeset in Interstate
by Apex CoVantage, LLC

CONTENTS

ILLUSTRATIONS

ACKNOWLEDGEMENTS

We would like to thank Thomas Sutton and the production team at Routledge/ Taylor & Francis for their assistance and patience.

PART I

SETTING THE STAGE

1 Introduction

In 2013, we published our first collaborative work on the consequences of victimization (Turanovic & Pratt, 2013). In this study we began with the idea that not everyone will experience victimization in the same way, and that a person's choice of coping strategy—one that could be either positive or negative (in the case of this study, substance use)—was heavily influenced by their level of self-control, which ultimately influenced the odds that they would engage in offending later on down the line. This study was important because it forced the field of victimization studies to look at the relationship between victimization and offending in a different way.

But we did not stop there. We followed that research up with quite a lengthy roster of empirical studies that we would be guilty of false modesty if we said that they did not push victimization research forward. This work included studies related to patterns of repeat victimization (Turanovic & Pratt, 2014), the relationship between self-control and victimization (Pratt et al., 2014), how strong social ties among youth can mitigate the potential long-term negative consequences of victimization into adulthood (Turanovic & Pratt, 2015), gendered pathways to victimization (Turanovic, Reisig, & Pratt, 2015), theoretical developments in the study of victimization (Pratt & Turanovic, 2016), the long-term consequences of violent victimization among Native American youth (Turanovic & Pratt, 2017), how a classic study concerning the "cycle of violence" did not replicate very well (Myers et al., 2018), and how structural conditions influence patterns of risky lifestyles and victimization (Turanovic, Pratt, & Piquero, 2018).

What the study includes

All of this work challenged much of the conventional wisdom in the field of victimization studies, and once you have produced a body of research such as this, it is natural to want to step back and "take stock" of what it all means. Doing so would be particularly useful for our students, since we have both taught courses at the undergraduate and graduate levels on victimization.

The problem was that we saw little in the way of book-length treatments of victimization that we felt comfortable using. The key problem as we saw it was that texts tend to be light on both theory and empirical evidence, if they even cover either of them at all. We thought this was a mistake, since theories are critically important (they are intended to organize in a systematic way what we know about a topic), and covering the research is absolutely essential if we are to ever be in a position to develop "evidence-based" approaches for addressing the causes and consequences of victimization.

So we set about writing our own book on the subject, and this is it. Neither of us likes big, clunky, expensive textbooks, so we did not write one of those. We instead wanted something more brief and to the point; a book that did not shy away from either theory or research; and one that would be written in an accessible style—free from the kind of unnecessary jargon that academics seem to be so fond of—that would be easy to understand without losing any critical content. This book will not bore you or talk down to you; we suspect that it will, however, challenge some of your assumptions about why victimization happens and what we should do about it.

The plan of the book

The book is organized into four parts, Part I of which is "Setting the stage." In addition to this introductory chapter, Chapter 2 relates to key aspects of the nature and measurement of victimization. Specifically, Chapter 2 focuses on the multiple places from which we draw victimization data to illustrate the scope of criminal victimization and to highlight victimization rates around the world. This discussion includes an overview of various official and self-report sources (e.g., the Uniform Crime Reports, and the National Crime Victimization Survey), as well as international data sources (e.g., the International Crime Victimization Survey, the Crime Survey for England and Wales), and what they each have to say about the nature of victimization. In addition, Chapter 2 presents a detailed discussion of the "dark figure" of crime, sampling procedures, and the potential biases that may come in information gleaned from both official and self-reported estimates of victimization. The key here is that readers will develop an appreciation for how important measurement is, particularly when different measurement strategies produce different pictures of the scope of the victimization problem.

The book then moves on to the three chapters that comprise Part II, "The sources of victimization." Chapter 3 addresses the individual sources of victimization, and includes a discussion of key demographic (e.g., age, gender, race), psychological (e.g., levels of self-control), behavioral (e.g., risky lifestyles), and biosocial correlates of victimization. This chapter also discusses the theoretical perspectives that have been set forth to explain these patterns, as well as what the empirical research has to say about the level of support afforded to these perspectives.

Building on the research on these individual-level correlates, Chapter 4 addresses an issue that is virtually absent from the victimization literature: victimization from the offender's perspective. Indeed, the offender's perspective is perhaps the most overlooked component of victimization theory and research. We discuss the reasons behind this omission in Chapter 4, as well as the consequences of failing to consider the offender's perspective. In addition, we review the criminological theory and research concerning how offenders make decisions about who and how they will victimize others. The key theme in this chapter, then, is the importance of bringing the offender back into how we think about victimization.

We then move on in Chapter 5, "Situations and context," to present an overview of how victims and offenders converge in time and space. This chapter highlights how the behavior of both victims and offenders is shaped and conditioned by social context—both within the immediate situation the crime/victimization event is taking place, and also the broader social context that sets the stage for those very situations. Again, as with the previous chapters in Part II, we discuss both the theoretical perspectives and empirical research that have been set forth to explain these patterns.

The book then shifts gears to the three chapters that comprise Part III: the consequences of victimization. Chapter 6 presents a detailed discussion of the personal consequences of victimization. In the process, this chapter covers the large and interdisciplinary literature on how individuals respond to their victimization experience. Some victims experience much more harm than others (e.g., psycho-emotional distress, behavioral problems), and some are better able to cope more effectively with victimization, and the purpose of this chapter is to lay out the reasons behind why the consequences of victimization can vary so much from person to person. In illustrating these points, special attention is given to issues surrounding adverse childhood experiences, as well as the short- and long-term consequences of victimization for children and adolescents.

Chapter 7 focuses on the legal consequences of victimization. In particular, we discuss various issues related to the criminal justice system's responses to victimization. These include victims' services as well as how victims are treated during the arrest, prosecution, and punishment processes of offenders. As well, we discuss the impact of victimization on legal reforms, including victim impact statements, and victim compensation. An important theme in this chapter concerns how some victims have greater access to legal assistance than others, and how some victims experience a form of dual victimization in the way they are treated throughout the legal process (e.g., differential access to compensation/restitution, as well as how victims of sexual assault are treated in the processing of offenders).

The final chapter in Part III, Chapter 8, addresses the broader social and political consequences of victimization. These include how victimization can result in elevated levels of fear of crime, which can in turn be a source of community change (e.g., residents withdrawing from neighborhood life or moving away to a different community). This chapter also covers how high-profile instances of victimization—those that have a way of stoking fear among citizens—have been used by policy makers to generate support for a wide array of punitive policies that have done little to enhance public safety.

The final part of the book, Part IV, contains four chapters related to special topics in victimization. Chapter 9 discusses violence against women. In doing so, we note the important role that data and research on intimate partner violence (IPV) and sexual assault have played in the development of victimization theory and policy. We discuss what the major data sources have to say about the extent and nature of these problems, and we discuss in more detail contemporary issues related to sexual assault on college campuses, misconceptions about false reporting, and issues with responding to intimate partner violence.

Next, Chapter 10 addresses victimization in prison. In this chapter, we note that the growth of incarceration is a global concern, and as prison populations swell, there will inevitably be more and more prisoners who will eventually be released back into the community. Thus, this chapter presents an overview of the research regarding prison victimization in an effort to provide a better understanding of how these experiences may influence whether prisoners either will or will not successfully navigate their re-entry into the community.

Chapter 11 then reviews the research related to the growing issue of cybervictimization. We examine this issue from the standpoint of both the victim (e.g., what factors place people at risk to be victimized) as well as the offender (e.g., how offenders target victims and complete their crimes). The key here is that we discuss how various forms of cybervictimization are either essentially "unique," or instead resemble other forms of personal victimization in terms of their causes and consequences.

We then end the book (Chapter 12) with a discussion of some of the important emerging issues in victimization theory, research, and policy. These topics will include victimization by legal authorities (e.g., police violence), state-sponsored violence/terrorism (i.e., those that result in widespread deaths and displacement of citizens), and the role that public concern about victimization plays in discussions regarding immigration policy both in the U.S. and in Europe. The key takeaway is that theory and research both matter—neither should be

key takeaway: theory and research both matter

neglected when studying something as important as victimization, and both are important if we want to put ourselves in the position of addressing the sources and consequences of victimization in a meaningful way.

A note on chapter structure

You will notice that each of the following chapters is structured in the same way. This was not a happy accident; we totally did it on purpose. Each chapter begins with an opening anecdote—a true "story" of a victimization event (or events) that actually occurred, and this will place "real world" context around the content that will be covered in the relevant chapter. These chapter openers are vivid, sometimes heartbreaking, sometimes funny, and sometimes all of the above. Either way, they stick with you. Each chapter then moves on to its substantive content, whatever this may be for that specific chapter. The chapters then end with three sections designed to help readers organize their thoughts on what they have just read: *gaps and challenges*, where we detail the missing pieces in our knowledge base on a particular topic and where we give our thoughts as to where the research should go in the future; *key readings*, where we specify a small handful of "key works" that address each chapter's substantive focus if readers want to dig a little deeper into the subject; and *discussion questions*, designed to keep readers' minds centered on the major issues covered in each chapter. We hope you will find this structure helpful and that the book is informative, compelling, and one that you will want to keep on your bookshelf long after you have read it.

References

Myers, W., Lloyd, K., Turanovic, J.J., & Pratt, T.C. (2018). Revisiting a criminological classic: The cycle of violence. *Journal of Contemporary Criminal Justice, 34*, 266-286.

Pratt, T.C. & Turanovic, J.J. (2016). Lifestyle and routine activity theories revisited: The importance of "risk" to the study of victimization. *Victims and Offenders, 11*, 335-354.

Pratt, T.C., Turanovic, J.J., Fox, K.A., & Wright, K.A. (2014). Self-control and victimization: A meta-analysis. *Criminology, 52*, 87-116.

Turanovic, J.J. & Pratt, T.C. (2013). The consequences of maladaptive coping: Integrating general strain and self-control theories to specify a causal pathway between victimization and offending. *Journal of Quantitative Criminology, 29*, 321-345.

Turanovic, J.J. & Pratt, T.C. (2014). "Can't stop, won't stop": Self-control, risky lifestyles, and repeat victimization. *Journal of Quantitative Criminology, 30*, 29-56.

Turanovic, J.J. & Pratt, T.C. (2015). Longitudinal effects of violent victimization during adolescence on adverse outcomes in adulthood: A focus on prosocial attachments. *Journal of Pediatrics, 166*, 1062-1069.

Turanovic, J.J. & Pratt, T.C. (2017). Consequences of violent victimization for Native American youth in early adulthood. *Journal of Youth and Adolescence, 46*, 1333-1350.

Turanovic, J.J., Pratt, T.C., & Piquero, A.R. (2018). Structural constraints, risky lifestyles, and repeat victimization. *Journal of Quantitative Criminology, 34*, 251–274.

Turanovic, J.J., Reisig, M.D., & Pratt, T.C. (2015). Risky lifestyles, low self-control, and violent victimization across gendered pathways to crime. *Journal of Quantitative Criminology, 31*, 183–206.

2 Measuring victimization

By the early 1970s, the United States was experiencing a period of sustained turmoil. The previous decade had seen civil rights marches, riots in the streets and on college campuses, protests over the Vietnam War, the Watergate scandal, the Attica prison riots, and dramatic increases in violent crime. Rates of aggravated assault, robbery, and rape more than tripled, striking fear into many law-abiding Americans. Power differentials were shifting between and within groups in society, and concerns were growing over problems such as child abuse, sexual assault, and domestic violence. The women's liberation movement was in full swing, increasing awareness of victims' rights and pushing for the establishment of rape crisis centers.

It was also at this time that trepidation over the validity of official report data and the "dark figure" of unreported crime was at an all-time high. Scholars criticized police-generated crime statistics for reflecting levels of social control rather than "actual" deviance (Black, 1970), and for unduly skewing crime in the direction of minorities and the poor (Quinney, 1970). Growing distrust in law enforcement spurred the need for data to be collected that was independent from, and not influenced by, police policies and practices.

In light of these sociopolitical shifts and the recommendations of Presidential Commissions charged with addressing the nation's crime problem (President's Commission on Law Enforcement and Administration of Justice, 1967), in 1972, the National Crime Survey (NCS) on victimization was rolled out. Equipped with a sophisticated sampling design, the NCS was a nationally representative survey of U.S. households that captured a wealth of information on criminal incidents directly from victims. Not only did the NCS confirm that self-report data could provide reliable estimates of crime, but it also helped instill legitimacy and scientific merit in the study of victimization. Today, the NCS continues (as the National Crime Victimization Survey, or the NCVS) to be the primary source of information on aggregate trends in victimization and on the number and types of crimes not reported to U.S. law enforcement agencies (Addington & Rennison, 2014).

Armed with new NCS data, scholars had the opportunity to develop and test new explanations of criminal events from the viewpoint of victims. The NCS helped spark the real explosion in contemporary victimization research, which was the introduction of Hindelang, Gottfredson, and Garofalo's (1978) lifestyle, and Cohen and Felson's (1979) routine activity theories. Since their inception, these ideas have dominated the study of victimization. These perspectives, while different in certain key ways, each emphasize the importance of thinking about victimization in terms of the convergence in time and space of a motivated offender, an attractive target/victim, and the absence of capable guardianship. These principles have informed policing policies and situational crime prevention efforts, and a host of crime control policies that range all the way from using video surveillance in public places, to reducing graffiti in New York subway cars (Sloan-Howitt & Kelling, 1990), to reinforcing order and civility at Disney World (Shearing & Stenning, 1984), and to curbing public drunkenness in Swedish resort towns (Björ, Knutsson, & Kühlhorn, 1992).

Across the pond a few years later, in 1982, the British Crime Survey (BCS) first went into the field. Like the NCS, the BCS was a national crime survey of victimization that developed over similar concerns about official report data. When the BCS hit the scene, it created even more opportunities for scholars to answer pressing criminological questions on topics ranging from repeat victimization (Farrell & Pease, 1993), to fear of crime (Maxfield, 1987), to attitudes toward police (Skogan, 1994), and community-level sources of violence (Sampson & Wooldredge, 1987). All of this was facilitated by the availability of large-scale, reliable victimization data.

When the NCS and BCS data were first made available, we gained tremendous knowledge about crime and victimization—both theoretically and empirically. Before then, virtually all we knew about these issues was through law enforcement records and arrest data. Now, victimization surveys are about 40 years old, and during that time they have evolved from a novelty to a mainstay of crime statistics. Their purpose has also evolved over time: when they were first developed in the 1970s and 1980s, they were used as a rigorous check on police crime statistics (Lynch & Addington, 2006), and to answer cutting-edge questions facing the field. Today, however, the role that these large-scale data sources can play in pushing forward victimization research is a little less clear.

Accordingly, in this chapter, we discuss several key issues related to the major sources of victimization data from the U.S., England and Wales, and elsewhere in the world. We will review some major "official" data sources—namely the U.S. based Uniform Crime Reports (UCR) and the National Incident-Based

Reporting System (NIBRS)—as well as several prominent crime and victimization surveys, including the NCVS, the Crime Survey of England and Wales (formerly known as the BCS), and the International Crime Victims Survey. We will conclude with some gaps and challenges with respect to advancing research on victimization using the data that we have available.

Official sources of victimization data

limitation: not all crimes are reported

The so-called "official" sources of victimization data are those that capture crime known to the police. To an extent, these data are limited by the fact that not *all* crimes are reported or come to the attention of law enforcement. These unreported or undiscovered crimes are known as the "dark figure of crime." Although there are harsh critics of the use of official statistics to capture crime—with some arguing that police records and arrests reflect the activity of criminal justice agencies, and not true criminal behavior (Elliott, 1995)—others maintain that they can be useful for learning about crime and its distribution over time and across cities (Skogan, 1974).

Uniform Crime Reports

The Uniform Crime Reporting Program (UCR) represents the oldest running source of crime data in the U.S., with information dating back to 1931. Crime data are compiled annually from jurisdictions throughout the country, and, each year, the UCR releases a report—published by the Federal Bureau of Investigation (FBI)—entitled *Crime in the United States*. This report provides information such as: (1) the number of offenses known or reported to police; (2) the number of arrests made by police for specific offenses; (3) the amount of crime known to police and arrests made in different regions, states, cities, towns, and areas under tribal law enforcement; (4) the number of police officers killed in the line of duty; and (5) the number of hate or bias crimes known to police. There are eight different types of crimes captured in this report, known as "Part I index offenses": murder and non-negligent manslaughter, forcible rape, robbery, aggravated assault, burglary, larceny-theft, motor vehicle theft, and arson. The definitions of these crimes are standardized, making it possible to draw comparisons across different jurisdictions, and across many different years. Currently, over 18,000 city, university/college, county, state, tribal, and federal law enforcement agencies across all 50 states participate in the UCR, where crime data are submitted either through a state UCR Program or directly to the FBI.

Still, the UCR is not without its limitations. For starters, it does not provide very much information on the types of crimes that occur in society outside of

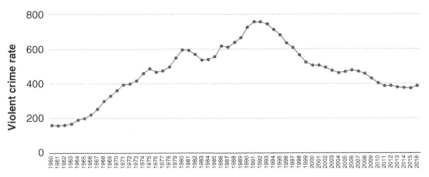

Figure 2.1 Violent crime in the United States, UCR 1960-2016
Source: FBI Uniform Crime Reporting Program.

the Part I offenses–like simple (non-aggravated) assaults, sexual abuse other than forcible rape, or kidnappings. Furthermore, the UCR uses the "hierarchy rule," meaning that if more than one Part I offense occurs within the same incident report, the UCR only counts the most serious one. These issues–coupled with the fact that the UCR only reports on crime known to the police–likely result in an underestimation of the crime problem. Figure 2.1 shows the violent crime rate in the U.S. between 1960 and 2016, using UCR data.

National Incident-Based Reporting System

To overcome some of the limitations of the UCR, the FBI set up the National Incident-Based Reporting System (NIBRS). While the NIBRS still captures only those crimes known to law enforcement, it contains a lot more detailed information. In particular, agencies participating in the NIBRS program collect information on crime and arrest in 22 different categories, rather than just the eight index offenses in the UCR (shown in Table 2.1). Moreover, the NIBRS dataset does not abide by the hierarchy rule. Instead, it counts all offenses that occurred during a criminal incident. And for each of those incidents, the NIBRS records information on 53 different data elements, most of which are not found in the UCR data–including the victim-offender relationship, injuries, property loss, the presence of weapons, the number of victims and offenders, and other arrestee information. This level of detail is clearly an improvement over the UCR.

Outside of the fact that it still suffers from the "dark figure of crime," the only other major downside to the NIBRS dataset is that many states and law enforcement agencies are not included in the program. Participation is voluntary, and currently only about 37 percent of all U.S. law enforcement agencies

Table 2.1 NIBRS offense categories

Crimes against persons
  Assault offenses
  Homicide offenses
  Human trafficking offenses
  Kidnapping/abduction
  Sex offenses
  Sex offenses, non-forcible
Crimes against property
  Arson
  Bribery
  Burglary/breaking and entering
  Counterfeiting/forgery
  Destruction/damage/vandalism
  Embezzlement
  Extortion/blackmail
  Fraud offenses
  Larceny/theft offenses
  Motor vehicle theft
  Robbery
  Stolen property offenses
Crimes against society
  Animal cruelty
  Drug/narcotic offenses
  Gambling offenses
  Pornography/obscene material
  Prostitution offenses
  Weapon law violations

Source: Federal Bureau of Investigation (FBI). (2017). *2016 National Iincident-based reporting system*. Retrieved from https://ucr.fbi.gov/nibrs/2016/resource-pages/nibrs-2016_summary.pdf.

contribute to the NIBRS data (FBI, 2017). Although the plan is to transition the UCR program to a NIBRS-only data collection effort by 2021 (Strom & Smith, 2017), moving over to the new system can be troublesome for many law enforcement agencies. Some worry about the costs and training requirements for data entry, and—because of the greater level of detail captured—others are concerned that their agency may appear to have higher levels of crime after switching over to the NIBRS model. Currently, states such as Florida, New York, California, New Mexico, Nevada, and Wyoming do not participate in the NIBRS program (FBI, 2017).

As a research platform, the NIBRS dataset has been gaining more traction in recent years. Studies have used these data to examine issues of co-offending—such as how offenses committed by groups of offenders are more likely to involve a weapon and to result in injury (Lantz, 2018)—as well as how the situational characteristics of violence vary by victim characteristics, such as age (Kelsay et al., 2017). Indeed, there are many opportunities to enrich the study of crime and victimization with these data.

Victimization surveys

The first victimization surveys were developed over concerns about the "dark figure of crime" and the need for more information on victims themselves. These surveys captured self-reported information on crime directly from individuals. While the advent of these surveys was momentous to the study of victimization, it is important to note that not everyone was open to the possibility of using "self-report" data to study crime. Originally, there were concerns about whether self-report surveys were accurate (Hindelang, Hirschi, & Weis, 1979), and Gibbons (1979: 84) went so far as to call self-report studies "a criminological fad" that could not fulfill their "early promise." Well, Gibbons' (1979) prediction did not exactly pan out, and today self-reported data on crime and victimization are a staple of criminological research (Thornberry & Krohn, 2000).

National Crime Victimization Survey (NCVS)

The NCVS—formerly known as the NCS—has been the premier source of information on victimization that occurs each year in the U.S. since it started in 1973. Importantly, this data source—like the other victimization surveys that we will discuss—does not rely on victim reporting behaviors or police practices. The NCVS is administered to a nationally representative sample of households, and each member of the household who is 12 years or older participates in the survey. Households remain in the study for three years at a time, and respondents complete a total of seven interviews at six-month intervals. In 2016, approximately 134,690 households and 224,520 persons aged 12 or older were interviewed for the NCVS (Bureau of Justice Statistics, 2017).

The NCVS primarily collects information on non-fatal personal victimization (i.e., rape or sexual assault, robbery, aggravated and simple assault, and personal larceny) and household property victimization (i.e., burglary, motor vehicle theft, and other theft). As well, the NCVS captures information about the offender for each victimization incident (e.g., age, race and Hispanic origin, sex, and victim-offender relationship), along with characteristics of the crime (e.g., time and place of occurrence, use of weapons, nature of injury, and economic consequences), whether the crime was reported to police, the reasons the crime was (or was not) reported, and the victim's experiences with the criminal justice system. Demographic information is also collected from victims (e.g., age, sex, race and Hispanic origin, marital status, education level, and income), along with some very basic features of their daily routines and lifestyles (e.g., how often they go grocery shopping, or spend the night away from home).

Relative to the UCR, the NCVS captures a lot more crime—nearly double the amount (Morgan & Kena, 2017). Even though the general trends in crime between the UCR and the NCVS are similar—with crime peaking in the 1990s and declining thereafter—the gap between the two datasets is large with respect to the volume of crime reported. Clearly, people reveal to interviewers their experiences with victimization that they do not tell the police. Figure 2.2 shows that, for most offenses, approximately half or fewer than half of victims report their crimes to law enforcement. As can be seen, the most under-reported crime is rape or sexual assault, with only 22.9 percent of such crimes coming to the attention of police.

Although these reporting statistics may seem relatively low, the research actually shows that, over time, crime reporting has increased. Using NCS/NCVS data from 1973 to 2005, Baumer and Lauritsen (2010) found that significant increases occurred in the likelihood of police notification for sexual assault crimes as well as for other forms of assault. These increases were observed for violence against women, violence against men, stranger and non-stranger violence, as well as crimes experienced by members of different racial and

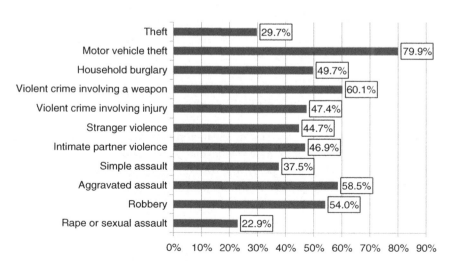

Figure 2.2 Percentage of victimizations reported to police, NCVS 2016
Source: National Crime Victimization Survey (NCVS); Morgan & Kena (2017).

ethnic groups. The reporting of property victimization was also found to have increased (Baumer & Lauritsen, 2010). Even though there is much to improve, reporting rates are actually getting better (even if only gradually).

In addition to estimating rates of reporting to police, the NCVS has proven to be useful in other contemporary research that examines aggregate changes in victimization rates over time. For example, looking at the years 1989 to 2004, Xie, Lauritsen, and Heimer (2012) found that women's rates of intimate partner violence were lower in areas that had more sworn police officers per capita and larger social service workforces—suggesting that both law enforcement and social service agencies play important roles in addressing rates of intimate partner violence. In another study using the NCVS (1973-2005), Lauritsen and Heimer (2010) found that the rates of serious violent victimization among Latino and Black males increased during periods of economic downturn—a pattern not seen for White males. These findings helped emphasize that the NCVS has major advantages for studying victimization against Latinos, because, until 2012, the UCR did not capture data on Hispanic ethnicity.

Crime Survey for England and Wales

Formerly known as the British Crime Survey (BCS), the Crime Survey for England and Wales (CSEW) is the British counterpart to the NCVS. Back in 1982 when it began, it was primarily intended to provide estimates of the dark figure of crime, fear of crime, police contact, and risk factors for victimization in England, Wales, and Scotland (Hough et al., 2007). The BCS was carried out every two to four years between 1982 and 2000, and then every year since then. In 2012, Scotland commissioned its own Scottish Crime and Victimization Survey, and thus the BCS was renamed to reflect its focus on England and Wales exclusively. Similar to the NCVS, the CSEW uses a stratified, cluster-based sampling design to obtain a representative sample of residents of England and Wales aged 16 and older (and since 2009 it has also included children aged 10 to 15 living in private settings).

Unlike the NCVS—which has always had the primary goal of providing accurate and nationally representative estimates of crime—the BCS (now the CSEW) has been viewed as more of a supplementary metric of crime in the U.K. Because the CSEW is "freed somewhat" from the requirement to be a precise and consistent measure of crime, Hough et al. (2007: 16) state that it has "always had a broader range of objectives to the NCVS," and evolved as a "flexible tool for criminological research and policy development."

Each sweep of the CSEW includes bundles of items designed to capture the antecedents and consequences of victimization, and many of these have been developed from criminological theories. The survey even includes measures of self-reported offending, which allows for the study of the vic-tim–offender overlap (Lauritsen & Laub, 2007). Various sweeps of the BCS/CSEW have also included supplemental questions on special topics of domes-tic violence, drug misuse, fraud and technology-based offenses, and atti-tudes toward criminal justice agencies (Tseloni & Tilley, 2016). These data are therefore useful for examining victimization at aggregate levels, as well as at the individual level. In recent years, the CSEW has been used to study diverse topics such as the effectiveness of alarms in reducing burglaries (Tilley et al., 2015), violent and non-violent crimes against adults with severe mental ill-ness (Khalifeh et al., 2015), hate crime attacks (Williams & Tregidga, 2014), and the predictors of trust and confidence in the police and criminal justice system (Hough et al., 2013).

International Crime Victims Survey

The International Crime Victims Survey (ICVS) is the main source of cross-national data available for the study of non-lethal victimization. It has been administered five times between 1989 and 2005 (van Dijk, 2008), and various pilots have taken place since 2010. By the end of 2005, over 320,000 indi-viduals had been surveyed in 78 different countries (although the countries included in the survey can vary each time), with approximately 2,000 respond-ents included in each nation's survey. Like the NCVS, the ICVS samples house-holds, but only a single respondent in each household who is age 16 or older is included in the survey.

In nations where landline telephones are widely used, households are selected through random-digit dialing, and participants are interviewed over the phone. In nations where landline telephones are less common, a multi-stage stratified sampling method is used to select households primarily from the nation's capital or largest city. Under these circumstances, the survey is administered to respondents via face-to-face interviews. Research on the ICVS has generally shown that victimization rates on the survey do not significantly vary by telephone ownership, or whether the interview was face-to-face or over the phone (see van Dijk, 2008). However, it is possible that the victimization experiences of individuals residing in the capital or largest cities are not repre-sentative of others in their country.

The ICVS measures victimization according to 11 "conventional" crimes included in the questionnaire. A first group of crimes deals with the vehicles owned by the respondent or the respondent's household; a second group refers to breaking and entering (burglaries); and a third group of crimes refers to victimization experienced by the respondent personally, including pickpock-eting and violent crimes (van Dijk, 2007). Respondents are asked to report victimization within the past 12 months, as well as in the past 5 years. Those who report having been personally victimized are asked about the incident, and whether they were injured. The ICVS also captures information on the socio-demographic characteristics of the victim and the perpetrator, the location of the incident, whether a weapon was used or present (e.g., a gun, a knife, a club, a bottle, or rocks), as well as victim reporting practices, satisfaction with police, and the consequences of crime for victims.

The dataset is useful for comparative research because it does not rely on official government sources (which may be an issue in countries that face prob-lems with political corruption) and because results are not affected by whether or not crime is reported to the police or leads to arrest. The questions about victimization in the survey also focus on specific behaviors rather than legally defined crime labels, in order to increase comparability across nations. The ICVS includes crimes such as theft (including theft of cars, motorcycles, and bicycles), vandalism, burglary, attempted burglary, robbery, simple and aggra-vated assault, sexual assault, consumer fraud, and bribery/corruption. The ICVS therefore offers unique opportunities to compare national rates, characteris-tics, and correlates of self-reported victimization across nations (see, e.g., Fel-son, Berg, & Rogers, 2014; van Wilsem, 2004).

Summing it up: when to trust data

At this point, the big debates about which approach to measure victimization is "best"—through official records or through self-reports—have all been (mostly) resolved for a long time now (Thornberry & Krohn, 2000). This does not, how-ever, mean that both approaches are always equally as good under all con-ditions. Depending on what kind of victimization is in question, and how the results associated with that victimization are intended to be interpreted, some sources of data are likely to be more trustworthy and useful than others.

For example, studies of the prevalence of sexual violence that use official records (e.g., arrest data from police departments; reporting data to univer-sities)—whether a snapshot at one point in time or if tracked over multiple time points—are likely to significantly underestimate the extent of victimiza-tion (Fisher et al., 2003). On the one hand, there could be good reasons to use official records in this case, such as if there was a new policy or practice put into place that was intended to increase the reporting of sexual violence—using data from official records would totally be useful in that context. On the other hand, if the purpose of the research is to gather an accurate estimate of the prevalence of sexual violence, self-reported victimization data would definitely be our best bet.

If, however, someone is interested in forms of victimization like homicide, residential burglary, robbery, or auto theft, data drawn from official records are likely to work well. When it comes to homicide victimization, of course, the reason why is rather obvious: we cannot call people up and ask them: "In the past six months have you been killed by another person?" But with respect to burglary, robbery, and auto theft victimization, research has shown that these are offenses with higher rates of reporting to the police (Baumer & Lauritsen, 2010). This should come as no surprise—if someone breaks into your house and steals your stuff, or if a man comes up to you on the street with a gun and takes your wallet, or if you walk out of a restaurant after eating tacos to find that your car has been stolen, calling the police may be one of the first things you will do.

Alternatively, there is a wide array of less serious offenses for which victims are unlikely to call the police, making official records of their prevalence problematic. For instance, if a person finds out that there was a fraudulent charge on their ATM card for $25, they are likely to call their bank instead of the police, even though that person was clearly the victim of fraud and likely identity theft. And if a father finds out that his 14-year-old son has been sneaking beers out of the refrigerator in the garage, he may ground the boy or take away his video game privileges for a while, but he is unlikely to call the police to have his son charged with underage drinking and theft (after all, the father was the victim).

The broader point here is that measuring victimization through official records or self-reports will never *always* be either inherently good or bad, nor inherently more or less valid. Context will always be critically important, where we need to think hard about what kind of victimization we are interested in knowing about, and then we need to think just as hard about what approach to measuring that victimization will be the most appropriate. Put simply, when it comes to victimization, we need to take measurement seriously, however it is done.

Gaps and challenges

In recent years, advances in theory, longitudinal surveys, and statistical methods have raised the bar with respect to the quality of information that we have come to expect from victimization research—and it is unclear whether the major data sources discussed here can be used to meet those demands (Pratt & Turanovic, 2016). Indeed, over 40 years ago—in their landmark study using the NCS—Hindelang et al. (1978: 271) argued that:

> In relation to victimization events, there is . . . a need for data about factors that immediately preceded the victimization (e.g., were the victim and

offender drinking together in a bar?) and for more detailed information about the victim–offender relationship (e.g., was the offender a co-worker, a fellow student, a rival gang member?). Data of these sorts would be helpful for understanding the links between lifestyle and victimization.

Still to this day, we can rarely capture this sort of information with the data that we have.

In many ways, victimization research is still lagging behind the work on offending, which, in part, may have to do with the data available. Many of the datasets that criminologists use to study crime simply cannot be used to study victimization in the same way (Turanovic, 2018). For instance, the National Longitudinal Survey of Youth (NLSY) 1997—an ongoing study that captures a wealth of information on men and women born in the U.S. between 1980 and 1984—includes detailed and repeated information on offending, but not on victimization (with the exception of being a victim of "bullying" between the ages of 12 and 18, and having been threatened at school). In addition, the NLSY 1979—which follows people born between 1957 and 1964 in the U.S.—also includes limited information on victimization, and records only whether respondents were physically harmed by their parents prior to the age of 18. The Cambridge Study in Delinquent Development is another data source that has hugely influenced the study of crime over the life course but does not measure victimization (with the exception of whether respondents were injured due to "fighting or horseplay" when they were 18 or 19 years old). The reality is that many of the longitudinal datasets that criminologists have access to cannot be used to study victimization with the same rigor as criminal offending.

Our hope is that victimization continues to move to the forefront of criminologists' attention, and that new data-collection efforts are undertaken to collect more detailed information on the sources of victimization, and the conditions under which victimization is most likely to occur.

Key readings

Baumer, E.P. & Lauritsen, J.L. (2010). Reporting crime to the police, 1973-2005: A multivariate analysis of long-term trends in the National Crime Survey (NCS) and the National Crime Victimization Survey (NCVS). *Criminology, 48,* 131-185.

Black, D.J. (1970). Production of crime rates. *American Sociological Review, 35,* 733-748.

Skogan, W.G. (1974). The validity of official crime statistics: An empirical investigation. *Social Science Quarterly,* 25-38.

Thornberry, T.P. & Krohn, M.D. (2000). The self-report method for measuring delinquency and crime. In *Criminal Justice 2000,* Vol. 4 (pp. 33-83). Washington, DC: National Institute of Justice.

Discussion questions

1. What are some advantages and disadvantages of the NCVS and the UCR?
2. What types of crimes are most likely to go undetected by police, and why?
3. If you had the opportunity to include three new questions in the NCVS, what would you ask, and why?

References

Addington, L.A. & Rennison, C.M. (2014). US National Crime Victimization Survey. In G. Bruinsma & D. Weisburd (Eds.), *Encyclopedia of criminology and criminal justice* (pp. 5392-5401). New York: Springer.

Baumer, E.P. & Lauritsen, J.L. (2010). Reporting crime to the police, 1973-2005: A multivariate analysis of long-term trends in the National Crime Survey (NCS) and the National Crime Victimization Survey (NCVS). *Criminology, 48*, 131-185.

Björ, J., Knutsson, J. & Kühlhorn, E. (1992). The celebration of Midsummer Eve in Sweden– a study in the art of preventing collective disorder. *Security Journal, 3*, 169-174.

Black, D.J. (1970). Production of crime rates. *American Sociological Review, 35*, 733-748.

Bureau of Justice Statistics. (2017). *Data collection: National Crime Victimization Survey (NCVS)*. Washington, DC. Retrieved from www.bjs.gov/index.cfm?ty=dcdetail&iid=245 #Methodology.

Cohen, L.E. & Felson, M. (1979). Social change and crime rate trends: A routine activity approach. *American Sociological Review, 44*, 588-608.

Elliott, D.S. (1995). *Lies, damn lies, and arrest statistics*. Boulder, CO: Center for the Study and Prevention of Violence.

Farrell, G. & Pease, K. (1993). Once bitten, twice bitten: Repeat victimisation and its implications for crime prevention. Crime Prevention Unit Series Paper no. 46. London: Home Office Police Department.

Federal Bureau of Investigation (FBI). (2017). *2016 National Incident-Based Reporting System*. Retrieved from: https://ucr.fbi.gov/nibrs/2016/resource-pages/nibrs-2016_sum mary.pdf.

Felson, R.B., Berg, M.T., & Rogers, M.L. (2014). Bring a gun to a gunfight: Armed adversaries and violence across nations. *Social Science Research, 47*, 79-90.

Fisher, B.S., Daigle, L.E., Cullen, F.T., & Turner, M.G. (2003). Reporting sexual victimization to the police and others: Results from a national-level study of college women. *Criminal Justice and Behavior, 30*, 6-38.

Gibbons, D.C. (1979). *The criminological enterprise: Theories and perspectives*. Upper Saddle River, NJ: Prentice Hall.

Hindelang, M.J., Gottfredson, M.R., & Garofalo, J. (1978). *Victims of personal crime: An empirical foundation for a theory of personal victimization*. Cambridge, MA: Ballinger.

Hindelang, M.J., Hirschi, T., & Weis, J.G. (1979). Correlates of delinquency: The illusion of discrepancy between self-report and official measures. *American Sociological Review, 44*, 995-1014.

Hough, M., Bradford, B., Jackson, J., & Roberts, J.V. (2013). *Attitudes to sentencing and trust in justice: Exploring trends from the crime survey for England and Wales*. London: Ministry of Justice Analytical Series.

Hough, M., Maxfield, M., Morris, B., & Simmons, J. (2007). The British Crime Survey over 25 years: Progress, problems, and prospects. *Crime Prevention Studies, 22*, 7-31.

Khalifeh, H., Johnson, S., Howard, L.M., Borschmann, R., Osborn, D., Dean, K., & Moran, P. (2015). Violent and non-violent crime against adults with severe mental illness. *The British Journal of Psychiatry, 206*(4), 275-282.

Lantz, B. (2018). The consequences of crime in company: Co-offending, victim-offender relationship, and quality of violence. *Journal of Interpersonal Violence*. doi: 10.1177/0886260518786497.

Lauritsen, J.L. & Heimer, K. (2010). Violent victimization among males and economic conditions: The vulnerability of race and ethnic minorities. *Criminology and Public Policy, 9*, 665-692.

Lauritsen, J.L. & Laub, J.H. (2007). Understanding the link between victimization and offending: New reflections on an old idea. *Crime Prevention Studies, 22*, 55-75.

Lynch, J.P. & Addington, L.A. (2006). *Understanding crime statistics: Revisiting the divergence of the UCR and the NCVS*. New York: Cambridge University Press.

Maxfield, M.G. (1987). *Explaining fear of crime: Evidence from the 1984 British Crime Survey*, Vol. 43. London: Home Office.

Morgan, R.E. & Kena, G. (2017). *Criminal victimization, 2016*. Washington, DC: U.S. Department of Justice, Bureau of Justice Statistics.

Pratt, T.C. & Turanovic, J.J. (2016). Lifestyle and routine activity theories revisited: The importance of "risk" to the study of victimization. *Victims & Offenders, 11*, 335-354.

President's Commission on Law Enforcement and Administration of Justice. (1967). *The challenge of crime in a free society*. Washington, DC: U.S. Government Printing Office.

Quinney, R. (1970). *The social reality of crime*. Boston, MA: Little, Brown.

Sampson, R.J. & Wooldredge, J.D. (1987). Linking the micro- and macro-level dimensions of lifestyle-routine activity and opportunity models of predatory victimization. *Journal of Quantitative Criminology, 3*(4), 371-393.

Shearing, C.D. & Stenning, P.C. (1984). From the panopticon to Disney World: The development of a discipline. In A.N. Doob & E.L. Greenspan (Eds.), *Perspectives in criminal law* (pp. 335-349). Aurora, Ontario: Canada Law Books.

Skogan, W.G. (1974). The validity of official crime statistics: An empirical investigation. *Social Science Quarterly*, 25-38.

Skogan, W.G. (1994). *Contacts between police and public: Findings from the 1992 British Crime Survey*. Norwich, UK: Her Majesty's Stationery Office.

Sloan-Howitt, M. & Kelling, G. (1990). Subway graffiti in New York City: "Gettin' up" vs. "meanin' it and cleanin' it." *Security Journal, 1*, 131-136.

Strom, K.J. & Smith, E.J. (2017). The future of crime data: The case for the National Incident-Based Reporting System (NIBRS) as a primary data source for policy evaluation and crime analysis. *Criminology and Public Policy, 16*, 1027-1048.

Thornberry, T.P. & Krohn, M.D. (2000). The self-report method for measuring delinquency and crime. In *Criminal Justice 2000*. Vol. 4 (pp. 33-83). Washington, DC: National Institute of Justice.

Tilley, N., Thompson, R., Farrell, G., Grove, L., & Tseloni, A. (2015). Do burglar alarms increase burglary risk? A counter-intuitive finding and possible explanations. *Crime Prevention and Community Safety, 17*, 1-19.

Tseloni, A. & Tilley, N. (2016). Choosing and using statistical sources in criminology: What can the crime survey for England and Wales tell us? *Legal Definition Management, 16*, 78-90.

Turanovic, J.J. (2018). Toward a life-course theory of victimization. In S.H. Decker & K.A. Wright (Eds.), *Criminology and public policy: Putting theory to work (2nd ed.)* (pp. 85-103). Philadelphia, PA: Temple University Press.

van Dijk, J. (2007). The International Crime Victims Survey and complementary measures of corruption and organized crime. *Crime Prevention Studies, 22*, 125-144.

van Dijk, J. (2008). *The world of crime: Breaking the silence on problems of security, justice, and development across the world*. Thousand Oaks, CA: Sage.

van Wilsem, J. (2004). Criminal victimization in cross-national perspective. *European Journal of Crimiology, 1,* 89-109.

Williams, M.L. & Tregidga, J. (2014). Hate crime victimization in Wales: Psychological and physical impacts across seven hate crime victim types. *British Journal of Criminology, 54*(5), 946-967.

Xie, M., Lauritsen, J.L., & Heimer, K. (2012). Intimate partner violence in US metropolitan areas: The contextual influences of police and social services. *Criminology, 50,* 961-992.

PART II

THE SOURCES OF VICTIMIZATION

3 Individual sources of victimization

One of the most popular places around college campuses is the beloved college bar. Always a hit with students (and alumni), there are places like "The Coug" at Washington State University, the row of beer joints that line Mill Avenue at Arizona State University, and countless others that inevitably accommodate large groups of people between the ages of 18 and 22 who are experiencing new-found freedom for the first time in their lives. These are the places that we tend to remember with fondness long after we have received our diplomas, and that serve as a well-spring for some of our lives' most colorful stories—both good and bad; funny and tragic.

Anyone who has ever spent a significant amount of time in these kinds of places knows that however a bar "feels" at, say, 7 o'clock in the evening, is quite different than it feels at 1:30 in the morning. At 7 p.m. the crowd is full of people with a diverse set of plans for the evening. There are those who will only be there for an hour or so to have a quick drink after school or work before heading home; those who plan on having a couple of cocktails with friends before a night of studying; those who plan on having a few beers while watching the game on television; and yes, those who fully intend to be there until closing time. There is usually a lot of laughter and conversation, no small amount of flirting, and the atmosphere is generally happy and content, with a little hint of excited energy from the collective crowd. But as the night wears on, the previously diverse crowd starts to narrow itself down to those who probably got there earlier and who plan on staying later. The more studious and responsible have left already, leaving behind those less concerned about what they have to do (or how they will feel) tomorrow morning. In the process, more and more drinks are consumed. That fourth beer would have been okay on its own, for example, but once that one is down the hatch what seemed like a stupid idea a couple hours before—having a round of Irish whiskey shots perhaps—seems all of a sudden like a great idea now! And as midnight passes and the clock keeps ticking, the collective judgment of those who remain in the bar starts to become more and more questionable. Inhibitions are eased, voices get louder, guys will develop "beer muscles," and interpersonal slights are viewed through a more antagonistic lens. This is what a college bar feels like at 1:30 in the morning.

So it is at about this time that something like this will happen: a young guy (it's almost always a young guy) commits some late night offense that elicits the anger of another young guy (or perhaps even a group of young guys). Maybe he bumped someone's shoulder and a beer got spilled; or maybe he was wearing a Florida State University football jersey and a rabid University of Miami fan took issue with it; or maybe he made the mistake of making eye contact for too long with a girl whose boyfriend didn't like it. Either way, a young man is now angry, and he is dead set on making that anger known. And so, through some slurred speech, he proceeds to confront the offender—a process that usually begins with profanity-laced accusations and "peacocking" (getting all puffed up in an attempt to show physical dominance). But the peacock doesn't stop there—he instead gives the object of his anger a little shove in the chest, thus forfeiting what might have been a great opportunity to de-escalate things and just sit back down. And upon getting shoved, the original shoulder bumper/jersey wearer/girlfriend poacher proceeds to give the peacock a good, solid ass kicking. Punches are thrown, bones are broken, and blood gets spilled. Many of us have seen something just like this play out, and we would usually describe it as merely a "bar fight"; yet, in a strictly legal context, the peacock is now officially the victim of an assault, and maybe even an aggravated assault depending on the level of injury involved.

The point of telling you this story is to highlight the reality—however uncomfortable it may make us feel—that some people are placed (or place themselves) in harm's way a lot more often than others. This idea is not new, and it was recognized a long time ago by early victimization scholars (von Hentig, 1948). But the notion that some victims might play a role in their own victimization can be a taboo subject over concerns about "victim blaming" (George & Martinez, 2002; Gracia & Tomas, 2014; Hayes, Lorenz, & Bell, 2013). And this concern is understandable given that victimization is not voluntary, and from a legal and moral standpoint we are not trying to assign fault when it comes to someone being victimized. We are instead trying to understand *why* victimization happens, and to do that we need to take a careful look at the behavior of victims themselves.

The bottom line is that some people go places and behave in ways that put them at an elevated risk of being victimized. We are not saying that this is okay or that such folks deserve to be victimized—not at all. But shying away from looking closely at how people's personal characteristics may contribute to their victimization does us all a disservice (Pratt & Turanovic, 2016). We can use an empirical approach to understand why some people are more likely to be victimized without blaming them for it.

Accordingly, this chapter focuses on the key individual sources and correlates of victimization. This will include a discussion of certain demographic (e.g., age, gender, race), psychological (e.g., particular personality traits), and behavioral (e.g., lifestyles) factors that have been demonstrated in the research to be associated with various forms of victimization. In the process, we also cover the major theories that have been developed in an effort to explain these patterns and correlates (e.g., routine activity and risky lifestyle theories, as well as those that focus on self-control and biosocial processes), and how much empirical merit these theories currently have. We end this chapter with a discussion of some of the important gaps and challenges in the literature that still need to be addressed if we are to reach a better understanding of the nature of criminal victimization.

The demographic dimensions of victimization

Criminology is not like other scientific fields (e.g., physics or chemistry) in that we are not really a discipline of "facts." Indeed, light moves at a known speed and an atom with two protons, two neutrons, and two electrons is helium. These are not guesses that may be right or wrong; they simply are what they are. But in criminology we do not have the same level of certainty about that which we study. Focusing on human behavior—particularly negative behavior like crime that hurts other people—is messy, complicated, and hard to predict (Weisburd & Piquero, 2008). In short, compared to other scientific disciplines, we have little in the way of solid "facts" about crime and its consequences. We do, however, have a few well-established patterns that may at least pass as "criminological facts"—among them the associations that age, gender, and race have with crime and victimization.

Age

Being young is tough. Youths—particularly those going through adolescence—are smack-dab in the middle of all kinds of new physical and social transitions (Turanovic & Young, 2016). They face a whole new set of social and cultural expectations, their peer groups start to take on added importance to their lives, and they find themselves with new levels of autonomy while at the same time still being subjected to many of the same old constraints (e.g., still having to obey their parents and listen to their teachers: see Steinberg & Morris, 2001; Warr, 2002). It is therefore not surprising that children have been the focus of so much social science research in general, and that they have been the main-stay of virtually all modern criminological theory and research (Agnew, 1992; Hirschi, 1969; Shaw & McKay, 1942)—and some would say with good reason (Gottfredson & Hirschi, 1990; cf. Cullen, 2011).

To be sure, if the past 100 years of criminological theory and research have taught us anything, it is that criminal behavior tends to follow a relatively clear "age-crime curve" (Loeber & Farrington, 2014). Indeed, across different decades, different nations, and multiple sources of data (both new and old), a similar pattern tends to emerge: people's enthusiasm (or at least willingness) to engage in criminal and deviant behavior tends to increase during adolescence, peaking at around age 17 or so, and then to decline steadily after that (Piquero, Farrington, & Blumstein, 2003). Of course, not everyone fits this pattern and exceptions certainly exist (e.g., early starters, late starters, people who continue to offend at a high rate well into adulthood: Nagin, 2005; Moffitt, 1993). But the departures from the age-crime curve are just that: exceptions. Most of us fit the pattern.

What is interesting for us is that rates of victimization over the life course tend to follow relatively closely the same age-crime curve (Turanovic & Pratt, 2016). According to the National Crime Victimization Survey (NCVS), rates of victimization are highest among those between the ages of 12 and 17 (Truman & Langton, 2015). Again, exceptions certainly exist, particularly with respect to certain forms of victimization like child abuse and intimate partner violence (Finkelhor et al., 2015; Johnson et al., 2015). But when the full spectrum of victimization is considered—everything from being punched and shot at, to being stalked and harassed online, and to having your belongings stolen or destroyed by vandals—the broad pattern that emerges is that the age-victimization curve closely resembles the age-crime curve (Figure 3.1). So clearly there is something about being young that puts people at an elevated risk to be on both the giving and receiving end of criminal behavior. Why this is the case is far less clear, but, before we can get to that, we have to face the reality that age alone is far from the only thing that predicts one's odds of victimization.

Gender

Similar to the age-crime curve, another rather well-established "criminological fact" involves the gender gap in offending. When it comes to most kinds of offenses—from violent to property crimes, and from those that occur up close and personal to those that happen remotely (e.g., online and on social media)— the overwhelming majority are committed by males (Broidy & Agnew, 1997; Mears, Ploeger, & Warr, 1998; Steffensmeier, Schwartz, & Roche, 2013). This pattern occurs across nations and cultures (both Western and non-Western),

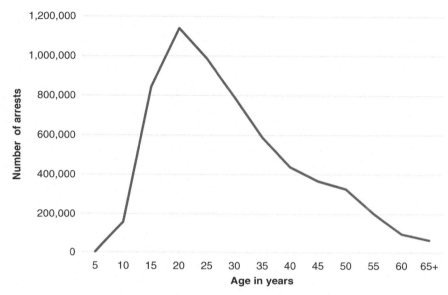

Figure 3.1 Total arrests by age in the United States, 2016
Source: FBI Uniform Crime Reports (2016).

where young boys behave badly more often than do young girls, adolescent boys engage in more deviance than do their female counterparts, and adult males continue to offend at rates significantly higher than women (Houghton et al., 2013; Loeber, Capaldi, & Costello, 2013; Thijs et al., 2015).

There are, of course, exceptions to this pattern, where women are more likely than men to engage in offenses such as prostitution (Finn, Muftic, & Marsh, 2015). Females are also more likely than males to engage in certain forms of peer victimization, such as relational aggression (Crick & Grotpeter, 1995). It is important to note that the differences in the rates of offending between males and females have been narrowing steadily since the 1970s (Estrada, Backman, & Nilsson, 2016; Kruttschnitt, 2013; Vieraitis, Britto, & Morris, 2015)—so much so that calls for "gender-specific" theories and explanations of female offending have been made repeatedly (Daly, 1994; DeKeseredy, 2015; Ferraro, 2006). That is all true—and the exceptions and changes over time are important—but the broad pattern persists: there is most often a sizeable gender gap in antisocial behavior.

As with age, there is a significant and observable gender gap with respect to victimization. In the United States, for example, the NCVS tends to find higher rates of victimization overall for males (Truman & Morgan, 2016). This gap tends to be even more pronounced when it comes to forms of violent victimization

(Turanovic, Reisig, & Pratt, 2015; Zaykowski & Gunter, 2013). Again, there are notable exceptions to this pattern in that females are disproportionately victims of certain kinds of offenses like intimate partner violence (IPV) and sexual assault (Hamby, 2014), as well as crimes like identity theft (Harrell, 2015). Similar patterns emerge when examining data from the International Crime Victims Survey (ICVS) and the European Survey on Crime and Safety (EU ICS) as well, where, with the notable exception of sexual violence, males are more often the victims of crime (Van Dijk, Van Kesteren, & Smit, 2007). So, once again, the pattern makes it clear that, overall, males tend to be at greater risk for victimization than females. We therefore now see that it is not just being young that matters when it comes to increasing the odds of being victimized, but being young and male. And that is not all—there is still one last "criminological fact" to cover.

Race

In the United States, members of particular racial minority groups often live in what has been described as "divergent social worlds" (Peterson & Krivo, 2010). These are worlds that are often characterized by economic deprivation and social isolation (Krivo et al., 2013; Sharkey, 2013). Such communities are often plagued by multiple problems, including high rates of family disruption and parental incarceration, chronic unemployment, poor educational opportunities, and limited access to quality health care (Sampson, Morenoff, & Earls, 1999; Turanovic, Rodriguez, & Pratt, 2012; Wilson, 1996). These are also communities where members of racial/ethnic minority groups are disproportionately at risk of being victimized (Pratt & Cullen, 2005).

In the United States, African-Americans have long been recognized as experiencing rates of victimization—particularly violent victimization—that far exceed those of their White counterparts (Lauritsen, Rezey, & Heimer, 2014). Specifically, rates of serious violent victimization for African-Americans (offenses like sexual assault, robbery, and aggravated assault) are nearly 50 percent higher than they are for Whites (Truman & Langton, 2015). This disparity gets even wider when we look at homicide victimization, where African-Americans are eight times more likely than Whites to be the victim of a homicide (Federal Bureau of Investigation, 2016). Indeed, no other developed nation has a homicide rate that comes close to African-Americans' homicide rate of 19.4 deaths per 100,000 persons—we would have to look to nations like Rwanda and Myanmar to find comparable rates (Silver, 2015).

While these figures are certainly alarming, it is important to note that, as a group, African-Americans are not even the most frequently victimized citizens in the U.S. That designation goes to Native Americans, who experience violent victimization at rates—for crimes involving sexual violence, intimate partner violence, physical violence, stalking, and even overall exposure to violence—that are roughly double those of African-Americans and Whites (Rosay, 2016; see also Truman & Langton, 2014). Other marginalized minority groups—for example, Hispanics—tend to have safer communities than other minority groups who are similarly situated socioeconomically (Martinez, Stowell, & Iwama, 2016). And yet, taken together, what this all means is that, in the United States, victimization risk is far from evenly distributed throughout the population—being a member of particular racial/ethnic minority groups comes with an added victimization cost.

These patterns tend to persist in other developed nations as well. Research reveals, for example, that members of minority immigrant communities in democratic nations in Western Europe are disproportionately targeted for hate crimes (Van Kesteren, 2016). The same holds true for research conducted in Australia (Johnson, 2005) and Canada (Millar & Owusu-Bempah, 2011), where members of minority groups face elevated levels of racially/ethnically motivated victimization. Even among the less well-developed parts of the world we seem to see the same thing. Indeed, recent work in South Africa shows that members of racial minority groups must take on the added responsibility of blending in culturally as they move from place to place in order to avoid victimization—a practice that White citizens really do not have to worry about (Lindegaard, Miller, & Reynald, 2013).

So, when we add all this up, a relatively clear picture starts to emerge. In particular, we find that a couple of key conclusions are warranted: (1) within any given society, not everybody is at equal risk of being victimized; and (2), despite some notable and important exceptions, there is something about being young, male, and a member of a racial/ethnic minority group that seems to come with an elevated risk of experiencing all kinds of victimization. The question, then, is why that is the case—the very issue we turn to now.

Thinking theoretically: individual sources of victimization

So why *do* these demographic patterns exist with respect to criminal victimization? To put it more concretely: why are some people at greater risk of being victimized than others? Criminologists have taken this question up—in one form or another—over a long period of time (Daigle & Muftic, 2016). As you might expect, there has been a considerable amount of disagreement as to what the answer to that question is. But one common thread that seems to unite most theories of victimization—particularly those we will cover here—may be found in the story we told at the beginning of this chapter: that people's actions, wittingly or unwittingly, can contribute to their own victimization (Pratt & Turanovic, 2016). Most of the theoretical disagreement tends to surround which kinds of people and which kinds of actions are most important.

So to take you through how these ideas have emerged and shifted over time to get to where we are now, the rest of this chapter traces the development of the key theories of victimization that focus on individual characteristics. In the process, we lay out the studies that either support or call into question these various theories. Not all ideas about victimization are created equal—some are really well supported and others simply wish that they were. But by the end of this chapter you will know exactly what we do and do not know about the role that individual characteristics play in victimization.

Early theoretical perspectives

Early theoretical perspectives on the causes of victimization can be quite entertaining (or infuriating!) to read. The first serious theoretical statement of victimization came from von Hentig's (1948) *The Criminal and His Victim*. Note the use of the gender-specific pronoun: his. This was no accident, and much of von Hentig's discussion is unabashedly male-centered, which of course fits with the long-standing demographic pattern associated with crime and victimization. And when it is not male-centered, his language often drifts comfortably into blatant sexism, such as when he characterizes being female as a "form of weakness" (p. 406). But keep in mind that it was 1948 and he was German (although we do not offer that up as an excuse). However, in looking past his "tone" and focusing on his ideas, his explanation for what puts people at risk to be victimized is relatively clear and straightforward: by and large, victims are not very smart.

For von Hentig, this intelligence-victimization link plays itself out in predictable ways. Those who are not very bright, for example—people who he referred to with labels like "dull normals"—are usually not very good at evaluating the consequences of their actions. They wander into sticky situations all the time— they get drunk in public, leave easily stolen goods in plain view, and are too dimwitted to know when they are being conned. At the same time they lack the common sense to even know they are doing something that makes them a target of victimization. They are therefore "easy marks" for offenders, who themselves do not need to be smart either. But von Hentig did not limit his typology of victims to those who lack intelligence or had the misfortune of being female; he also held some overtly racist views about minorities and immigrants, and he argued that the elderly make easy targets for victimization because they tend to be "feeble."

While these ideas may be viewed as either entertaining or highly offensive, they never really caught on in any significant way. Not only were they largely unconfirmed empirically, but criminological theory and research continued in the 1950s and 1960s to focus much more heavily on the offender side of the equation (Kornhauser, 1978; Matza, 1964). Indeed, strain theories (Agnew, 1985, 1992), the social learning perspective (Burgess & Akers, 1966), and social control theory (Hirschi, 1969)–the perspectives that dominated criminological theory and research during that time and continue to represent the core theories covered in criminology textbooks to this day–really had nothing to say about the criminal event from the perspective of the victim.

One exception, though, was Wolfgang's (1958) seminal work on homicides. In looking closely at the data on homicide victimization from Philadelphia–particularly the demographic patterns that surround homicide events (those very demographic factors reviewed in this chapter)–he argued that such events often involved what he termed "victim precipitation" (see also Wolfgang, 1957). What this means is that victims of a homicide event–who are often young minority males–often started the whole thing themselves by engaging in their own criminal behavior. And it is that criminal behavior–from attempting to rob or assault others, and to being verbally and physically aggressive–that elicits an escalated response from the intended victim that ends up getting the initial offender killed in the process. In short, the victim precipitation argument holds that many victims of homicide essentially bring it upon themselves (Felson & Messner, 1998).

So, to sum up much of the early thinking about victimization, the key explanations seemed to range from one that viewed victims of crime as being dumb to one that viewed them as being jerks (categories that are not, of course, mutually exclusive). But again, neither of these ideas really caught on with respect to mainstream criminology (Lilly, Cullen, & Ball, 2014). An oft-cited reason for this inattention is that these ideas seemed to engage in "victim blaming," which scholars argue became increasingly distasteful in the 1970s over growing concerns about problems like child abuse and domestic violence (Karmen, 2013). Most contemporary victimization textbooks will give this as the core reason, and it is not necessarily wrong on its face. But the real explanation for why these ideas did not catch on until much later was this: they were too hyper-individualistic. Indeed, von Hentig's perspective (1948), for example, was set forth as a "sociobiological" study of crime–an idea that was at odds with the theoretical norms of sociological criminology which focused more heavily on social structure and process as opposed to individual differences. Thus, these early perspectives were void of social context and seemed to be blind to broader structural concerns. It was therefore not until the late 1970s that theory and research about criminal victimization really took off.

Risky lifestyles and routine activities

On the heels of the "crime spike" of the late 1960s in the United States, where nearly all forms of crimes reached a long-time peak, criminologists were faced with an unexpected paradox. Here was the United States—an economically prosperous nation that experienced both exceptional affluence and exceptionally high crime rates (Cullen & Gilbert, 1982). This was a combination that was not supposed to exist. To be sure, the prevailing social science wisdom of the time held that problems like crime were intimately tied to economic conditions, and that when things improved economically—as they did in post-World War II America—crime was supposed to go down (Blau, 1977). But it didn't. What, then, was going on?

In an attempt to answer this question, two closely related theoretical statements emerged—what have become known as lifestyle (Hindelang, Gottfredson, & Garofalo, 1978) and routine activity (Cohen & Felson, 1979) theories. Both perspectives started with the idea that crime and victimization are the result of broad patterns of human interactions. In particular, the ways that people move around in social space can affect whether offenders and victims will come into contact with each other (Felson & Cohen, 1980). These ideas did, however, differ with respect to one key element: what constitutes "risky" behavior in the context of victimization (Pratt & Turanovic, 2016).

In the first of these perspectives, Hindelang et al.'s lifestyle theory (1978) emphasized how the risk of victimization varied according to certain demographic characteristics. Like the key factors discussed in this chapter, it is young minority males who are—at least overall—at the greatest risk of victimization. Hindelang et al. (1978) used data from the National Crime Survey (NCS) to reveal these very patterns. The reason these patterns existed, according to Hindelang et al. (1978), was because demographic variations are correlated with "structural constraints" (e.g., economic deprivation tied to particular racial/ ethnic groups), which then translate into behavioral differences among community members. Young males, for example, tend to behave, spend their time, and arrange their "routine activities" in ways that are likely very different from, say, elderly women. Teenage boys, for example, are more likely to engage in verbal and physical confrontations with one another—particularly in public spaces—as a means of earning the respect of their peers (Anderson, 1999), whereas grandmothers are more likely to stay close to the home and watch CBS. So the argument went that young minority males are more likely to spend time participating in high-risk activities (like engaging in deviant behaviors), in high-risk situations (where they are unsupervised or unguarded), at high-risk times (like at night), with high-risk people (such as others who may be inclined to offend). Thus, the key component of lifestyle theory is that, when it comes to victimization, some situations are much riskier than others, and one of the best ways to elevate one's risk of being victimized is to do risky things in risky settings.

There was, however, a potential problem with this explanation. Specifically, a clever insight came around at about the same time: you do not have to be doing something risky to get victimized. And it was with that insight in mind that Cohen and Felson (1979) developed their routine activity perspective. Like Hindelang et al. (1978), Cohen and Felson (1979) were concerned with macro-level social processes that created more movement of citizens away from the safety of their houses. A stronger and more equitable economy, for example, meant greater opportunities for female labor force participation which, in turn, meant more houses left unguarded during the day and more potential female "targets" out in public spaces who could be vulnerable to victimization (Chiricos, 1987).

In the process, Cohen and Felson (1979) also gave the criminological community a tidy, three-part, triangular heuristic to explain the victimization event, which occurs when there is a convergence in time and space of: (1) a motivated offender, (2) a suitable target, and (3) the absence of capable guardianship. What was most important, however, was the notion provided by Cohen and Felson (1979) that it was not the risky stuff which Hindelang et al. (1978) talked about that elevates the odds of the three points of the triangle coming together. It was instead the normal elements of going about our daily routines that puts us all at risk to be victimized. Thus, rather than view victimization through the lens of risky behaviors like engaging in violence, consuming alcohol in public spaces, or associating with violent people, the routine activity perspective held that:

> College enrollment, female labor force participation, urbanization, suburbanization, vacations, and new electronic durables provide various opportunities to escape the confines of the household while they increase the risk of predatory victimization.
>
> (Cohen & Felson, 1979: 605)

At the macro-level, there seemed to be at least a modest amount of empirical support for Cohen and Felson's (1979) perspective. Rates of unemployment, for example, were found to have a protective effect against burglary rates, conceivably because unemployed people were more likely to be home during the day, guarding their houses (Pratt & Cullen, 2005). Rates of female labor force participation were also found to be positively associated with victimization rates—particularly among women (Cohen & Land, 1987; Felson, 1993). And perhaps most important, a new macro-level measure developed by Cohen and Felson (1979)—the household activity ratio—showed that the dispersion of activities away from the home (for things like going to work and going shopping) were also associated with higher rates of victimization (Cohen, Felson, & Land, 1980).

The problem began when criminologists started to try to translate these macro-level concepts and measures into individual-level ones—a problem known as the "ecological fallacy" (the erroneous assumption that broad patterns found among large groups of people should apply to all individuals within that group: see Robinson, 1950). Studies in this tradition generally entailed surveys that would contain measures of individuals' mundane routine activities—like how often they go shopping or to the movies—in an effort to try to approximate one's risk of victimization (Kennedy & Forde, 1990; Miethe, Stafford, & Long, 1987; Osgood et al., 1996). The appearance of these measures was compounded by another development: the merger of lifestyle and routine activities into a single perspective, which was done in a lazy way that failed to appreciate just how differently Hindelang et al. (1978) and Cohen and Felson (1979) viewed the concept of risk. As a result of this merger, a whole slew of studies started to appear that had completely forgotten about Hindelang et al.'s concept of risk, and instead attempted to correlate victimization with behavioral routines like buying groceries and clothes (Averdijk, 2011; Bunch, Clay-Warner, & McMahon-Howard, 2014), to spending time in public places like a garden or a café (Felson et al., 2013), to watching soccer matches on television (Kirby, Francis, & O'Flaherty, 2014), to spending time on the yearbook committee (Popp & Peguero, 2011), and even to sleeping (Lemieux & Felson, 2012).

But why would we expect any of these kinds of mundane routine activities to actually put us at risk of being victimized? As we have noted in our previous work, "There is nothing about these kinds of daily activities that is either dangerous or should inherently enhance anyone's risk of victimization beyond that of simply being in the presence of others" (Pratt & Turanovic, 2016: 343). Indeed, even routine activity theory's obsession with how leaving the home is somehow inherently risky seems badly overblown. Pratt et al. (2014: 104, emphasis in original) recently argued, for example, that:

> it is not simply going outside of the house that matters, but it is instead the differential risks associated with *what one is actually doing outside*—such as planting flowers in a garden versus selling drugs on a street corner—that influence one's susceptibility to victimization.

Even if we want to concede that leaving the home at night is more risky than during the day—a possibility that has been raised within the routine activity literature on victimization (Bunch et al., 2014; Klevens, Duque, & Ramirez, 2002)— we still view such an idea as dangerously imprecise. To be sure, as Pratt and

Turanovic (2016: 344) put it:

> Surely, some people leave home at night to do things like watch the latest episode of *The Bachelor* and eat bonbons at a friend's place—not everyone who goes out after dark does piles of cocaine at a biker bar.

Thankfully, some criminologists still appreciate these distinctions, and have conducted research that shows rather clearly that some behavioral routines are, in fact, riskier than others when it comes to the likelihood of being victimized. Committing crimes, using substances, and behaving aggressively toward others, for example, are strongly associated with victimization (Stewart, Schreck, & Simons, 2006; Turanovic & Pratt, 2014). There is no longer any doubt that individuals who act in these ways are engaging in behaviors that are risky. It is this revival of the lifestyle perspective as originally envisioned by Hindelang et al. (1978)—one that is quite distinct from the routine activity perspective—that is currently producing some of the most important and relevant victimization research. And in its most current form, a key individual characteristic—one's level of self-control—has been incorporated into the risky lifestyle–victimization discussion in an important way.

Individual differences revisited

One of the key factors where individuals differ is their levels of self-control. Defined generally as the ability to control one's impulses, to delay gratification, and to think about the long-term consequences of one's actions, volumes of research across a wide array of academic fields now recognize that people with higher levels of self-control typically have a significantly higher quality of life (De Ridder et al., 2012). They tend to live longer, to have better jobs, and to enjoy more fulfilling social relationships (Pratt, 2016). And with respect to crime and victimization, those with higher levels of self-control tend to do a better job of staying out of trouble (Pratt & Cullen, 2000; Pratt et al., 2014).

To be sure, bad things happen when people lack self-control. Some of the negative outcomes associated with low self-control include being in poor health, being involved in accidents and getting injured, losing jobs, squandering money, and failing in romantic relationships (De Ridder et al., 2012). What is more, those with low self-control are also more quick to grow angry and to feel like they have been treated unfairly (Ellwanger & Pratt, 2014; Piquero, Gomez-Smith, & Langton, 2004), they are more likely to be rude interpersonally and to offend others through their behavior (Reisig & Pratt, 2011), they are more prone to taking unnecessary risks both personally and financially (Reisig, Pratt, & Holtfreter, 2009; Schreck, Stewart, & Fisher, 2006), and they are much more likely to engage in a wide range of aggressive and criminal behaviors (Pratt & Cullen, 2000). And if you think that all these consequences might raise an individual's risk of victimization, you would be exactly right.

The idea that self-control is an important factor for criminologists to consider was first brought to the field by Gottfredson and Hirschi (1990). But the idea that self-control could be related to victimization was introduced explicitly for the first time by Schreck (1999). The gist of the theory was relatively straightforward: people who lack self-control are more likely to self-select into certain risky lifestyles; those lifestyles, in turn, tend to lead to victimization. Criminologists wasted no time in putting this idea to the test, and as a result this perspective has a lot of support in the research. Indeed, studies have shown that those who lack self-control are more likely to be victims of all kinds of crimes, including violent crimes (Schreck, Wright, & Miller, 2002; Turanovic & Pratt, 2014), property crimes (Averdijk & Loeber, 2012), and even forms of "remote victimization" like identity theft and fraud (Holtfreter, Reisig, & Pratt, 2008; Holtfreter et al., 2015). And as Pratt et al. (2014) noted, the effects of self-control on victimization operate largely through their influence on the risky lifestyle choices on the part of victims—lifestyles that are often characterized by things like substance use and criminal behavior.

This pattern of behavior that leads to victimization has come as no surprise to developmental psychologists. Indeed, for years scholars have been discussing the "dual systems" model whereby personality factors like a preference for "risk seeking" tend to follow a particular developmental pathway, one that peaks during the prime "crime prone years" of late adolescence (Steinberg et al., 2008). At this same time in the life course, one's ability to control one's impulses is on a delayed trajectory, and the two personality dimensions (risk seeking and impulsivity) tend not to "square up" with each other (particularly among males) until the early to mid-twenties, when we tend to see a decline in risky and impulsive behavior (Steinberg, 2010). Thus, the age–crime curve may reflect an age-specific preference for risk, which makes those at the peak of the curve most vulnerable to victimization.

This biological/developmental idea is certainly insightful, but it does not provide much of an explanation as to why some people are still more at risk of victimization even after they have passed through their crime-prone years. Some more recent thoughts within the self-control tradition in criminology, however, may help fill in the blanks here. In particular, Pratt (2016) recently noted that those with low self-control tend to self-select into a wide array of negative life events well into adulthood. He noted that:

> people who lack self-control are often really unpleasant to be around. These are people who victimize others, who have a tough time recognizing when

they are being insensitive and socially inappropriate, and who are often too self-centered to understand that quality relationships require the reciprocal investment of time, care, and energy. As a result, such people tend to make lousy friends, husbands, and wives, and prosocial others rarely want to have anything to do with them.

(Pratt, 2016: 138)

Thus, even adults can still lack self-control, and when they do they still tend to behave badly and to elicit the worst behavior in others. This, combined with having likely burned up whatever social capital they might have otherwise had to insulate them from experiencing negative life events, places them at an elevated risk of victimization.

Gaps and challenges

So where does this leave us? On the one hand, the study of the individual sources of victimization has come a long way. We can now say with confidence, for example, that victimization doesn't happen just because someone is "dull" or because they brought it on themselves. Yet we can also recognize that people with certain personality traits, like low self-control, are more likely to engage in the kinds of risky behaviors—including offending—that tend to place them at risk of being victimized. We do, however, still have important tasks in front of us if we want to gain a better understanding of the nature and sources of victimization. We have our work cut out for us in two respects.

First, we need to make a more concerted effort to develop and test better measures of risky lifestyles. This is not a small problem. As it sits right now the victimization literature is still dominated by the use and reuse of lifestyle measures drawn from the 1970s that merely tap into the amount of time people spend away from their homes. Hindelang et al. (1978) first used such measures not because they were ideal, but because they were making the best of what they had available in the NCS data (e.g., major daytime activity; frequency of nighttime activities). In the process, they noted that better measures would be those that tap into what constitute high-risk times, places, and people. Some scholars took them up on this in the 1990s (Mustaine & Tewksbury, 1998), but for the most part there seems to have been a regression in recent years back toward measures of the more mundane routines which we have no real reason to think actually place people at risk. Some scholars are bucking this trend and revisiting workable concepts of risk (Berg et al., 2012; Stewart, Elifson, & Sterk, 2004; Turanovic et al., 2015), but a more complete understanding of the sources of victimization will continue to elude us until the field of victimization studies as a whole decides that we should measure risky lifestyles (and not just mundane routine activities).

Second, and relatedly, as we go about developing these improved measures of the factors that place people at risk of being victimized, we need to keep in mind that such measures would be most useful if they were what might be termed "domain-specific." What this means is that particular forms of victimization may be the consequence of particular risky behaviors. For instance, the role that excessive alcohol use may play in victimization will likely depend on when and where someone does their drinking. Someone who gets drunk in public at night in a crowd of people, for example, may be placing themselves at a much greater risk of being robbed or assaulted than the person who gets drunk in his living room alone while watching reruns of *Family Guy*. Similarly, what might not be considered to be much of a risky lifestyle choice for someone in their early twenties—like having a few beers and smoking cigarettes—might be considered extremely risky for a 10-year-old. Thus, we may also need to think of risky behaviors as being *age-graded* (Turanovic, 2018). Either way, we know a lot more about victimization than we used to, but we still have a lot to learn.

Key readings

Cohen, L.E. & Felson, M. (1979). Social change and crime rate trends: A routine activity approach. *American Sociological Review, 44,* 588–608.
Gottfredson, M.R. (1981). On the etiology of criminal victimization. *Journal of Criminal Law and Criminology, 72,* 714–726.
Pratt, T.C. & Turanovic, J.J. (2016). Lifestyle and routine activity theories revisited: The importance of "risk" to the study of victimization. *Victims and Offenders, 11,* 335–354.
Pratt, T.C., Turanovic, J.J., Fox, K.A., & Wright, K.A. (2014). Self-control and victimization: A meta-analysis. *Criminology, 52,* 87–116.

Discussion questions

1. What are the core "criminological facts" concerning the demographic correlates of victimization?
2. How did early criminologists think about the sources of victimization?
3. How are lifestyle and routine activity theories similar, and how are they different?
4. How does the concept of self-control fit into the lifestyle model of victimization?

References

Agnew, R. (1985). A revised strain theory of delinquency. *Social Forces, 64,* 151–167.
Agnew, R. (1992). Foundation for a general strain theory of crime and delinquency. *Criminology, 30,* 47–88.

Agnew, R. (2006). *Pressured into crime: An overview of general strain theory*. Los Angeles, CA: Roxbury.

Anderson, E. (1999). *Code of the street: Decency, violence, and the moral life of the inner city*. New York: Norton.

Averdijk, M. (2011). Reciprocal effects of victimization and routine activities. *Journal of Quantitative Criminology, 27,* 125-149.

Averdijk, M. & Loeber, R. (2012). The role of self-control in the link between prior and future victimization: An indirect test. *International Review of Victimology, 18,* 189-206.

Berg, M.T., Stewart, E.A., Schreck, C.J., & Simons, R.L. (2012). The victim-offender overlap in context: Examining the role of neighborhood street culture. *Criminology, 50,* 359-390.

Blau, P.M. (1977). *Inequality and heterogeneity: A primitive theory of social structure*. New York: Free Press.

Broidy, L. & Agnew, R. (1997). Gender and crime: A general strain theory perspective. *Journal of Research in Crime and Delinquency, 34,* 275-306.

Bunch, J., Clay-Warner, J., & McMahon-Howard, J. (2014). The effects of victimization on routine activities. *Criminal Justice and Behavior, 41,* 574-592.

Burgess, R.L. & Akers, R.L. (1966). A differential association-reinforcement theory of criminal behavior. *Social Problems, 14,* 128-147.

Chiricos, T.G. (1987). Rates of crime and unemployment: An analysis of aggregate research evidence. *Social Problems, 34,* 187-212.

Cohen, L.E. & Felson, M. (1979). Social change and crime rate trends: A routine activity approach. *American Sociological Review, 44,* 588-608.

Cohen, L.E. & Land, K.C. (1987). Age structure and crime: Symmetry versus asymmetry and the projection of crime rates through the 1990s. *American Sociological Review, 52,* 170-183.

Cohen, L.E., Felson, M., & Land, K.C. (1980). Property crime rates in the United States: A macrodynamic analysis, 1947-1977. *American Journal of Sociology, 86,* 90-117.

Crick, N.R. & Grotpeter, J.K. (1995). Relational aggression, gender, and social-psychological adjustment. *Child Development, 66,* 710-722.

Cullen, F.T. (2011). Beyond adolescence-limited criminology: Choosing our future—the American Society of Criminology 2010 Sutherland Address. *Criminology, 49,* 287-330.

Cullen, F.T. & Gilbert, K.E. (1982). *Reaffirming rehabilitation*. Cincinnati, OH: Anderson.

Daigle, L.E. & Muftic, L.R. (2016). *Victimology*. Thousand Oaks, CA: Sage.

Daly, K. (1994). *Gender, crime, and punishment*. New Haven, CT: Yale University Press.

DeKeseredy, W.S. (2015). New directions in feminist understandings of rural crime. *Journal of Rural Studies, 39,* 180-187.

De Ridder, D.T.D., Lensvelt-Mulders, G., Finkenauer, C., Stok, F.M., & Baumeister, R.F. (2012). Taking stock of self-control: A meta-analysis of how trait self-control relates to a wide range of behaviors. *Personality and Social Psychology Review, 16,* 76-99.

Ellwanger, S.J. & Pratt, T.C. (2014). Self-control, negative affect, and young driver aggression: An assessment of competing theoretical claims. *International Journal of Offender Therapy and Comparative Criminology, 58,* 85-106.

Estrada, F., Backman, O., & Nilsson, A. (2016). The darker side of equality? The declining gender gap in crime: Historical trends and an enhanced analysis of staggered birth cohorts. *British Journal of Criminology, 56,* 1272-1290.

Federal Bureau of Investigation. (2016). *Crime in the United States, 2015*. Washington, DC: U.S. Department of Justice.

Felson, M. (1993). Social indicators for criminology. *Journal of Research in Crime and Delinquency, 30,* 400-411.

Felson, M. & Cohen, L.E. (1980). Human ecology and crime: A routine activity approach. *Human Ecology, 8,* 389-406.

Felson, R.B. & Messner, S.F. (1998). Disentangling the effects of gender and intimacy on victim precipitation in homicide. *Criminology, 36,* 405-424.

Ferraro, K.J. (2006). *Neither angels nor demons: Women, crime, and victimization.* Lebanon, NH: Northeastern University Press.

Finkelhor, D., Turner, H.A., Shattuck, A., & Hamby, S.L. (2015). Prevalence of childhood exposure to violence, crime, and abuse: Results from the National Survey of Children's Exposure to Violence. *JAMA Pediatrics, 169,* 746–754.

Finn, M.A., Muftic, L.R., & Marsh, E.I. (2015). Exploring the overlap between victimization and offending among women in sex work. *Victims and Offenders, 10,* 74–94.

George, W.H. & Martinez, L.J. (2002). Victim blaming in rape: Effects of victim and perpetrator race, type of rape, and participant racism. *Psychology of Women Quarterly, 26,* 110–119.

Gottfredson, M.R. & Hirschi, T. (1990). *A general theory of crime.* Palo Alto, CA: Stanford University Press.

Gracia, E. & Tomas, J.M. (2014). Correlates of victim-blaming attitudes regarding partner violence against women among the Spanish general population. *Violence Against Women, 20,* 26–41.

Hamby, S. (2014). Intimate partner and sexual violence research: Scientific progress, scientific challenges, and gender. *Trauma, Violence, and Abuse, 15,* 149–158.

Harrell, E. (2015). *Victims of identity theft, 2014.* Washington, DC: Bureau of Justice Statistics.

Hayes, R.M., Lorenz, K., & Bell, K.A. (2013). Victim blaming others: Rape myth acceptance and the just world belief. *Feminist Criminology, 8,* 202–220.

Hindelang, M.J., Gottfredson, M.R., & Garofalo, J. (1978). *Victims of personal crime: An empirical foundation for a theory of personal victimization.* Cambridge, MA: Ballinger.

Hirschi, T. (1969). *Causes of delinquency.* Berkeley, CA: University of California Press.

Holtfreter, K., Reisig, M.D., & Pratt, T.C. (2008). Low self-control, routine activities, and fraud victimization. *Criminology, 46,* 189–220.

Holtfreter, K., Reisig, M.D., Pratt, T.C., & Holtfreter, R.E. (2015). Risky remote purchasing and identity theft victimization among older internet users. *Psychology, Crime and Law, 21,* 681–698.

Houghton, S., Tan, C., Khan, U., & Carroll, A. (2013). Rates of self-reported delinquency among Western Australian male and female high school students: The male–female gender gap. *International Journal of Disability, Development and Education, 60,* 74–84.

Johnson, H. (2005). *Experiences of crime in two selected migrant communities.* Canberra: Australian Institute of Criminology.

Johnson, W.L., Giordano, P.C., Manning, W.D., & Longmore, M.A. (2015). The age-IPV curve: Changes in the perpetration of intimate partner violence during adolescence and young adulthood. *Journal of Youth and Adolescence, 44,* 708–726.

Karmen, A. (2013). *Crime victims: An introduction to victimology* (8th edn). Belmont, CA: Wadsworth.

Kennedy, L.W. & Forde, D.R. (1990). Routine activities and crime: An analysis of victimization in Canada. *Criminology, 28,* 137–152.

Kirby, S., Francis, B., & O'Flaherty, R. (2014). Can the FIFA World Cup football (soccer) tournament be associated with an increase in domestic abuse? *Journal of Research in Crime and Delinquency, 51,* 259–276.

Klevens, J., Duque, L.F., & Ramirez, C. (2002). The victim–perpetrator overlap and routine activities: Results from a cross-sectional study in Bogota, Colombia. *Journal of Interpersonal Violence, 17,* 206–216.

Kornhauser, R.R. (1978). *Social sources of delinquency: An appraisal of analytic models.* Chicago, IL: University of Chicago Press.

Krivo, L.J., Washington, H.M., Peterson, R.D., Browning, C.R., Calder, C.A., & Kwan, M.P. (2013). Social isolation of disadvantage and advantage: The reproduction of inequality in urban space. *Social Forces, 92,* 141–164.

Kruttschnitt, C. (2013). Gender and crime. *Annual Review of Sociology, 39,* 291–308.

Lauritsen, J.L., Rezey, M.L., & Heimer, K. (2014). Violence and economic conditions in the United States, 1973-2011: Gender, race, and ethnicity patterns in the National Crime Victimization Survey. *Journal of Contemporary Criminal Justice, 30,* 7-28.

Lemieux, A.M. & Felson, M. (2012). Risk of violent victimization during major daily activities. *Violence and Victims, 27,* 635-655.

Lilly, J.R., Cullen, F.T., & Ball, R.A. (2014). *Criminological theory: Context and consequences* (6th edn). Thousand Oaks, CA: Sage.

Lindegaard, M.R., Miller, J., & Reynald, D.M. (2013). Transitory mobility, cultural heterogeneity, and victimization risk among young men of color: Insights from an ethnographic study in Cape Town, South Africa. *Criminology, 51,* 967-1008.

Loeber, R. & Farrington, D.P. (2014). Age-crime curve. In Bruinsma, G., & Weisburd, D. (Eds.), *Encyclopedia of criminology and criminal justice* (pp.12-18). New York: Springer.

Loeber, R., Capaldi, D.M., & Costello, E. (2013). Gender and the development of aggression, disruptive behavior, and delinquency from childhood to early adulthood. In *Advances in development and psychopathology: Brain research foundation symposium series Vol 1* (pp.137-160). New York: Springer.

Matza, D. (1964). *Delinquency and drift.* New York: Wiley.

Martinez, R., Stowell, J.I., & Iwama, J.A. (2016). The role of immigration: Race/ethnicity and San Diego homicides since 1970. *Journal of Quantitative Criminology, 32,* 471-488.

Mears, D.P., Ploeger, M., & Warr, M. (1998). Explaining the gender gap in delinquency: Peer influence and moral evaluations of behavior. *Crime and Delinquency, 35,* 251-266.

Miethe, T.D., Stafford, M.C., & Long, J.S. (1987). Social differentiation in criminal victimization: A test of routine activities/lifestyle theories. *American Sociological Review, 52,* 184-194.

Millar, P. & Owusu-Bempah, A. (2011). Whitewashing criminal justice in Canada: Preventing research through data suppression. *Canadian Journal of Law and Society, 26,* 653-661.

Moffitt, T.E. (1993). Adolescence-limited and life-course persistent antisocial behavior: A developmental taxonomy. *Psychological Review, 100,* 674-701.

Mustaine, E.E., & Tewksbury, R. (1998). Predicting risks of larceny theft victimization: A routine activity analysis using refined lifestyle measures. *Criminology, 36,* 829-858.

Nagin, D.S. (2005). *Group-based modeling of development over the life course.* Cambridge, MA: Harvard University Press.

Osgood, D.W., Wilson, J.K., O'Malley, P.M., Bachman, J.G., & Johnston, L.D. (1996). Routine activities and individual deviant behavior. *American Sociological Review, 61,* 635-655.

Peterson, R.D. & Krivo, L.J. (2010). *Divergent social worlds: Neighborhood crime and the racial-spatial divide.* New York: Russell Sage Foundation.

Piquero, A.R., Farrington, D.P., & Blumstein, A. (2003). The criminal career paradigm. *Crime and Justice: A Review of Research, 30,* 359-506.

Piquero, A.R., Gomez-Smith, Z., & Langton, L. (2004). Discerning unfairness where others may not: Low self-control and unfair sanction perceptions. *Criminology, 42,* 699-733.

Popp, A.M. & Peguero, A.A. (2011). Routine activities and victimization at school: The significance of gender. *Journal of Interpersonal Violence, 26,* 2413-2436.

Pratt, T.C. (2016). A self-control/life-course theory of criminal behavior. *European Journal of Criminology, 13,* 129-146.

Pratt, T.C. & Cullen, F.T. (2000). The empirical status of Gottfredson and Hirschi's general theory of crime: A meta-analysis. *Criminology, 38,* 931-964.

Pratt, T.C. & Cullen, F.T. (2005). Assessing macro-level predictors and theories of crime: A meta-analysis. *Crime and Justice: A Review of Research, 32,* 373-450.

Pratt, T.C. & Turanovic, J.J. (2016). Lifestyle and routine activity theories revisited: The importance of "risk" to the study of victimization. *Victims and Offenders, 11,* 335-354.

Pratt, T.C., Turanovic, J.J., Fox, K.A., & Wright, K.A. (2014). Self-control and victimization: A meta-analysis. *Criminology, 52,* 87-116.

Reisig, M.D. & Pratt, T.C. (2011). Low self-control and imprudent behavior revisited. *Deviant Behavior, 32,* 589-625.

Reisig, M.D., Pratt, T.C., & Holtfreter, K. (2009). Perceived risk of internet theft victimization: Examining the effects of social vulnerability and financial impulsivity. *Criminal Justice and Behavior, 36*, 369–384.

Robinson, W.S. (1950). Ecological correlations and the behavior of individuals. *American Sociological Review, 15*, 351–357.

Rosay, A.B. (2016). *Violence against American Indian and Alaska Native women and men*. Washington, DC: National Institute of Justice.

Sampson, R.J., Morenoff, J.D., & Earls, F. (1999). Beyond social capital: Spatial dynamics of collective efficacy for children. *American Sociological Review, 64*, 633–660.

Schreck, C.J. (1999). Criminal victimization and low self-control: An extension and test of a general theory of crime. *Justice Quarterly, 16*, 633–654.

Schreck, C.J., Stewart, E.A., & Fisher, B.S. (2006). Self-control, victimization, and their influence on risky lifestyles: A longitudinal analysis using panel data. *Journal of Quantitative Criminology, 22*, 319–340.

Schreck, C.J., Wright, R.A., & Miller, J.M. (2002). A study of individual and situational antecedents of violent victimization. *Justice Quarterly, 19*, 159–180.

Sharkey, P. (2013). *Stuck in place: Urban neighborhoods and the end of progress toward racial equality*. Chicago, IL: University of Chicago Press.

Shaw, C.R. & McKay, H.D. (1942). *Juvenile delinquency and urban areas*. Chicago, IL: University of Chicago Press.

Silver, N. (2015). Black Americans are killed at 12 times the rate of people in other developed countries. *FiveThirtyEight.com*, June 18.

Steffensmeier, D.J., Schwartz, J., & Roche, M. (2013). Gender and twenty-first century corporate crime: Female involvement and the gender gap in Enron-era corporate frauds. *American Sociological Review, 78*, 448–476.

Steinberg, L. (2010). A dual systems model of adolescent risk-taking. *Developmental Psychobiology, 52*, 216–224.

Steinberg, L. & Morris, A.S. (2001). Adolescent development. *Journal of Cognitive Education and Psychology, 2*, 55–87.

Steinberg, L., Albert, D., Cauffman, E., & Banich, M. (2008). Age differences in sensation seeking and impulsivity as indexed by behavior and self-report: Evidence for a dual systems model. *Developmental Psychology, 44*, 1764–1778.

Stewart, E.A., Elifson, K.W., & Sterk, C.E. (2004). Integrating the general theory of crime into an explanation of violent victimization among female offenders. *Justice Quarterly, 21*, 159–181.

Stewart. E.A., Schreck, C.J., & Simons, R.L. (2006). I ain't gonna let no one disrespect me: Does the code of the street reduce or increase violent victimization among African American adolescents? *Journal of Research in Crime and Delinquency, 43*, 427–458.

Thijs, P.E., van Dijk, I.K., Stoof, R., & Notten, N. (2015). Adolescent problem behavior: The gender gap in European perspective. *European Journal of Criminology, 12*, 598–615.

Truman, J.L. & Langton, L. (2014). *Criminal victimization, 2013*. Washington, DC: Bureau of Justice Statistics.

Truman, J.L. & Langton L. (2015). *Criminal victimization, 2014*. Washington, DC: Bureau of Justice Statistics.

Truman, J.L. & Morgan, R.E. (2016). *Criminal victimization, 2015*. Washington, DC: Bureau of Justice Statistics.

Turanovic, J.J. (2018). Toward a life-course theory of victimization. In S.H. Decker & K.A. Wright (Eds.), *Criminology and public policy: Putting theory to work (2nd ed.)* (pp. 85–103). Philadelphia, PA: Temple University Press.

Turanovic, J.J. & Pratt, T.C. (2014). "Can't stop, won't stop": Self-control, risky lifestyles, and repeat victimization. *Journal of Quantitative Criminology, 30*, 29–56.

Turanovic, J.J. & Young, J.T.N. (2016). Violent offending and victimization in adolescence: Social network mechanisms and homophily. *Criminology, 54*, 487–519.

Turanovic, J.J., Reisig, M.D., & Pratt, T.C. (2015). Risky lifestyles, low self-control, and violent victimization across gendered pathways to crime. *Journal of Quantitative Criminology, 31,* 183-206.

Turanovic, J.J., Rodriguez, N., & Pratt, T.C. (2012). The collateral consequences of incarceration revisited: A qualitative analysis of the effects on caregivers of children of incarcerated parents. *Criminology, 50,* 913-959.

Van Dijk, J., Van Kesteren, J., & Smit, P. (2007). *Criminal victimisation in international perspective: Key findings from the 2004-2005 ICVS and EU ICS.* The Hague: Ministry of Justice, WODC.

Van Kesteren, J. (2016). Assessing the risk and prevalence of hate crime victimization in Western Europe. *International Review of Victimology, 22,* 139-160.

Vieraitis, L.M., Britto, S., & Morris, R.G. (2015). Assessing the impact of changes in gender equality on female homicide victimization, 1980-2000. *Crime and Delinquency, 61,* 428-453.

von Hentig, H. (1948). *The criminal and his victim: Studies in the sociobiology of crime.* New Haven, CT: Yale University Press.

Warr, M. (2002). *Companions in crime: The social aspects of criminal conduct.* Cambridge: Cambridge University Press.

Weisburd, D. & Piquero, A.R. (2008). How well do criminologists explain crime? Statistical modeling in published studies. *Crime and Justice: A Review of Research, 37,* 453-502.

Wilson, W.J. (1996). *When work disappears: The world of the new urban poor.* New York: Alfred A. Knopf.

Wolfgang, M.E. (1957). Victim precipitated criminal homicide. *Journal of Criminal Law, Criminology, and Police Science, 48,* 1-11.

Wolfgang, M.E. (1958). *Patterns of criminal homicide.* Oxford: Oxford University Press.

Zaykowski, H. & Gunter, W.D. (2013). Gender differences in victimization risk: Exploring the role of deviant lifestyles. *Violence and Victims, 28,* 341-356.

4 Victimization from the offender's perspective

In 2015 the State of New York began to show orientation videos put together by The Marshall Project to incoming prison inmates entitled "Ending sexual abuse behind the walls." Partially in response to the Prison Rape Elimination Act (see Jenness et al., 2010), the purpose of the videos (23 minutes for the men, 19 minutes for the women) is to equip inmates with strategies to avoid being sexually assaulted (by other inmates and by staff) as they serve out their sentences, and to provide information about how to report sexual victimization. Following a brief introduction by the head of the New York State Department of Corrections and Community Supervision, the rest of the videos feature inmates themselves talking candidly about their experiences—either personally or vicariously—of sexual violence in prison and how to avoid becoming a victim.

Some of the strategies that the inmates offer up are cognitive. Their advice was to "trust no one" and to make sure that new inmates "don't fall for the subtle trickery, deception, and manipulation," since sexual victimization often involves a process of gaining trust from those who are scared or vulnerable (Hensley, Tewksbury, & Castle, 2003; Struckman-Johnson et al., 2013). The inmates in the video are also quick to advise new prisoners to be wary when someone is "too anxious to be your friend, who offers things to you without any prompting," since such things can translate into feeling indebted to the predatory inmates. And a common theme within both videos was an effort at cognitive reframing to convey the idea that reporting sexual victimization "is not snitching."

Other strategies that the inmates provide are more behavioral in nature. In recognizing that some places are more risky than others, new inmates were given the advice: "Don't take a shower with no underclothes on" and "Never have a conversation with an inmate in an adjacent shower." The exercise yard was also recognized as another high-risk location, and inmates shared the advice that "You need to be smart about what you do on the weight pile," to

"Choose your workout partner wisely," and when doing exercises like bench presses or squats, "don't let your spotter invade your space."

There were also certain "symbolic" strategies that inmates were advised to either adopt or avoid. A common theme, for example, was "Don't appear to be weak" (which implicitly included to avoid being young or small in stature, as if that is something a new inmate can do anything about). And in recognizing that going to prison can be a traumatic event in a person's life, with respect to such trauma, inmates are told "don't show it," because "predators know when you're traumatized." Instead, new inmates are told to "be comfortable with who you are," because if so it is less likely that a predator will see you as vulnerable.

All of these strategies are offered up as necessary because the threat of sexual violence in prison is assumed to be ever-present, constantly looming over everyone at all times. This is not mere subtext in the videos, but is instead stated explicitly: "Predators come in all shapes, sizes, and races . . . predators look like us." Thus, the whole point behind the videos is that everyone is always at risk.

The anecdote presented above is meant to convey two things—one of which is true, the other of which is a dangerous exaggeration. Here is the true thing: when it comes to the criminal event, much of it on the part of the offender is simply impulsive and unplanned, where the opportunity to victimize someone—whether it be the person themselves or their property—presents itself unexpectedly (Gottfredson & Hirschi, 1990; Pratt, 2016). And even when an offense *is* actually planned, offenders tend to drift toward easy opportunities (St. John, 2007). They look for easy targets, those that are likely to offer up little resistance and will not make them work too hard to accomplish their intended offense, and will abandon the whole idea if it all looks as though it will take too much energy (Jacques, 2010; Wright & Decker, 1994, 1997). Put simply: most offenders are not masterminds, nor are they relentless in their pursuit to victimize others.

So while all of that is true, implicitly embedded within the narrative above—one that is not limited to the prison environment—was also a dangerous exaggeration, and here it is: that offenders are everywhere and that all of us are always at risk of being victimized all of the time. The message is that there are potential criminals "out there" at all times and that none of us is ever safe (Bennett, DiIulio, & Walters, 1996)—a message that policy makers have found to be enormously useful for gaining political capital by appearing to be "tough on crime" (Ogle & Turanovic, 2016; Pratt, 2019). It is also an idea that resonates rather well with the notion that any time and place is equally as risky as any other and that we can all be victimized as we go about our normal, mundane daily routines of going to work, buying stuff, and entertaining ourselves (Felson, 1987).

Taking this a step further, there is an embedded notion—sometimes even stated explicitly—that we are all potential criminals and that if the opportunity is good enough we can all become sufficiently motivated to engage in criminal behavior (Felson & Boba, 2010). While there may be a kernel of truth to this statement (or at least to the sentiment behind it), the data from decades of criminological research show rather clearly that over half of all crimes committed are carried out by a small (less than 10 percent) portion of the population (Piquero, Farrington, & Blumstein, 2003). So yes, while all (or most) of us may *theoretically* engage in crime if pushed hard enough, in reality there is only a small handful of the population that generally has a tough time behaving itself.

So the problem, then, is that most of us do not engage in crime—even when the "opportunity" to do so seems to be really easy. When we see a stranger's *i*Phone unattended on the table at the coffee shop, most of us are never going to swipe it; if we are upset with a friend for voting for a Presidential candidate whom we dislike, most of us are never going to punch that friend in the face for having done so; if a pre-approved credit card for our neighbor accidentally arrives in our mailbox, most of us are never going to open it and use it to buy beer and chips. But some people do—given the same "opportunity structures" that face all of us, they respond to them very differently. Why is that? In our obsession with focusing on concepts like "target attractiveness" and "capable guardianship," where did the offender and the decisions that they make go in the victimization equation?

The offender's perspective is perhaps the most overlooked component of victimization theory and research (see, e.g., Pratt & Turanovic, 2016). Thus, in this chapter, we discuss the reasons behind this omission, as well as the consequences for victims of failing to consider the offenders' perspective. In addition, we review the criminological theory and research concerning how offenders make decisions about who (and what) they will victimize and how they will go about doing it. The key theme in this chapter, then, is the importance of bringing the offender back into how we think about victimization.

The vanishing offender in victimization theory and research

An offender's "motivation" to victimize someone else has always been a fundamental part of criminological theory. To be sure, the criminological literature is full of reasons as to why offenders are motivated to commit crimes, steal other people's stuff, and to act violently toward them. And if we were to look closely at the "criminal event"—that which results in the victimization of one person at the hands of another—through the lens of the perspectives that make up the "core" of criminological theory (Lilly, Cullen, & Ball, 2010), we would likely come away with the impression that victimization cannot be fully understood without an understanding of the offender's perspective.

For example, one of the perspectives that comprises the core of criminology is social learning theory. This perspective begins with the assumption that criminal behavior—like virtually all other forms of behavior—is learned through a process of reinforcement (Akers, 2009). Indeed, the reasons why we wear the clothes we wear, use the slang terminology we use, or pitch a fit when we do not get what we want is because those behaviors have likely been positively reinforced at some point in time (e.g., via compliments we receive about our wardrobe, the laughter we elicit from others when we use certain words, and others eventually giving us what we want in the hope that we will stop pitching a fit when we get it). Not surprisingly, peers play a pivotal role in this process of reinforcement, helping to "push" people into potentially problematic behaviors (like crime) by encouraging them, providing them with cognitive justifications to excuse the behavior, and even teaching others techniques in how to actually commit certain offenses that may require at least a smidgen of skill (McGloin & Thomas, 2016). The key idea here is that the desire to victimize others is not "natural" or innate in individuals; it has to be put there.

A second idea within the core of criminology—one that also deals in how criminal "motivation" gets established—is what has come to be known as strain/anomie theory (Merton, 1938). This uniquely American perspective begins with the assumption that everyone generally aspires to the same goal: economic success (or at least economic comfort). The problem is that some people face structural barriers to achieving that goal (e.g., limited educational opportunities, poor employment prospects, depleted economic/social networks; Merton, 1968). This is upsetting. And since—at least in America—there is a far greater emphasis placed on the goal of economic success than there is on "playing fair" to reach that goal, it exerts pressure on the norms that guide our behavior. Put differently, the norms that should keep our behavior in check (e.g., don't steal, don't cheat, don't punch people) are weakened, which results in more crime. Thus, at its heart the strain/anomie perspective views the choice to commit a crime as being rooted in various forms of frustration, coupled with limited avenues for dealing with that frustration in prosocial ways (Agnew, 2006).

Within the control tradition we are assumed to all be born with the motivation to behave badly and we just need something in our lives—punishments, social bonds, or some sort of system of surveillance—to tell us not to (Gottfredson & Hirschi, 1990; Hirschi, 1969).

So while the offender's perspective is a fundamental part of mainstream criminological theory, it is curiously absent from much of the victimization literature. From the presentation of symbolic interactionist models and the rise of feminist perspectives on victimization in the 1970s, to the revival of the deterrence/rational choice tradition in the 1980s, to routine activity theory in its current modern form, these perspectives have all fallen short when it comes to being able to explain why, even when faced with the same potential situational dynamics, certain people are willing to victimize their fellow citizens while others are not. We review these perspectives here as a way of transitioning into a discussion of how we might bring the offender back into thinking about and understanding victimization.

When theories cannot explain variation

The 1970s was a unique time in the social sciences. During this time, the field that long "owned" the study of crime and victimization was sociology (Laub, 2004). Thus, the working assumption was that individual differences (e.g., variations in people's personalities, intelligence, and other predispositions) were not really all that important in determining human behavior (Hirschi & Hindelang, 1977; Laub & Sampson, 1991). Instead, focusing on macro-level factors was all the rage—things like structured inequality, patterns of employment, and race/gender stratification—and how they shape interactions between people (Blau, 1977). At its best this perspective shone a light (and often a politically inconvenient one) on inequality and its consequences; at its worst it portrayed humans as "blank slates" to be determined purely by socialization and context (Pinker, 2002). But for better or worse, this was the scholarly landscape of the time.

It was at this time that Luckenbill (1977: 176) set forth his *situated transaction perspective* on homicide. He began by noting that "By definition, criminal homicide is a collective transaction. An offender, victim, and possibly an audience engage in an interchange which leaves the victim dead." What this means is that pre-situation characteristics of individuals are largely irrelevant when it comes to homicide. Instead, the situation itself defines the event by creating "roles" and a "character contest" (Luckenbill, 1977: 177) between individuals to appear tough in the presence of others. The event then unfolds like a script, where what begins as low-level conflict goes through an exchange-induced process of escalation (taunts, shoves, mouthing off)—typically on the part of both the offender and the victim—which ultimately ends up with someone dead.

This idea made sense in that it was built upon previous work on "victim-precipitated homicide" (Wolfgang, 1958). The key contribution was thus the notion that "criminal homicide does not appear as a one-sided event with an unwitting victim assuming a passive, non-contributory role" (Luckenbill, 1977: 185). This was an extremely insightful observation, yet the situated transaction perspective fell short in being able to explain why some negative interactions between people end up in a homicide while others do not. Why, for example, do only some situations with what appear to include all the "ingredients" never result in a victimization event? To his credit, Luckenbill (1977: 181) acknowledged this issue:

> The apparent affront could have evoked different responses. The offender could have excused the violation because the victim was judged to be drunk, crazy, or joking. He could have fled the scene and avoided further interaction with the victim by moving into interaction with other occasioned participants or dealt with the impropriety through a retaliatory move aimed at restoring face and demonstrating strong character.

The problem is that by portraying people as "blank slates" who carry with them nothing of real importance (predispositions, preferences, or experiences) from situation to situation, there is no substantive explanation for why some people will find themselves in these kinds of encounters way more often than others. Neither can this perspective explain why—when faced with the same general situation—some people will excuse, flee, and live, while others will escalate, become violent, and die. In short, when examining victimization through a situated transaction lens, there really is no offender—there is only the situation.

At around the same time, another major development was happening in the social sciences: feminist scholars were gaining substantial visibility and in the process were highlighting the consequences of gender inequality and patriarchy (Daly, 1997). In general, this *feminist perspective* focused on how men exert power over women (e.g., financially, socially, and physically), how the broader culture comes to reflect this pattern where the male way of doing things is "normal" and female roles are secondary, and how the control over women is viewed as legitimate (Heimer & De Coster, 1999). A core part of this theoretical tradition emphasizes how adhering to traditional gender roles—those where men feel entitled to their position of privilege—encourages (or "motivates") men to engage in violence when that power is threatened (Hood-Williams, 2001).

Accordingly, when it came to victimization, much of this feminist literature focused most closely on violence against women and intimate partner violence—offenses where gender-based power differentials were most likely to play out in violent ways (Simon, 1975). This is a compelling idea, and one that made sense in the1970s—a time when the U.S. and other nations experienced rapid changes in their labor markets where more and more women were entering the workforce, and traditional gender roles and inequalities seemed to be breaking down (Adler, 1975). Women's greater earning power in the economy meant greater access to legal protection as well (Simpson, 1989). This was an important development because this was also a time when scholars pointed out how male violence against women–particularly sexual violence and that which occurs in the home–went virtually unpunished by the state (Daly & Chesney-Lind, 1988). This reality provided persuasive evidence of how men are able to maintain dominance over women and how the patriarchal system is able to reproduce itself by failing to protect female victims of crime (Belknap, 1996).

Nevertheless, a key problem still remained: feminists' view of men was essentially one-dimensional in that there was little room for patriarchy to affect men in different ways (Messerschmidt, 1993). Put simply, this perspective predicted that there should be a lot more violence on the part of men than actually occurs. It thus offered no real explanation as to why only some men engage in gender-based violent behavior while others do not, and so once again the victimization literature failed to provide a compelling explanation as to why there is variation in violent behavior among men. Indeed, if they are all entrenched in the same system of structured patriarchy, why do only some of them choose to embrace violence, while others–even most–seem to have no interest in it? So, once again, structure and context are implicated in offending, but the offenders themselves have been left out of the discussion. This is not to say that structure and context are unimportant when it comes to facilitating violence against women (a subject discussed in more detail in Chapter 9), but rather that it is still important to examine the role that individual offenders play in victimization events.

The offender becomes irrelevant

The idea that some people may be more prone to offend–that they may be more aggressive, violent, or impulsive than other people–virtually disappeared from discussions of victimization with the introduction of routine activity theory. This happened with the introduction of a couple of key pieces of research in the field of criminology. First, armed with new data–the National Crime Survey (NCS, discussed in Chapter 2)–Hindelang, Gottfredson, and Garofalo (1978) found that people who shared certain demographic characteristics were most likely to be victimized. In particular, young black males–especially those residing in impoverished social contexts–were most at risk of being victimized. The assumption was that those who share this combination of demographic characteristics were also the most likely to have made certain lifestyle choices (e.g., committing crimes and participating in other risky behaviors) and to have engaged in patterns of social interaction that placed them in close proximity to offenders.

In the second key piece of work, Cohen and Felson (1979) ran with Hindelang et al.'s (1978) idea and took it a step further. Cohen and Felson (1979) first noted that structural and economic changes in the 1960s and 1970s–mainly more women entering the labor force—meant greater social mobility. This also meant that more people would be leaving the home during the day (particularly women) as a matter of their "routine activities" (see also Felson & Cohen, 1980). These new routine activities, in turn, resulted in more homes being left unattended during the day and more people finding themselves out and about in public spaces, rubbing shoulders with other people—including potential offenders. "Opportunities" for victimization in all manner of ways—from residential burglary to assault and homicide—thus increased (Cohen, Felson, & Land, 1980).

What do such opportunities look like within the routine activity theoretical framework? In a stroke of simple elegance, Cohen and Felson's (1979) conceptualization of "routine activity theory" noted that for a criminal event to occur, three things needed to converge in time and space at the same time: (1) a motivated offender, (2) a suitable target, and (3) the absence of capable guardianship (as discussed in Chapter 3). What was particularly insightful about this idea was the notion that these three elements can converge not because people are doing risky things like offending (as Hindelang et al. (1978) said would be important for understanding patterns of victimization), but instead the elements can come together as a result of people going about their normal, mundane lives. To be sure, when people go to work, when they go about their normal economic activities like shopping, and when they engage in all manner of legal and legitimate attempts to entertain themselves, they all risk running into potential offenders who might victimize them in all manner of ways (Kennedy & Forde, 1990). Indeed, empty houses are burgled all the time, shopping bags full of newly purchased stuff are regularly stolen, and people get into fights at concerts often enough for such events to be rarely even newsworthy (Wittebrood & Nieuwbeerta, 2000).

But it is important to note that routine activity theory's conceptualization of opportunities for victimization emphasizes the role of "exposure" and "target attractiveness" for victimization. Targets become attractive to potential offenders in a variety of ways. Carjacking victims, for example, become more attractive when they do not look like they will put up much of a fight and when the car itself has an automatic transmission (it turns out that car thieves have trouble driving a stick; see Jacobs & Cherbonneau, 2017); drug dealers are more attractive to steal from when the offender thinks that the potential retaliation from the victim can be managed without much difficulty (Jacques & Reynald, 2012); and property is more attractive to steal if it is small, easy to conceal and carry, and can be traded in for cash with little or no trouble (Clarke, 1999).

Looking at victimization through this kind of lens has proven to be wildly popular in crime control circles. Indeed, the routine activity perspective has spawned a virtual cottage industry of strategies that fall under the heading of "situational crime prevention" efforts (Clarke, 1995). This approach emphasizes making things more difficult for potential offenders, often referred to as "target hardening" (Nee & Taylor, 2000). This includes things like: putting locks on previously unlocked doors, using tamper-proof packaging on goods, placing call boxes in apartment complex lobbies, putting anti-theft detection scanners at the exits to retail stores, and putting gates on alleys to prevent people from getting in (Hirschfield, Newton, & Rogerson, 2010). This idea has also crept into architecture and urban planning in the form of "crime prevention through environmental design" (CPTED) where the physical environment is constructed in a way that reduces opportunities to offend (fewer hiding/ambush spots and escape routes; see Reynald, 2015).

What is implicit in all of this, however, is that the motivation to offend is largely irrelevant within the routine activity model. This is no accident. To be sure, the offender—with his or her preferences, personality characteristics, and experiences—could effectively be taken out of the victimization equation. This is because the routine activity perspective assumes that good people do bad things all the time and that if the target is attractive enough, there will be a motivated offender somewhere around who will want to take advantage of the situation. Taking this logic one step further is the idea that if the situation is "good enough" anyone is capable of committing a crime (Clarke & Felson, 1998). This is akin to the idea that "all dogs bite." But we believe that thinking about victimization in this way is a mistake because it provides no explanation as to why—when faced with the same potential "target"—only some people choose to become offenders while for others it would never even cross their minds.

So the bottom line is that we cannot really count on the routine activity perspective—or those perspectives that came before it either—to help us understand why only some people take on the role of motivated offender and others choose to pass on it. We also cannot count on routine activity theory to tell us why only some people approach a certain situation—like an unlocked car with the keys in the ignition—and see it as a good "opportunity" to commit a crime while others just see a car. So if we want to understand why that kind of variation exists, we need to look elsewhere.

Taking offender decision making seriously

It is a safe bet that all of us want to believe that we are "rational" people. We like to think that when it comes to making choices we weigh our options carefully and do a thorough job of thinking through the relative costs and benefits of choosing one option over another (Cornish & Clarke, 2014). Entire academic disciplines are rooted in this very idea (e.g., economics), as well as the American system of laws and punishments (Pratt, 2008). After all, what would be the point of ratcheting up penalties for crimes if doing so failed to cause would-be criminals to "think twice" about engaging in unlawful behavior?

But the reality of how we all make decisions is much more complex than a pure "rational choice" model would have us believe. It turns out that when we make choices, we use a wide array of cognitive short cuts to make things easier on ourselves, and we import a host of biases into our decision-making process (Kahneman & Tversky, 2000). In particular, instead of being purely rational and weighing all of our options, we often only do a limited search in our minds for potential consequences and we tend to make choices according to what is "good enough" in the moment—not what might be most advantageous in the long run (Simon, 1997). We also tend to be plagued by things like "confirmation bias" (paying attention to information we already agree with and filtering out the rest; see Nickerson, 1998) and the "gambler's fallacy" (where even if we suffered the cost of a certain behavior in the past, we think we were simply unlucky to have been caught and the odds of getting nailed again must be lower this time; see Ayton & Fischer, 2004; Croson & Sundali, 2005). So, as it turns out, we engage in behaviors all the time—we eat things that we know are bad for us; we drink too much; we throw things at the television when our baseball team loses—that seem, at least upon further reflection, to be decidedly irrational.

The decision to victimize others is no different. While there is a long tradition of "rational choice"-based literature in criminology (Loughran et al., 2016), it turns out that the idea that offenders are careful weighers of costs and benefits does not fit very well with reality (Pratt & Turanovic, 2018). Instead, volumes of data from criminological studies (Pratt & Cullen, 2005; Pratt et al., 2006) and the literature on correctional interventions (Cullen, Pratt, & Turanovic, 2016; Lipsey & Wilson, 1993) all demonstrate that the potential "costs" of victimizing someone else rarely even enter offenders' minds. Because here is the fundamental problem: offenders generally lack self-control (Gottfredson & Hirschi, 1990), which means they tend to be impulsive (acting on the spur of the moment without even thinking of the consequences), and they tend to be present-oriented (focusing on the immediate benefits of crime that they see right in front of them, not the potential costs—should they even come—down the road) (Pratt & Cullen, 2000). The "cost" of victimizing someone must be just as present if it is to matter at all (e.g., there is "natural guardianship": the other person is bigger than they are; some physical barrier that prevents access to a crime; or police are plainly in view; see Cullen & Pratt, 2016).

The problem is that such costs are rarely present during a criminal event. First of all, it needs to be recognized that, among the general public, there is little awareness of what the penalties for various crimes actually are (Kleck & Barnes, 2013). Most of us really have no idea what kind of prison time we would be looking at for breaking into a house or stealing a car. This lack of awareness is then coupled with the fact that most people have rather low "certainty estimates" of punishment, meaning that they feel as though the odds of getting caught for any manner of offenses is not all that high (Paternoster, 1987). Such low estimates are understandable, however, given that the odds of getting caught for crimes like driving under the influence of alcohol are actually exceedingly low, with some estimates at around 1 in 200 (Beitel, Sharp, & Glauz, 2000). Then there is the fact that for punishment to be effective it needs to be immediately delivered—its power tends to diminish if it is delayed even a few seconds after the bad behavior (Pratt & Turanovic, 2018)—which is a practical impossibility when it comes to formal punishments by the criminal justice system. In some cases days or weeks may pass before an offender is arrested, and after that it may be several months or even years before an offender is sentenced to prison for a crime. What this all means is that offenders rarely spend time mulling over in their minds whether or not they should victimize someone else, and even if they do, the idea that they may be punished for it is, at best, buried deep in the backs of their minds.

What is in the front of their minds is usually what is in front of their faces—the immediate situation and how they interpret it through their own set of values and preferences. For example, if a person harbors attitudes that it is perfectly all right to use violence as a way of settling disagreements, then that person will be more likely to act violently than someone who harbors more prosocial ideas about how to solve conflicts (Akers, 2009). If a person feels that they are entitled to something—property, respect, sex—they are more likely to try to gain access to it illegally (Anderson, 1999). And if youth feel as though their social status might be enhanced among their peers if they were to victimize others, then they are certainly more likely to do it (Turanovic & Young, 2016). Things become even more complicated when intense emotions (e.g., anger) and chemical intoxication are entered into the mix, where individuals' judgments get even more blurry about acceptable ways to behave and to resolve conflicts (Nagin, 2007). The point here is that there are a host of attitudes and cognitions that can motivate a person to break the law and we need to consider their role in the victimization event.

We also need to consider the fact that offenders—like most people—can also generally be quite lazy when given the opportunity. And the average offender tends not to be very good at the harder things in life, such as holding down a job, maintaining healthy romantic relationships, paying their bills, and staying physically healthy (Pratt et al., 2016). All of that takes work, which can be made even more difficult for those who grew up and were socialized within structural contexts characterized by economic hardship, impoverished educational systems, and a lack of legitimate economic opportunities. What this means in the context of crime is that offenders rarely put in much effort in their quest to victimize others. To be sure, an offender will pass up the group of sober people in favor of robbing the intoxicated person who is alone in a public space because of the perception that they will not put up much resistance (Wright & Decker, 1997); the burglar will walk past the locked house with people clearly inside of it in favor of the empty one with an open side window at waist height (Wright & Decker, 1994); the underage kid will chug the beer when his friends are egging him on to do it (Thomas & McGloin, 2013); and big people will continue to prefer hitting little people (Felson, 1996). None of this is done as the result of some deliberate calculus of the full set of potential costs and benefits on the part of the offender—one where the pros and cons are carefully tallied and a cold, rational, dispassionate decision is settled upon. It is instead done to satisfy an urge for immediate gratification that can be accomplished without expending too much energy.

What, then, is the big picture here concerning the role of the offender when thinking about victimization? The bottom line is that when some of us see a kid who is small for his age we see a kid who we want to protect, while others see someone they want to pick on; when most of us pass by a parked car it would never occur to us to check if it is unlocked and whether there is stuff inside of it we can take, but the thought certainly occurs to others; and while the majority of us have at some point become very angry while driving, only a select few decide that shooting someone over it is the smart thing to do. Yet if we are to ever reach a good understanding of why such variation exists, the motivation people carry with them and the decision-making processes they go through all need to come back into how we look at victimization.

Gaps and challenges

Taking the offender out of the explanation of victimization has not proven to be a good idea. By emphasizing only (or even primarily) the situational elements of the victimization event—things like exposure or target attractiveness— we have fallen into what Matza (1964) referred to as an "embarrassment of riches": our current crop of theories collectively predicts way more offending and victimization than actually happens (see also Pratt, 2017). But the reality is that most people—even people who offend at a higher rate than others— control themselves most of the time (even chronic offenders do not start breaking the law the moment they wake up, keep doing it all day long, and only take a break from crime when it is time to go to bed; see also Gottfredson, 2011). What this means is that variability concerning why one person is victimized in a given situation and another somehow escapes it is currently not very well understood. And popular perspectives like routine activity theory have no way of explaining why, when faced with what seems to be a good "opportunity" for crime, only some people grab the opportunity. And taking the offender out of the discussion altogether is not going to help us find that explanation.

But we do have some promising places to look. Recent research on self-control "depletion," for example, is helping us understand how people are able to muster up sufficient restraint to avoid exhibiting bad behavior at one point in time and then lose it in others (Baumeister, 2002; Hagger et al., 2010). This work treats self-control like a muscle—one that can get tired if it is being used all the time and needs sufficient rest to get ready to use again. There is even evidence that our levels of self-control fluctuate during the day, and when we get tired or hungry (and our blood sugar drops) we tend to be at a much greater risk of losing self-control than if we were well rested and well fed (Pratt, 2016). This is all still somewhat in the early stages, yet the core implication for us has to do with how offenders' level of motivation may be influenced by certain victim or situational characteristics. Either way, the bottom line is that how offenders make decisions needs to once again become a core part of discussions about the causes of victimization.

Key readings

Belknap, J. (1996). *The invisible woman: Gender, crime, and justice*. Belmont, CA: Wadsworth.

Cornish, D.B. & Clarke, R.V. (2014). *The reasoning criminal: Rational choice perspectives on offending*. New Brunswick, NJ: Transaction.

Felson, R.B. (1996). Big people hit little people: Sex differences in physical power and interpersonal violence. *Criminology, 34*, 433-452.

Jacques, S. & Reynald, D.M. (2012). The offenders' perspective on prevention: Guarding against victimization and law enforcement. *Journal of Research in Crime and Delinquency, 49*, 269-294.

Wright, R. & Decker, S.H. (1994). *Burglars on the job: Streetlife and residential break-ins*. Boston, MA: Northeastern University Press.

Discussion questions

1. How did Luckenbill's situated transaction perspective leave the offender's motivation out of the explanation of victimization?
2. Why did the feminist perspectives of the 1970s fail to explain why only some women are victimized and others are not?
3. How did routine activity theory leave the offender out of the victimization explanation altogether?
4. Why is offender decision making not really all that "rational"?

References

Adler, F. (1975). *Sisters in crime: The rise of the new female criminal*. New York: McGraw-Hill.

Agnew, R. (2006). *Pressured into crime: An overview of general strain theory*. Los Angeles, CA: Roxbury.

Akers, R.L. (2009). *Social learning and social structure: A general theory of crime and deviance*. New Brunswick, NJ: Transaction.

Anderson, E. (1999). *Code of the street: Decency, violence, and the moral life of the inner city*. New York: Norton.

Ayton, P. & Fischer, I. (2004). The hot hand fallacy and the gambler's fallacy: Two faces of subjective randomness? *Memory and Cognition, 32*, 1369-1378.

Baumeister, R.F. (2002). Ego depletion and self-control failure: An energy model of the self's executive function. *Self and Identity, 1*, 129-136.

Beitel, G.A., Sharp, M.C., & Glauz, W.D. (2000). Probability of arrest while driving under the influence of alcohol. *Injury Prevention, 6*, 158-161.

Belknap, J. (1996). *The invisible woman: Gender, crime, and justice*. Belmont, CA: Wadsworth.

Bennett, W., DiIulio, J.J., & Walters, J. (1996). *Body count*. New York: Simon & Schuster.

Blau, P.M. (1977). *Inequality and heterogeneity: A primitive theory of social structure*. New York: Free Press.

Clarke, R.V. (1995). Situational crime prevention. *Crime and Justice: A Review of Research, 19*, 91-150.

Clarke, R.V. (1999). *Hot products: Understanding, anticipating and reducing demand for stolen goods*. Police Research Series, Paper 112. London: Home Office.

Clarke, R.V. & Felson, M. (1998). *Opportunity makes the thief: Practical theory for crime prevention*. Police Research Series, Paper 98. London: Home Office.

Cohen, L.E. & Felson, M. (1979). Social change and crime rate trends: A routine activity approach. *American Sociological Review, 44*, 588-608.

Cohen, L.E., Felson, M., & Land, K.C. (1980). Property crime rates in the United States: A macrodynamic analysis, 1947-1977. *American Journal of Sociology, 86*, 90-117.

Cornish, D.B. & Clarke, R.V. (2014). *The reasoning criminal: Rational choice perspectives on offending*. New Brunswick, NJ: Transaction.

Croson, R. & Sundali, J. (2005). The gambler's fallacy and the hot hand: Empirical data from casinos. *Journal of Risk and Uncertainty, 30*, 195-209.

Cullen, F.T. & Pratt, T.C. (2016). Toward a theory of police effects. *Criminology and Public Policy, 15*, 799-811.

Cullen, F.T., Pratt, T.C., & Turanovic, J.J. (2016). It's hopeless: Beyond zero-tolerance supervision. *Criminology and Public Policy, 15*, 1215-1227.

Daly, K. (1997). Different ways of conceptualizing sex/gender in feminist theory and their implications for criminology. *Theoretical Criminology, 1*, 25-51.

Daly, K. & Chesney-Lind, M. (1988). Feminism and criminology. *Justice Quarterly, 5*, 497-535.

DeKeseredy, W.S. (2015). New directions in feminist understandings of rural crime. *Journal of Rural Studies, 39*, 180-187.

Felson, M. (1987). Routine activities and crime prevention in the developing metropolis. *Criminology, 25*, 911-932.

Felson, M. & Boba, R.L. (2010). *Crime and everyday life*. Thousand Oaks, CA: Sage.

Felson, M. & Cohen, L.E. (1980). Human ecology and crime: A routine activity approach. *Human Ecology, 8*, 389-406.

Felson, R.B. (1996). Big people hit little people: Sex differences in physical power and interpersonal violence. *Criminology, 34*, 433-452.

Gottfredson, M.R. (2011). Sanctions, situations, and agency in control theories of crime. *European Journal of Criminology, 8*, 128-143.

Gottfredson, M.R. & Hirschi, T. (1990). *A general theory of crime*. Palo Alto, CA: Stanford University Press.

Hagger, M.S., Wood, C., Stiff, C., & Chatzisarantis, N.L.D. (2010). Ego depletion and the strength model of self-control: A meta-analysis. *Psychological Bulletin, 136*, 495–525.

Heimer, K,. & De Coster, S. (1999). The gendering of violent delinquency. *Criminology, 37*, 277–318.

Hensley, C., Tewksbury, R., & Castle, T. (2003). Characteristics of prison sexual assault targets in male Oklahoma correctional facilities. *Journal of Interpersonal Violence, 18*, 595–606.

Hindelang, M.J., Gottfredson, M.R., & Garofalo, J. (1978). *Victims of personal crime: An empirical foundation for a theory of personal victimization*. Cambridge, MA: Ballinger.

Hirschfield, A., Newton, A., & Rogerson, M. (2010). Linking burglary and target hardening at the property level: New insights into victimization and burglary protection. *Criminal Justice Policy Review, 21*, 319–337.

Hirschi, T. (1969). *Causes of delinquency*. Berkeley, CA: University of California Press.

Hirschi, T. & Hindelang, M.J. (1977). Intelligence and delinquency: A revisionist review. *American Sociological Review, 42*, 571–587.

Hood-Williams, J. (2001). Gender, masculinities, and crime: From structures to psyches. *Theoretical Criminology, 5*, 37–60.

Jacobs, B.A. & Cherbonneau, M. (2017). Nerve management and crime accomplishment. *Journal of Research in Crime and Delinquency, 54*, 617–638.

Jacques, S. (2010). The necessary conditions for retaliation: Toward a theory of non-violent and violent forms in drug markets. *Justice Quarterly, 27*, 186–205.

Jacques, S. & Reynald, D.M. (2012). The offenders' perspective on prevention: Guarding against victimization and law enforcement. *Journal of Research in Crime and Delinquency, 49*, 269–294.

Jenness, V., Maxson, C.L., Sumner, J.M., & Matsuda, K.N. (2010). Accomplishing the difficult but not impossible: Collecting self-report data on inmate-on-inmate sexual assault in prison. *Criminal Justice Policy Review, 21*, 3–30.

Johnson, H. (2005). *Experiences of crime in two selected migrant communities*. Canberra: Australian Institute of Criminology.

Kahneman, D. & Tversky, A. (2000). *Choices, values, and frames*. Cambridge: Cambridge University Press.

Kennedy, L.W. & Forde, D.R. (1990). Routine activities and crime: An analysis of victimization in Canada. *Criminology, 28*, 137–152.

Kleck, G. & Barnes, J.C. (2013). Deterrence and macro-level perceptions of punishment risks: Is there a "collective wisdom"? *Crime and Delinquency, 59*, 1006–1035.

Laub, J.H. (2004). The life course of criminology in the United States: The American Society of Criminology 2003 Presidential Address. *Criminology, 42*, 1–26.

Laub, J.H. & Sampson, R.J. (1991). The Sutherland–Glueck debate: On the sociology of criminological knowledge. *American Journal of Sociology, 96*, 1402–1440.

Lilly, J.R., Cullen, F.T., & Ball, R.A. (2010). *Criminological theory: Context and consequences* (5th edition). Thousand Oaks, CA: Sage.

Lipsey, M.W. & Wilson, D.B. (1993). The efficacy of psychological, educational, and behavioral treatment: Confirmation from meta-analysis. *American Psychologist, 48*, 1181–1209.

Loughran, T.A., Paternoster, R., Chaflin, A., & Wilson, T. (2016). Can rational choice be considered a general theory of crime? Evidence from individual-level panel data. *Criminology, 54*, 86–112.

Luckenbill, D.F. (1977). Criminal homicide as a situated transaction. *Social Problems, 25*, 176–186.

Matza, D. (1964). *Delinquency and drift*. New York: Wiley.

McGloin, J.M. & Thomas, K.J. (2016). Considering the elements that inform perceived peer deviance. *Journal of Research in Crime and Delinquency, 53*, 597–627.

Merton, R.K. (1938). Social structure and anomie. *American Sociological Review, 3,* 672-682.

Merton, R.K. (1968). *Social theory and social structure.* New York: The Free Press.

Messerschmidt, J.W. (1993). *Masculinities and crime: Critique and reconceptualization of theory.* Lanham, MD: Rowman & Littlefield.

Nagin, D.S. (2007). Moving choice to center stage in criminological research and theory: The American Society of Criminology 2006 Sutherland Address. *Criminology, 45,* 259-272.

Nee, C. & Taylor, M. (2000). Examining burglars' target selection: Interview, experiment or ethnomethodology? *Psychology, Crime and Law, 6,* 45-59.

Nickerson, R.S. (1998). Confirmation bias: A ubiquitous phenomenon in many guises. *Review of General Psychology, 2,* 175-220.

Ogle, M.R. & Turanovic, J.J. (2016). Is getting tough with low-risk kids a good idea? The effect of failure to appear detention stays on juvenile recidivism. *Criminal Justice Policy Review.* doi: 10.1177/0887403416682299.

Paternoster, R. (1987). The deterrent effect of the perceived certainty and severity of punishment: A review of the evidence and issues. *Justice Quarterly, 4,* 173-217.

Pinker, S. (2002). *The blank slate: The modern denial of human nature.* New York: Penguin.

Piquero, A.R., Farrington, D.P., & Blumstein, A. (2003). The criminal career paradigm. *Crime and Justice: A Review of Research, 30,* 359-506.

Pratt, T.C. (2008). Rational choice theory, crime control policy, and criminological relevance. *Criminology and Public Policy, 7,* 43-52.

Pratt, T.C. (2016). A self-control/life-course theory of criminal behavior. *European Journal of Criminology, 13,* 129-146.

Pratt, T.C. (2017). Delinquency and drift: Challenging criminology then and now. In Blomberg, T.G., Cullen, F.T., Carlsson, C., & Jonson, S.L (Eds.), *Delinquency and drift revisited: The criminology of David Matza and beyond* (pp.13-31). New Brunswick, NJ: Transaction.

Pratt, T.C. (2019). *Addicted to incarceration: Corrections policy and the politics of misinformation in the United States* (2nd edition). Thousand Oaks, CA: Sage.

Pratt, T.C. & Cullen, F.T. (2000). The empirical status of Gottfredson and Hirschi's general theory of crime: A meta-analysis. *Criminology, 38,* 931-964.

Pratt, T.C. & Cullen, F.T. (2005). Assessing macro-level predictors and theories of crime: A meta-analysis. *Crime and Justice: A Review of Research, 32,* 373-450.

Pratt, T.C. & Turanovic, J.J. (2016). Lifestyle and routine activity theories revisited: The importance of "risk" to the study of victimization. *Victims and Offenders, 11,* 335-354.

Pratt, T.C. & Turanovic, J.J. (2018). Celerity and deterrence. In Nagin, D.S., Cullen, F.T., & Jonson, C.L. (Eds.), *Deterrence, choice, and crime: Contemporary perspectives* (pp.187-209). New Brunswick, NJ: Transaction.

Pratt, T.C., Barnes, J.C., Cullen, F.T., & Turanovic, J.J. (2016). "I suck at everything": Crime, arrest, and the generality of failure. *Deviant Behavior, 37,* 837-851.

Pratt, T.C., Cullen, F.T., Blevins, K.R., Daigle, L.E., & Madensen, T.D. (2006). The empirical status of deterrence theory: A meta-analysis. In Cullen, F.T., Wright, J.P., & Blevins, K.R. (Eds.), *Taking stock: The status of criminological theory* (pp.367-396). New Brunswick, NJ: Transaction.

Reynald, D.M. (2015). Environmental design and crime events. *Journal of Contemporary Criminal Justice, 31,* 71-89.

Simon, H.A. (1997). *Administrative behavior* (4th edition). New York: The Free Press.

Simon, R.J. (1975). *Women and crime.* Lexington, MA: Lexington Books.

Simpson, S.S. (1989). Feminist theory, crime, and justice. *Criminology, 27,* 605-631.

St. John, P.K.B. (2007). *Pockets of crime: Broken windows, collective efficacy, and the criminal point of view.* Chicago, IL: University of Chicago Press.

Struckman-Johnson D., Struckman-Johnson, C., Kruse, J.D., Gross, P.M., & Sumners, B.J. (2013). A pre-PREA survey of inmate and correctional staff opinions on how to prevent prison sexual assault. *The Prison Journal, 93,* 429-452.

Thomas, K.J.& McGloin, J. M. (2013). A dual-systems approach for understanding differential susceptibility to processes of peer influence. *Criminology*, *51*, 435–474.

Turanovic, J.J.& Young, J.T.N. (2016). Violent offending and victimization in adolescence: Social network mechanisms and homophily. *Criminology*, *54*, 487–519.

Wittebrood, K.& Nieuwbeerta, P. (2000). Criminal victimization during one's life course: The effects of previous victimization and patterns of routine activities. *Journal of Research in Crime and Delinquency, 37,* 91–122.

Wolfgang, M.E. (1958). *Patterns of criminal homicide*. Oxford: Oxford University Press.

Wright, R. & Decker, S.H. (1994). *Burglars on the job: Streetlife and residential break-ins*. Boston, MA: Northeastern University Press.

Wright, R. & Decker, S.H. (1997). *Armed robbers in action: Stickups and street culture*. Boston, MA: Northeastern University Press.

5 Situations and context

Beginning with his campaign for the 2016 Presidential election, Donald J. Trump made it a habit to pick on Chicago. Part of his focus on Chicago was undoubtedly due to it being President Obama's hometown, and Trump was dead-set on defining himself as Obama's opposite in every way possible. But in any event, it became a campaign rallying cry—one that has extended into his term as President and Twitter enthusiast—to call attention to Chicago's "epidemic" problem with violence and "carnage" (McLaughlin& Chiacu, 2017). He was fond of saying that crime in Chicago was a "horror show" that was "out of control."

But why, according to Trump and to those in his Administration, was violence so "out of control?" Part of the problem, according to Attorney General Jeff Sessions, is that Chicago is a "sanctuary city,"one that is soft on illegal immigration, and the Trump Administration has long held that unchecked immigration sets the stage for an epidemic of violence (Tanfani, 2017). Another source of the problem has to do with lax gun laws, particularly with respect to weapons trafficking, with assault weapons and other firearms coming into Chicago from out of state (Berman & Lowery, 2017). This is, of course, an ironic position for the Trump Administration to hold, since they have also framed "mass shooting" events as having little or nothing to do with guns, but rather that such events are the consequence of a "morality problem" (Gorner, 2017).

Either way, the solution to the violence problem in Chicago is clear according to the Trump Administration: crack down on illegal immigration and stiffen up penalties for violations of gun laws (Hing, 2017). Trump has even suggested deploying federal troops into Chicago to address the problem (Samuelson, 2017). If that does not work, he has repeatedly made vague statements about a "rough cookie" police officer—a motorcycle cop, no less—who claims that he could rid the city of crime in "a couple of days" if he was just given the legal latitude to do what political leaders are too skittish to allow him to do (what exactly this would entail is never stated; see Janssen, 2017).

This kind of chest beating has always resonated well with a certain bloc of the American voting public (Pratt, 2019). Indeed, getting "tough on crime" is in America's political DNA (Ogle & Turanovic, 2016). After all, the United States gave the world Dirty Harry, all things Chuck Norris, and the world's highest incarceration rate. Getting tough is therefore as American as baseball—a sport that lent its language of "three strikes and you're out" to lifetime sentences in prison. But what Trump had to say is dangerously misleading in two important ways, the first of which is that it misrepresents the level of lethal violence Chicago has experienced over time. To be sure, Trump's claim that the murder rate in Chicago is the highest it has been in 47 years—a claim he has repeated often to whoever would listen—is actually patently false. Violent crimes, including murder, are still at historic lows in Chicago (and elsewhere) following the precipitous crime drop of the 1990s (McCray, 2017). So the bottom line is that crime and violence are not "out of control" in Chicago—at least not by historic standards. And in a time when "alternative facts" are allowed to flourish, it is important to remember that data still matter and the data clearly show that Trump has badly missed the mark on this one.

Nevertheless, the second misleading comment made by Trump may actually be even more consequential. Specifically, Trump's understanding of both the problem of crime and its potential solution grossly mischaracterizes the nature of the violence that occurs in Chicago by treating it as a simple problem in need of more law and order. It assumes that structural conditions like concentrated disadvantage, chronic unemployment, and racial inequality are irrelevant when it comes to crime, and it assumes that personal characteristics like self-control, antisocial attitudes, and deviant peer influences can all be scrubbed away as potential sources of crime and victimization. Instead, the crime problem—according to Trump and his disciples, who seem to have a nostalgic fondness for explanations of crime that were popular in the 1980s—is simply a function of lenient penalties for criminal behavior and the absence of a huge wall to keep out murderers, rapists, and other "bad hombres."

But the reality of violence is far more complex than that. The reality for Chicago, for example, was captured quite vividly in the documentary film *The Interrupters*. Focused on residents living in the most blighted communities in Chicago, the film follows a group of former criminal and gang members whose job it is to recognize potentially volatile situations and to interrupt them before violence can occur. One scene was particularly revealing when a young man said he had a gun and was threatening to shoot someone. Residents on the street were captured saying "the cops pulled up and they left," because "they're scared. They're scared of our community." So, rather than rely on the criminal justice system, a few other residents stepped in and knocked a few of the young man's teeth out. Immediately following that, the youth's two sisters came onto the scene and there was a shared understanding that the boy would have to retaliate with violence to "defend his honor." It was expected of him; expected by his friends and by his family. Indeed, these structural conditions—those where few legitimate economic opportunities exist and where there is a deep distrust of law enforcement—set the stage for cultural pressures to meet violence with violence.

But one of the "violence interrupters"—Ameena, a former gang member who herself now counsels youths in violent Chicago neighborhoods—stepped in. She physically grabbed the young man, tossed him into the back seat of her car, and drove around with him long enough talk to him about the consequences of what he might choose to do next, to give him time to cool down, and to let the situation go. She was even able to get him to laugh about it later—humor being a key strategy for avoiding losing face when walking away from a potentially violent situation (Dickinson & Wright, 2017). But what was so revealing was how much pressure was placed upon the young man to escalate things. It also shows how much effort it takes to successfully intervene in violent situations and, even when successful, it may only be successful "for now"—perhaps the inevitable has merely been delayed. Even more revealing is that situations like that depicted above happen all the time, and they will continue to occur whether federal prosecutors are threatening longer sentences or whether a huge wall exists between the United States and Mexico.

What the above example shows is the wide array of complex factors that often come together for a victimization event to occur. These include the choices victims make and the ways in which they evaluate information at hand and weigh the consequences of various behavioral alternatives; how offenders go through the exact same set of decision processes; how the structure of the environment sets the stage for the event itself; how cultural pressures and expectations push all parties toward a violent conflict; and finally, how ultimately the role of victim and offender is not preordained—it is easy to see how the final outcome could have gone either way for everyone had the interrupter not done the interrupting. In short, a lot of things have to happen in order for victims and offenders to converge in time and space, and the result of that convergence is often dictated by factors specific to the situation itself.

So, with that in mind, in bringing together the material presented in Chapters 3 and 4, this chapter will highlight how the behavior of both victims and offenders is shaped and conditioned by social context. Victimization events do not occur in a social or situational vacuum. They are instead influenced in important ways by context—both within the immediate situation that the crime/victimization event is taking place, and also the broader social context that provides the structural conditions and cultural scripts that guide expectations about how people are supposed to interact with one another (Wilson, 2009).

This is what this chapter addresses. And again, as with the previous chapters in Part II, we discuss both the theoretical perspectives and empirical research that have been set forth to explain the contextual patterns which surround victimization events. The purpose is to give readers an appreciation for how interactions between victims and offenders are often embedded in a larger set of circumstances—conditions of which victims and offenders may or may not even be fully aware themselves—that shape victimization events.

Risky routines and victimization revisited

In Chapter 3 we discussed how two different theoretical perspectives—lifestyle and routine activity theories—view the role that different kinds of behavioral routines play in elevating a person's odds of being victimized. Both perspectives are enormously popular (Reyns, Henson, & Fisher, 2016), so much so that the two have been treated as virtually one and the same in recent years (Schreck, Stewart, & Fisher, 2006; Wilcox et al., 2014). But also recall that we did not think that this theoretical merger was necessarily a good thing (Pratt & Turanovic, 2016) because the two theoretical traditions have very different ideas about what kinds of behavioral routines can result in victimization.

To be sure, routine activity theory holds that broad macro-structural changes following World War II resulted in greater social, economic, and geographic mobility in the United States (Cohen & Felson, 1979). This mobility happened at the same time that technological advances resulted in all kinds of gadgets and goods coming into the market, which meant that more people had more money to buy things (cars, televisions, credit cards) that could then be stolen (Cohen, Felson, & Land, 1980). Economic changes also meant that more women were entering the workforce, which took them out of the home (leaving houses unguarded for potential burglars) and into public spaces where they would be exposed to potential offenders (Felson, 1987). The bottom line is that victimization rates are being driven in large part by the legitimate, everyday routines in which people engage.

This idea sounds good at first blush, but on closer inspection it actually makes little sense. Yes, it is possible to be victimized when shopping for groceries, or while watching a movie at a theater, or while driving to work. But the reality is that there are other behaviors that are much more likely to result in a victimization event, and that is where lifestyle theory (Hindelang, Gottfredson, & Garofalo, 1978) comes in. According to this perspective, it is not the mundane, legal, and boring behavioral routines that elevate people's odds of being victimized, but is instead the more "high-risk" behaviors—such as getting drunk in public, hanging out with deviant friends, and committing crimes against other persons—that are more likely to place people in high-risk locations with other high-risk people (Pratt & Turanovic, 2016). But high-risk people (potential offenders) and high-risk (i.e., criminogenic) places are not randomly distributed in time and space (Weisburd, Groff, & Yang, 2012). What we need to understand, then, are the structural conditions that are most likely to lead to offenders and victims coming together and why those conditions matter.

Structural context and victimization

One of the most powerful predictors of what a community looks like and how residents experience daily life is tied to its level of structural disadvantage (Sampson, 2012). Communities characterized by structural disadvantage—particularly those in urban environments—are more likely to be isolated geographically and impoverished economically (Johnson & Kane, 2018), to be plagued by chronic joblessness and racial/ethnic segregation (Riley, 2018), where high rates of family disruption can be found, and where a transient and unstable population of residents is the norm (Riley, Hawkley, & Cagney, 2016).

Communities that face these levels of social and economic hardship also tend to experience elevated rates of a wide array of social problems. For example, those who reside in impoverished communities are more likely to experience adverse health problems such as heart disease, diabetes, cancer, and even suicide (Kubrin, Wadsworth, & DiPietro, 2006). They are also more likely to be exposed to pollution and other toxic environmental elements like lead and undrinkable water (Winter & Sampson, 2017). Rates of drug and alcohol abuse—and the deaths associated with them—are also higher (Fagan, Wright, & Pinchevsky, 2015). In addition, social and political institutions are weakened in such communities—institutions like schools, health care organizations, and law enforcement agencies—and community residents rarely possess enough collective political capital to strengthen them in a meaningful way (Vargas, 2016).

It should come as no surprise, then, that structural disadvantage is also one of the most powerful predictors of community-level crime rates (Pratt & Cullen, 2005). The reasons *why* structural disadvantage is so closely linked to crime rates has long been the source of intense theoretical debate. One early explanation—uniquely American in its flavor—comes from the social disorganization theoretical tradition (Shaw & McKay, 1942). This perspective argues that people who live in communities characterized by economic deprivation (and other problems like residential mobility and racial/ethnic heterogeneity) have a harder time exercising control over other community members—particularly young people (Sampson & Groves, 1989). They also have a harder time combating the spread of antisocial attitudes/values—those, for example, that reject traditional middle-class moral precepts of working hard and playing by the rules to get ahead in life in favor of values that support criminal behavior. The result is a breakdown in informal social control and the intergenerational transmission of criminal/delinquent attitudes—both of which tend to result in higher rates of crime and delinquency in the community (Sampson, Raudenbush, & Earls, 1997).

Another explanation for why structural disadvantage/economic deprivation and crime rates are so closely tied together—an explanation that is also uniquely American—comes from the strain/anomie theoretical tradition (Merton, 1938). This perspective argues that it is not the rejection of middle-class values that ultimately causes crime, but rather the rigid adherence to them. In particular, American culture universally holds up economic success as a core value, but there are structural barriers for those in disadvantaged communities (e.g., the absence of good jobs and quality education institutions) that make attaining economic success more difficult for some. And since American culture places a greater value on achieving the goal of economic affluence than on playing fair to get there, the mechanisms that keep people's bad behavior in check are weakened (Baumer & Gustafson, 2007).

Other explanations have followed, and our understanding of why disadvantaged communities experience a disproportionate share of crime and victimization has been enhanced substantially by contributions of scholars from European nations and other Western countries (Braithwaite, 1989; Young, 1999). And whether the explanation is targeted at the larger level of analysis (e.g., nation-level characteristics like inequality; see Savolainen, 2000) or smaller ones (e.g., individuals' levels of self-control and self-restraint; see Wikstrom & Loeber, 2000), a common thread running through nearly all of them is that structural disadvantage compromises a wide variety of control mechanisms. The bottom line, therefore, is that communities characterized by structural disadvantage tend to contain a greater proportion of people who are willing to victimize others. With that in mind, it is worth taking a closer look at how structural context—and the cultural responses to it—influence victimization events.

Economic deprivation and structural constraints

As stated above, rates of virtually all forms of victimization are higher in economically disadvantaged neighborhoods. This is due in no small part to the lifestyle patterns and routine activities in which community residents take part (Cohen & Felson, 1979). Variations in the lifestyles and routine activities in which people engage, in turn, carry different levels of risk for whether they will be putting themselves in particular places at particular times, and of coming into contact with particular people (Hindelang et al., 1978). And due to economic strains, subcultural norms that may encourage violence, and the weakening of formal and informal social controls, residents of disadvantaged communities will also face greater pressures to engage in certain lifestyles that are "risky," in that they expose individuals to situations conducive to crime and violence (Sampson et al., 1997).

These risky lifestyles come in many different forms, but the ones most closely linked to victimization are those that involve crime, violence, and substance use (Pratt & Turanovic, 2016). For example, people who engage in crime may put themselves at risk for retaliation from former victims (Jacobs & Wright, 2006). These same people may also be more likely to come into contact with violent persons while they commit offenses or use drugs and alcohol during high-risk times (e.g., after dark) and in high-risk settings (e.g., in the absence of capable guardianship). It is therefore not surprising that a large body of studies has found various forms of crime and delinquency to be some of the strongest cor-relates of victimization (Turanovic, Reisig, & Pratt, 2015). These risky lifestyles have also been closely linked to repeat victimization. For instance, Schreck, Stewart, and Fisher (2006) found that youth who engaged in delinquency (e.g., violent crime, property crime, and drug use) after being victimized were more likely to be victimized again.

It makes sense, then, that victims of violence who make *changes* to their risky lifestyles can reduce their likelihood of being victimized again in the future—what Hindelang et al. (1978: 129) referred to as the "once bitten, twice shy" hypothesis. Although the full body of research is somewhat mixed with respect to this proposition, Turanovic and Pratt (2014) found that adolescents who failed to make changes to their risky lifestyles after being victimized (e.g., by continuing to engage in risky socializing, substance use, violent offending, and hanging out with violent friends) were those most likely to experience repeat victimization.

The problem, however, is that not all victims of violence are able to make meaningful changes to their risky lifestyles—especially to their involvement in antisocial behavior. And for those who reside in conditions of economic depriva-tion, avoiding crime and victimization is made more difficult by the presence of certain "structural constraints." Hindelang et al. (1978) were among the first to put forth the idea of structural constraints in relation to personal victimization. They theorized that lifestyle patterns manifest as individual- and group-level *adaptations* to role expectations and to various aspects of the social structure. People learn attitudes and behaviors in response to their social environment and, once learned, they are incorporated into their routine activities. To be sure, Hindelang et al. (1978: 242) stated the following with respect to structural constraints:

> Structural constraints originating from [the social structure] can be defined as limitations on behavioral options that result from the particular arrangements existing within various institutional orders, such as the economic, familial, educational, and legal orders. For example, economic factors impose stringent limitations on the range of choices that individuals have with respect to such fundamentals as area of residence, nature of leisure activities, mode of transportation, and access to educational opportunities.

Accordingly, within economically deprived communities, there are structural constraints that shape daily life in important ways. These constraints can encourage criminal attitudes and beliefs, and they can limit the extent to which individuals are able to avoid coming into contact with risky people and risky settings (Bjarnson, Siguardardottir, & Thorlindsson, 1999). For victims of crime, structural constraints can also shape responses to victimization by influencing the degree to which victims are able (or even willing) to adopt the kinds of protective behaviors that might reduce their exposure to potential offenders. And due to the nature of these structural constraints, it is likely that they restrict the ability of victims to alter their deviant lifestyles in ways that reduce the risk of repeat victimization.

More specifically, structural constraints in disadvantaged communities can limit victims' ability to make changes to their risky lifestyles in that victims who reside in such contexts often do not have the power to change where they live, or where they go to school–factors that alone may be the source of victimization risk for some people (Carson, Esbensen, & Taylor, 2013). Furthermore, structural constraints upon economic opportunities, coupled with poor access to public transportation, may limit both the legitimate and illegal avenues of employment available to people in the area (Bellair & Kowalski, 2011). Dealing drugs, stealing things, and selling stolen property, for example, may be some of the most accessible ways to generate income in economically deprived neighborhoods (Rose & Clear, 1998). Thus, choices among behavioral alternatives are constrained by their availability.

Cultural responses to structural disadvantage

For those who reside in economically deprived communities, there is a cultural component to these structural constraints as well. In Elijah Anderson's (1999) research in impoverished neighborhoods in Philadelphia, for example, he found that citizens in such communities–and particularly young people–have little in the way of access to what we might think of as "traditional" indicators of social status. To be sure, he recognizes that certain community members live in a social context in which:

> family-sustaining jobs have become ever more scarce, public assistance has increasingly disappeared, racial discrimination is a fact of daily life, wider institutions have less legitimacy, legal codes are often ignored or not trusted, and frustration has been powerfully building for many residents.
>
> (Anderson, 1999: 11)

Thus, as an adaptation to these structural conditions, interpersonal respect becomes a primary source of social currency. A value system then emerges—one that Anderson referred to as the "code of the street"—where personal slights and even minor forms of disrespect are considered serious offenses. Accordingly, in places where a code of the street value system prevails, there are intense social pressures upon community residents to behave in certain ways. This includes acting tough and aggressively during interpersonal interactions, whether the substance of that interaction seems to call for it or not. It involves getting even with someone who you think has wronged you in order to avoid any loss of respect, and even calling on others to join you in retaliating against those who you think "have it coming" (Lindegaard, Miller, & Reynald, 2013). Residents will engage in these behaviors because they perceive that they do not have much choice in the matter, and that behaving in such a way will be self-protective (Turanovic, Pratt, & Piquero, 2018). Acting tough is thus intended to serve as a kind of "shield" or armor for when residents enter public spaces so that others will not view them as an easy target.

And yet there is a paradox here. People adopt these attitudes and behaviors in an effort to avoid being taken advantage of/victimized, yet doing so actually increases their risk of victimization. Stewart, Schreck, and Simons (2006), for example, found in their study of African-American adolescents that those kids who harbored attitudes consistent with the code of the street—attitudes that condone violence and retaliation—were more likely to be victims of violence themselves. This relationship is even exacerbated by neighborhood context, where the link between behaving aggressively/violently and being victimized is actually stronger among those who live in neighborhoods where the code of the street is more prominent (Berg et al., 2012). It is clear, therefore, that the cultural emphasis on the code of the street contributes significantly to victimization.

It is important to note that not everyone has been a fan of this "cultural" element surrounding the relationship between economic deprivation and crime/victimization. To be sure, while cultural and/or subcultural perspectives have long been popular in criminology (Lilly, Cullen, & Ball, 2014), they have also been the target of those skeptical of the role culture plays in shaping criminal events (Hirschi, 1969; Kornhauser, 1978). One of the most articulate critiques of cultural explanations of community dynamics has come from various work conducted by William Julius Wilson. Wilson has long argued that we often attribute problems in urban environments—problems such as the possession and transmission of problematic attitudes about work, education, and crime (including attitudes like the code of the street)—to the things we can see most easily; things like race and culture (Wilson, 1978). But the real culprits according to Wilson are structural and socioeconomic. To be sure, problems like broad economic changes that result in chronic joblessness among inner-city residents are hard to see clearly, and so they are often masked by the more visible urban troubles associated with street codes and violence among youth (Wilson, 1987, 1996).

Yet, even though Wilson's core argument that cultural explanations have been overplayed remains in place, even he has recently recognized the notion that urban culture is also important (Wilson, 2009), and one cultural element that has drawn increasing attention in recent years is the notion of "street efficacy." Unlike the code of the street—a code that emphasizes engaging in aggression and violence as a "strike-first" strategy for self-protection—street efficacy refers to a person's "ability to avoid violent confrontations and to be safe in one's neighborhood" (Sharkey, 2006: 826). Sharkey (2006) goes on to note that street efficacy "also involves a belief in one's own ability to manage such public interactions while avoiding violence" (p. 829). Recent work by Gibson, Fagan, and Antle (2014) using data from the Project on Human Development in Chicago Neighborhoods found that youth who scored higher on measures of street efficacy were less likely to be victims of violence, and that the effect of street efficacy was stronger among youths who lived in disadvantaged neighborhoods. So it is therefore safe to say that although street efficacy is a relatively new development in the victimization literature, it is an idea that looks like a promising explanation of why some people can avoid violence and others seem to fall victim to it, even in structural contexts where rates of victimization are higher overall.

Given all of the discussion above, the bottom line here is a relatively simple one: when it comes to victimization, context matters. Structural conditions in communities tend to shape social interactions in important ways; they have a way of constraining the kinds of behavioral alternatives to which people have access (or at least perceive that they have access to), and they can create pressure among community residents to buy into certain kinds of problematic cultural responses that may result in an elevated risk of victimization. Structural context is therefore a key factor that sets the stage for interactions—particularly violent ones—between potential offenders and victims.

Gaps and challenges

It is important to note that the structural conditions we have discussed in this chapter—those that are tied to what we have called "structural constraints"—will be more strongly linked to certain forms of victimization than others. In particular, these kinds of contextual conditions are more likely to influence victimization events that occur (or at least begin) in public spaces, where victim and offender have the opportunity to look each other in the eye; in short, what we typically think of as "personal" victimization (Turanovic, Pratt, & Piquero, 2018).

Accordingly, we still have little understanding of the contextual conditions that might influence other "non-contact" forms of victimization like computer hacking, fraud, or identity theft. This is not to say that we know nothing at all about these forms of victimization—to be sure, we will cover in detail the nature of "cybervictimization" in Chapter 11. It is just that the role structural conditions play in these forms of victimization may be quite different, especially given that non-contact forms of victimization (e.g., being the victim of fraud or of a computer phishing scam) tend to require rather more in terms of victim participation (or even cooperation; see Pratt et al., 2014) than the forms of personal victimization we have discussed in this chapter.

It is also important to note that there are other kinds of structural and contextual conditions that can constrain people's freedom to choose from among behavioral alternatives that may also influence their likelihood of victimization. For example, we do not yet have a firm understanding of how constraints imposed by age might operate to put someone at risk of being victimized. Those who are very young and very old are at a greater risk of certain kinds of victimization (e.g., child abuse/neglect and elder abuse), and yet we still know very little about the contextual conditions that surround these forms of victimization (Reisig, Holtfreter, & Turanovic, 2018; Wright et al., 2019). Similarly, there are constraints imposed by institutional context (e.g., schools and even prisons/jails (a subject we address in Chapter 10)) that limit people's choices concerning where they can go and how they can behave. In these environments, it is possible that forms of vulnerability (e.g., physical stature, disabilities, sexual orientation) may be more important than the behaviors we may think of as more traditionally "risky" when it comes to increasing the odds of being victimized (see, e.g., Kulig et al., 2017).

Yet, despite these gaps and challenges in our knowledge base, we should not forget the role of context in any of these forms of victimization (family context, school context, online context). Indeed, while the contextual conditions that surround things like identity theft or child abuse or assault in prison may be unique to that form of victimization, they are also no less important. Once again we are reminded that victimization does not occur in a vacuum. And context, as Sampson (2011: 83) says, "is everything."

Key readings

Anderson, E. (1999). *Code of the street: Decency, violence, and the moral life of the inner city*. New York: W.W. Norton.

Sharkey, P. (2006). Navigating dangerous streets: The sources and consequences of street efficacy. *American Sociological Review, 71*, 826–846.

Stewart. E.A., Schreck, C.J., & Simons, R.L. (2006). I ain't gonna let no one disrespect me: Does the code of the street reduce or increase violent victimization among African American adolescents? *Journal of Research in Crime and Delinquency, 43*, 427–458.

Turanovic, J.J., Pratt, T.C., & Piquero, A.R. (2018). Structural constraints, risky lifestyles, and repeat victimization. *Journal of Quantitative Criminology, 34*, 251–274.

Wilson, W.J. (2009). *More than just race: Being black and poor in the inner city*. New York: W.W. Norton.

Discussion questions

1. How did routine activity theory link victimization to the normal, everyday, mundane activities in which people engage?
2. How did Hindelang et al.'s (1978) lifestyle theory differ from the routine activity perspective with respect to what kinds of behaviors are most likely to put people at risk of victimization?
3. What are the key ways in which structural constraints—especially those imposed by economic deprivation—can lead to high rates of victimization in a community?
4. What are the forms of victimization that a "structural constraints" kind of argument may not be particularly well suited for explaining?

References

Anderson, E. (1999). *Code of the street: Decency, violence, and the moral life of the inner city*. New York: W.W. Norton.

Baumer, E.P. & Gustafson, R. (2007). Social organization and instrumental crime: Assessing the empirical validity of classic and contemporary anomie theories. *Criminology, 45*, 617–663.

Bellair, P.E. & Kowalski, B.R. (2011). Low-skill employment opportunity and Africa American-White difference in recidivism. *Journal of Research in Crime and Delinquency, 48*, 176–208.

Berg, M.T., Stewart, E.A., Schreck, C.J., & Simons, R.L. (2012). The victim–offender overlap in context: Examining the role of neighborhood street culture. *Criminology, 50*, 359–390.

Berman, M. & Lowery, W. (2017). Chicago police, federal officials to announce gun violence "strike force" on eve of July 4th weekend. *Washington Post*, June 30.

Bjarnason, T., Sigurdardottir, T.J., & Thorlindsson, T. (1999). Human agency, capable guardians, and structural constraints: A lifestyle approach to the study of violent victimization. *Journal of Youth and Adolescence, 28*, 105-119.

Braithwaite, J. (1989). *Crime, shame and reintegration*. Cambridge: Cambridge University Press.

Carson, D.C., Esbensen, F., & Taylor, T.J. (2013). A longitudinal analysis of the relationship between school victimization and student mobility. *Youth Violence and Juvenile Justice, 11*, 275-295.

Cohen, L.E. & Felson, M. (1979). Social change and crime rate trends: A routine activity approach. *American Sociological Review, 44*, 588-608.

Cohen, L.E., Felson, M., & Land, K.C. (1980). Property crime rates in the United States: A macrodynamic analysis, 1947-1977. *American Journal of Sociology, 86*, 90-117.

Dickinson, T. & Wright, R. (2017). The funny side of drug dealing: Risk, humor, and narrative identity. *Criminology, 55*, 691-720.

Fagan, A.A., Wright, E.M., & Pinchevsky, G.M. (2015). A multi-level analysis of the impact of neighborhood structural and social factors on adolescent substance use. *Drug and Alcohol Dependence, 153*, 180-186.

Felson, M. (1987). Routine activities and crime prevention in the developing metropolis. *Criminology, 25*, 911-932.

Gibson, C.L., Fagan, A.A., & Antle, K. (2014). Avoiding violent victimization among youths in urban neighborhoods: The importance of street efficacy. *American Journal of Public Health, 104*, e154-e161.

Gorner, J. (2017). As feds help Chicago on guns, Trump aide says city's crime more about "morality." *Chicago Tribune*, June 30.

Hindelang, M.J., Gottfredson, M.R., & Garofalo, J. (1978). *Victims of personal crime: An empirical foundation for a theory of personal victimization*. Cambridge, MA: Ballinger.

Hing, J. (2017). Despite "sanctuary city" status, Chicago police feed Trump's deportation machine. *Thenation.com*, October 12.

Hirschi, T. (1969). *Causes of delinquency*. Berkeley, CA: University of California Press.

Jacobs, B.A. & Wright, R. (2006). *Street justice: Retaliation in the criminal underworld*. New York: Cambridge University Press.

Janssen, K. (2017). Trump now says mystery cop claimed he could fix Chicago crime "immediately." *Chicago Tribune*, October 12.

Johnson, L.T. & Kane, R.J. (2018). Deserts of disadvantage: The diffuse effects of structural disadvantage on violence in urban communities. *Crime and Delinquency, 64*, 143-165.

Kornhauser, R.R. (1978). *Social sources of delinquency: An appraisal of analytic models*. Chicago, IL: University of Chicago Press.

Kubrin, C.E., Wadsworth, T., & DiPietro, S. (2006). Deindustrialization, disadvantage and suicide among young black males. *Social Forces, 84*, 1559-1597.

Kulig, T.C., Pratt, T.C., Cullen, F.T., Chouhy, C., & Unnever, J.D. (2017). Explaining bullying victimization: Assessing the generality of the low self-control/risky lifestyle model. *Victims and Offenders, 12*, 891-912.

Lilly, J.R., Cullen, F.T., & Ball, R.A. (2014). *Criminological theory: Context and consequences* (6th edition). Thousand Oaks, CA: Sage.

Lindegaard, M.R., Miller, J., & Reynald, D.M. (2013). Transitory mobility, cultural heterogeneity, and victimization risk among young men of color: Insights from an ethnographic study in Cape Town, South Africa. *Criminology, 51*, 967-1008.

McCray, R. (2017). How to stop the panic over violent crime. *Slate*, September 8.

McLaughlin, T. & Chiacu, D. (2017). Trump says he is sending federal help to fight Chicago crime. *Reuters*, June 30.

Merton, R.K. (1938). Social structure and anomie. *American Sociological Review, 3*, 672-682.

Ogle, M.R. & Turanovic, J.J. (2016). Is getting tough with low-risk kids a good idea? The effect of failure to appear detention stays on juvenile recidivism. *Criminal Justice Policy Review*, in press.

Pratt, T.C. (2019). *Addicted to incarceration: Corrections policy and the politics of misinformation in the United States* (2nd edition). Thousand Oaks, CA: Sage.

Pratt, T.C. & Cullen, F.T. (2005). Assessing macro-level predictors and theories of crime: A meta-analysis. *Crime and Justice: A Review of Research, 32*, 373–450.

Pratt, T.C. & Turanovic, J.J. (2016). Lifestyle and routine activity theories revisited: The importance of "risk" to the study of victimization. *Victims and Offenders, 11*, 335–354.

Pratt, T.C., Turanovic, J.J., Fox, K.A., & Wright, K.A. (2014). Self-control and victimization: A meta-analysis. *Criminology, 52*, 87–116.

Reisig, M.D., Holtfreter, K., & Turanovic, J.J. (2018). Criminal victimization, depressive symptoms, and behavioral avoidance coping in late adulthood: The conditioning role of strong familial ties. *Journal of Adult Development, 25*, 13–24.

Reyns, B.W., Henson, B., & Fisher, B.S. (2016). A gendered lifestyle-routine activity approach to explaining stalking victimization in Canada. *Journal of Interpersonal Violence, 31*, 1719–1743.

Riley, A.R. (2018). Neighborhood disadvantage, residential segregation, and beyond: Lessons for studying structural racism and health. *Journal of Racial and Ethnic Health Disparities, 5*, 357–365.

Riley, A.R., Hawkley, L.C., & Cagney, K.A. (2016). Racial differences in the effects of neighborhood disadvantage on residential mobility in later life. *The Journals of Gerontology: Series B, 71*, 1131–1140.

Rose, D.R. & Clear, T.R. (1998). Incarceration, social capital, and crime: Implications for social disorganization theory. *Criminology, 36*, 441–480.

Sampson, R.J. (2011). Communities and crime revisited. In Cullen, F.T., Jonson, C.L., Meyer, A.J., & Adler F. (Eds.), *The origins of American criminology–Advances in criminological Theory*, Vol.16. New Brunswick, NJ: Transaction.

Sampson, R.J. (2012). *Great American city: Chicago and the enduring neighborhood effect*. Chicago, IL: University of Chicago Press.

Sampson, R.J. & Groves, W.B. (1989). Community structure and crime: Testing social-disorganization theory. *American Journal of Sociology, 94*, 774–802.

Sampson, R.J., Raudenbush, S.W., & Earls, F. (1997). Neighborhoods and violent crime: A multilevel study of collective efficacy. *Science, 277*, 918–924.

Samuelson, K. (2017). President Trump says he is sending federal help to quell Chicago's violence problem. *Time*, June 30.

Savolainen, J. (2000). Inequality, welfare state, and homicide: Further support for the institutional anomie theory. *Criminology, 38*, 1021–1042.

Schreck, C.J., Stewart, E.A., & Fisher, B.S. (2006). Self-control, victimization, and their influence on risky lifestyles: A longitudinal analysis using panel data. *Journal of Quantitative Criminology, 22*, 319–340.

Sharkey, P. (2006). Navigating dangerous streets: The sources and consequences of street efficacy. *American Sociological Review, 71*, 826–846.

Shaw, C.R. & McKay, H.D. (1942). *Juvenile delinquency and urban areas*. Chicago, IL: University of Chicago Press.

Stewart. E.A., Schreck, C.J., & Simons, R.L. (2006). I ain't gonna let no one disrespect me: Does the code of the street reduce or increase violent victimization among African American adolescents? *Journal of Research in Crime and Delinquency, 43*, 427–458.

Tanfani, J. (2017). Atty. Gen. Sessions again attacks Chicago and other "sanctuary" cities. *Los Angeles Times*, August 16.

Turanovic, J.J. & Pratt, T.C. (2014). "Can't stop, won't stop": Self-control, risky lifestyles, and repeat victimization. *Journal of Quantitative Criminology, 30*, 29–56.

Turanovic, J.J., Pratt, T.C., & Piquero, A.R. (2018). Structural constraints, risky lifestyles, and repeat victimization. *Journal of Quantitative Criminology, 34*, 251–274.

Turanovic, J.J., Reisig, M.D., & Pratt, T.C. (2015). Risky lifestyles, low self-control, and violent victimization across gendered pathways to crime. *Journal of Quantitative Criminology, 31*, 183–206.

Vargas, R. (2016). *Wounded city: Violent turf wars in a Chicago barrio.* New York: Oxford University Press.

Weisburd, D., Groff, E.R., & Yang, S.M. (2012). *The criminology of place: Street segments and our understanding of the crime problem.* New York: Oxford University Press.

Wikstrom, P.O. & Loeber, R. (2000). Do disadvantaged neighborhoods cause well-adjusted children to become adolescent delinquents? A study of male juvenile serious offending, individual risk and protective factors, and neighborhood context. *Criminology, 38*, 1109–1142.

Wilcox, P., Sullivan, C.J., Jones, S., & Van Gelder, J. (2014). Personality and opportunity: An integrated approach to offending and victimization. *Criminal Justice and Behavior, 41*, 880–901.

Wilson, W.J. (1978). *The declining significance of race: Blacks and changing American institutions.* Chicago, IL: University of Chicago Press.

Wilson, W.J. (1987). *The truly disadvantaged: The inner city, the underclass, and public policy.* Chicago, IL: University of Chicago Press.

Wilson, W.J. (1996). *When work disappears: The world of the new urban poor.* New York: Alfred A. Knopf.

Wilson, W.J. (2009). *More than just race: Being black and poor in the inner city.* New York: W.W. Norton.

Winter, A.S. & Sampson, R.J. (2017). From lead exposure in early childhood to adolescent health: A Chicago birth cohort. *American Journal of Public Health, 107*, 1496–1501.

Wright, K.A., Turanovic, J.J., O'Neal, E.N., Morse, S.J., & Booth, E.T. (2019). The cycle of violence revisited: Childhood victimization, resilience, and future violence. *Journal of Interpersonal Violence, 34*, 1261–1286.

Young, J. (1999). *The exclusive society: Social exclusion, crime and difference in late modernity.* Thousand Oaks, CA: Sage.

PART III

THE CONSEQUENCES OF VICTIMIZATION

6 Personal consequences of victimization

One Saturday afternoon, a 53-year-old woman reluctantly made her way to a Walmart in semi-rural Nevada to get her eyeglasses replaced. She didn't want to go. It was the weekend, the store was likely to be crowded, and lately, large groups of people had become a source of high anxiety for her. But she really needed her glasses, and so she decided to forge through her discomfort and just get it done. She parked her car, entered the store, and immediately felt like it was a mistake to be there. The store seemed to be especially busy that day. Her chest tightened, her head started to throb, and the intruding sounds of people talking, babies crying, and shopping carts clanging seemed almost deafening. She almost cowered from the noise and covered her ears in distress, until she looked around and realized that all the other shoppers seemed happy and fine. Her stomach stared to churn.

Fighting off waves of panic and nausea, she managed to move through the store and navigate her way to the optical department. It too was crowded, and every clerk was busy with another customer. She started to get hot and sweaty, and to feel a sense of agitation rise up to her throat. The walls and ceiling seemed to be closing in on her. She considered leaving, but a clerk spotted her and let her know that someone would be assisting her in a moment. She stepped to the side and tried to take some deep breaths to relax. Some time passed, though, and no clerk assisted her. In fact, it appeared that newer customers were being helped before her. Confused and worried, the woman asked the clerk whether she had lost her place in line. The clerk glared in her direction and gave her an annoyed response, telling her again—somewhat aggressively—that someone would be assisting her in a moment. The woman felt threatened and misunderstood by the clerk's tone of voice. Her cheeks started to burn. She tried to maintain her composure.

Finally, the clerk approached the woman, asking how to assist her. The woman did her best to explain calmly that she was picking up a pair of replacement glasses, and that she had been told over the phone that the glasses would be provided free of charge. The clerk, visibly irritated, told the woman that replacement glasses are *not* free, and *nobody* would have *ever* said that. The clerk was not going to turn over the glasses without payment. The woman's heart started pounding. She felt unsteady on her feet, her arms and legs visibly trembling. She looked at the clerk's scowling face and thought, "Why am I being treated unfairly?" "I'm being called a liar!" "Why is the clerk being so mean to me?" "Why am I being blamed for something that isn't my fault?" "I'm not going to put up with this!" Unable to control herself, the woman lashed out at the clerk—yelling and demanding the glasses. She was making a scene, and people were staring.

The clerk disappeared into the back of the store to consult with other employees. A few minutes passed, which seemed like an eternity. The woman tried to calm herself down but it wasn't working very well—her breaths were sharp and shallow, her fists and jaw were clenched tight, and her body was shaking. But finally, the clerk emerged with the woman's glasses in hand. They were going to be provided free of charge as originally promised. The woman almost began to breathe a sigh of relief and feel the tension in her body fade away, until the clerk leaned into the woman and sneered, "I hope you know we're doing you a *big* favor here."

That was it. After that snarky comment, the woman went nuts. She doesn't remember much of what happened next, but she cussed out the clerk. Badly. Horrified at what was happening, a nearby female customer approached the cursing woman and yelled at her to *shut up*. Unable to stop herself, the woman turned her rage onto this customer and screamed nearly every curse word imaginable at her. A male customer tried to intervene by forcefully shoving the woman away and threatening that she back down, towering over her and pointing a finger in her face—actions that only served to escalate the situation. The woman began spewing even more profanities than before, this time at the male customer. People in the optical department started calling for security, and a crowd of onlookers began to form. The woman could not regain control of herself. She started to feel as though she was in a circus funhouse looking at dozens of mocking faces in a distortion mirror. She stared at the twisted, yelling faces of the clerk and the angry customers, which seemed to be amplified at least ten times larger than they actually were. She felt unsafe and threatened, as though she was under attack and everyone was out to get her.

Suddenly, the woman recalled that she had a can of pepper spray in her jacket pocket. She had never used pepper spray before, but she had purchased it recently in case she ever needed to use it to protect herself. In her sheer panic—without even pausing to think—she reached into her pocket, whipped out the canister, and started spraying.

First, she pepper sprayed the customers who were yelling at her. They fell to the floor, choking for air, their eyes burning. Next, she pepper sprayed the crowd of onlookers. Many collapsed, writhing and coughing. Then she tried to make a run for it. A number of other customers tried to tackle her in her path, but she pepper sprayed anyone who came close, chalking up more and more assault charges with each spray of the can. She felt like a wild animal, needing to fight for survival anyone who tried to restrain her. Eventually, several people wrestled her to the ground and managed to take her pepper spray away. On the floor, restrained under a small pile of customers, the woman remained crazed and completely disoriented—unsure of whether the whole ordeal lasted a few seconds, minutes, or hours.

At some point during the mayhem, a man emerged from the crowd and instructed everyone to get off of the woman. He approached her carefully, held her down firmly, and began talking to her in a soothing tone. He asked the woman what was bothering her. The woman immediately felt her body go limp in this strange man's arms, and she felt safe for the first time that day. She began sobbing, telling the man about the cruelty and unfairness of the staff and customers in the optical department, about her recent struggles with mental health issues, and her problems at work. It all came spewing out. The man listened and comforted the woman until the police arrived on the scene. She stayed calm as she was arrested and driven to jail. She spent the next three days on suicide watch, and eventually served several months behind bars.

Why did this woman behave in such a way, where she felt so panicked, threatened, and out of control? And why did she perceive that people were treating her so unfairly, or that they were out to get her?

What the woman didn't realize at the time was that she suffered from post-traumatic stress disorder (PTSD) that stemmed from her early life experiences with victimization. Throughout childhood, she was subject to profound physical and emotional abuse in the household, including overly harsh punishments and being tied up and gagged in front of family members. In adolescence, she was beaten up and bullied at school, and then blamed for her own victimization by teachers and administrators. For years, the woman had downplayed these traumas, not realizing that they could have lasting effects on her mood and mental health. Recently, the woman had been exposed to numerous instances of abusive behavior at work, where managers routinely berated and intimidated their subordinates. She became overly sensitive to situations that she perceived as unjust or bullying, and no longer wanted to spend time in public. That day in Walmart, she experienced a maladaptive stress response as a result of her PTSD. Once triggered, her executive thinking was hijacked by the "fight-or-flight" center of her brain, despite her better efforts to stop it happening (Sincerely, X, 2017; Staff Reports, 2016).

The point of this story is not to excuse the woman's behavior, but rather to highlight the ways in which experiences with violence, bullying, and abuse can have lasting effects on people's emotions and behaviors. For decades, researchers across various academic disciplines—criminology, psychology, social work, sociology, human development, and medicine—have documented that victimization can carry many negative and long-term harms to people's lives. Problems such as depression, anxiety, substance abuse, crime and violence, further victimization, and poor health have all been found disproportionately among adults who experience some form of abuse earlier in life. Especially when it happens during childhood or adolescence, victimization can alter brain structure and functioning, and compromise a person's ability to manage their negative emotions and responses to stress over the course of their lives.

And yet, despite the large body of evidence linking victimization to negative outcomes, the fact remains that not all victims of abuse or violence will ultimately experience these long-term problems or react to stress in maladaptive ways—such as the woman who went wild with her pepper spray in Walmart. So why do certain experiences with abuse or victimization affect some people more negatively than others? And why are some victims better equipped to cope with and overcome their experiences with trauma?

This chapter focuses on the personal consequences of victimization. We will discuss the various ways that victimization can impact people's lives in the short and long term, and highlight some explanations for why victimization often carries negative consequences. In the process, we will provide an overview of important research in this area (e.g., the Adverse Childhood Experiences study), and consider the various factors that might influence the severity of consequences that victims experience. We will also discuss the importance of coping responses and social support in helping victims recover and heal. The chapter will conclude with a discussion of remaining gaps and challenges in the literature.

Consequences of victimization

Victimization can be a frightening and unsettling experience. For many, it can be unexpected and unwelcomed, and its negative effects can linger long after the event occurred. Even if there are no injuries suffered, in the aftermath of a crime victims may feel confused, fearful, and angry, and suffer emotionally and psychologically. According to a recent NCVS report, in 2009 to 2012, 68 percent of victims of serious violent crime (sexual assault/rape, robbery, or aggravated assault) in the U.S. aged 12 years or older experienced socio-emotional problems as a result of their victimization (see Langton & Truman, 2014). Socio-emotional problems included feelings of moderate to severe distress, significant problems with work or school (such as trouble with a boss, co-workers, or peers), and significant problems with family members or friends (including more arguments than before the victimization, an inability to trust, or not feeling as close after the victimization). For nearly all of these victims (96%), their emotional distress lasted for a month or more (e.g., feeling worried or anxious, angry, unsafe, violated, vulnerable, distrustful, sad, or depressed). Symptoms were also found to be more severe for those victimized by someone they knew (e.g., an intimate partner, relative, or acquaintance) instead of a stranger (Langton & Truman, 2014).

These symptoms will lessen over time for some victims, but for others they may manifest into more serious and long-term problems. Part of the reason why this happens has to do with how victims cope with their experiences. Victimization elicits strong negative emotions (e.g., anxiety, depression, anger, and frustration) that victims will feel pressured to alleviate through some form of coping. Broadly speaking, coping may be defined as the process by which people regulate their behaviors and emotions under conditions of psychological distress (Agnew, 2006). Coping techniques may be cognitive or behavioral, and they seek to reduce or minimize the various demands of a stressful situation.

Coping strategies can vary widely in response to victimization, where healthy coping techniques—such as participating in therapy, seeking comfort from family or friends, or engaging in positive thinking—tend to be more successful at reducing long-term distress (Ong et al., 2006). Alternatively, unhealthy coping strategies may include behaviors like getting drunk or high on drugs, stealing things, beating people up, exacting revenge against the person who wronged you, withdrawing from school, work, or social settings, and engaging in negative self-talk—all of which may seem to make sense in the short run but can result in more problems in the long run. Due to the intensity of negative emotions that many victims feel, and because healthy coping can take more effort and resources, victims often cope with their experiences in unhealthy ways (Agnew, 2002). And while we might expect victimization to elicit these sorts of responses at any age, there are certain stages of the life course where individuals may be especially susceptible to coping poorly with victimization—such as when it happens early in life.

Consequences of victimization for youth

Throughout childhood and adolescence, victimization can have a profound developmental impact (Finkelhor, 2008). Between the ages of 3 and 16, youth are highly vulnerable to the harms of stress and trauma, such as violence (Romeo & McEwen, 2006). Being victimized during these years can violate one's sense of safety, control, and expectations for survival (Cicchetti & Toth, 2005) and can lead to distressing flashbacks, problems with insecure attachment, and difficulties with affective and emotional regulation—problems that are often carried into adulthood (Heim et al., 2010). Victimization can also influence the development of a "traumatized brain" (Hart & Rubia, 2012), where youth experience generalized states of fear, anxiety, and hyperarousal that can color how they interact with others, perceive their environments, and cope with stress (Caffo, Forresi, & Lievers, 2005).

To make matters worse, children and adolescents rarely develop the skills needed to cope with victimization in healthy, prosocial ways. Part of that development may be attributed to neurocognitive changes associated with aging. As people move into adulthood and their executive functioning increases, they become better at self-regulation (Smith, Steinberg, & Chein, 2014; Pratt, 2016). There is evidence that the prefrontal cortex—the part of the brain responsible for decision making, emotional regulation, and inhibitory responses—continues to develop until people are at least 20 years old (Romer, 2010). Thus, while most adolescents should be able to understand the risks associated with unhealthy coping behaviors by age 14, the inhibitory mechanisms required to resist them are not really equivalent to that of adults until after age 20 (Pharo et al., 2011). Therefore, young people are far more likely than adults to engage in maladaptive and risky forms of coping in response to victimization—forms of coping that can cause many psychological, behavioral, and health problems of their own (Turanovic & Pratt, 2013).

To help illustrate the significance of victimization early in life, some like to use the analogy of a tree—a "trauma tree"—such as that shown in Figure 6.1. Different parts of the tree represent their own stages of human development. The tree's roots represent prenatal development and infancy, the trunk represents childhood, the sturdy lower branches are adolescence, and the thinner upper branches are adulthood. The idea here is that, if something bad happens to the tree to compromise its roots and trunk (i.e., during infancy and childhood), the rest of the tree cannot thrive. However, if something happens to the thinner upper branches (i.e., during adulthood), the tree has a better chance of recovery. In other words, the earlier in life trauma and victimization happens, the greater potential it has to make a long-lasting impact on health and development over the life course.

Consistent with the idea of the "trauma tree," recent studies have demonstrated that the association between victimization and negative outcomes tends to be stronger earlier in life. For example, in their longitudinal study of low-income, minority children in Chicago, Topitzes, Mersky, and Reynolds

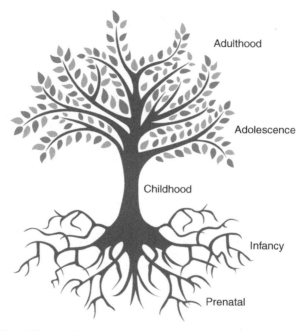

Figure 6.1 The "Trauma Tree"

(2012) found that youth who were victimized in childhood or adolescence were more likely to engage in crime and violence than non-victimized youth, and that childhood victimization was a stronger and more consistent predictor of crime in adulthood than adolescent victimization. Similarly, Russell, Vasilenko, and Lanza (2016) found that victimization was more strongly associated with depressive symptoms and heavy drinking when it occurred during the teen years rather than in people's early twenties; and Turanovic (2015) found that victimization in adolescence was linked to a much wider array of psychological, behavioral, and health problems than victimization in emerging or early adulthood.

The Adverse Childhood Experiences study

Some of the most compelling evidence that childhood experiences with trauma impact later life outcomes comes from the Adverse Childhood Experiences (ACE) study (Dube et al., 2001; Felitti et al., 1998). This study set out to determine how exposure to different negative events in childhood affected people's well-being later in life. Researchers surveyed over 17,000 adults in the United States (most over the age of 50) about their various health issues, as well as their exposure to ten categories of "adverse childhood experiences" (or "ACEs") prior to the age of 18. These ACEs included emotional abuse, physical abuse, sexual abuse, emotional neglect, physical neglect, household substance abuse, household mental illness, parental domestic violence, parental separation or divorce, and the incarceration of a household member. For every adverse childhood experience someone had, one point would be added to that person's total ACE score—ranging from a possible 0 to 10 points (see Table 6.1 to calculate your ACE score). Researchers then linked these ACE scores with the various health outcomes to see whether they were related.

Table 6.1. What is your ACE Score?

Check the corresponding box next to each question if your answer is "yes."

Before your 18th birthday, did a parent or other adult in the household often or very often:

1. Swear at you, insult you, put you down, or humiliate you? *or*   ☐
   Act in a way that made you afraid that you might be physically hurt?

2. Push, grab, slap, or throw something at you? *or*   ☐
   Ever hit you so hard that you had marks or were injured?

3. Touch or fondle you or have you touch their body in a sexual   ☐
   way? *or*
   Attempt or actually have oral, anal, or vaginal intercourse with you?

Before your 18th birthday, did you often or very often feel that:

4. No one in your family loved you or thought you were important   ☐
   or special? *or*
   Your family didn't look out for each other, feel close to each other, or support each other?

5. You didn't have enough to eat, had to wear dirty clothes, and had   ☐
   no one to protect you? *or*
   Your parents were too drunk or high to take care of you or take you to the doctor if you needed it?

Before your 18th birthday, was your mother or stepmother:

6. Often or very often pushed, grabbed, slapped, or had something   ☐
   thrown at her? *or*
   Sometimes, often, or very often kicked, bitten, hit with a fist, or hit with something hard? *or*
   Ever repeatedly hit for at least a few minutes or threatened with a gun or knife?

Check the corresponding box next to each question if your answer is "yes."

Before your 18th birthday:

7. Was a biological parent ever lost to you through divorce, abandonment, or other reason? ☐

8. Did you live with anyone who was a problem drinker or alcoholic, or who used street drugs? ☐

9. Was a household member depressed or mentally ill, or did a household member attempt suicide? ☐

10. Did a household member go to prison? ☐

For every box you checked "yes," you get 1 point added to your ACE score.

Source: Centers for Disease Control and Prevention (2016). Retrieved from www.cdc.gov/violenceprevention/acestudy/.

The results of this study were quite striking, and two key findings emerged. First, the study showed that ACEs were far more common and widespread than previously thought. The study found that around two-thirds of adults had experienced at least one ACE, and that one in eight had experienced four or more. Second, the study revealed a dose–response relationship between ACEs and health outcomes—meaning that the higher one's ACE score, the worse that person's health outcomes were. Compared to someone with an ACE score of zero, a person with an ACE score of four or higher was more than twice as likely to have a stroke, a sexually transmitted disease, or Hepatitis; four times more likely to have emphysema or to be diagnosed with Alzheimer's; five times more likely to suffer from depression; seven times more likely to be an alcoholic; ten times more likely to be an intravenous drug user; and twelve times more likely to attempt suicide. In addition, an ACE score of seven or more carried triple the lifetime risk of lung cancer, and three-and-a-half times the risk of ischemic heart disease—the leading cause of death in the United States.

The ACE study was conducted in the 1990s, but similar patterns have been reported in numerous follow-up studies conducted across the U.S. (Sacks, Murphey, & Moore, 2014) as well as in countries such as the United Kingdom, Canada, Australia, New Zealand, China, South Africa, Norway, Denmark, the Philippines, Brazil, Romania, and South Korea (see, e.g., Anda et al., 2010; Bellis et al., 2014; Danese et al., 2009). Subsequent research has also shown that some ACEs are more common among children who live in poverty (Halfon et al., 2017), and that black and Hispanic children tend to experience more ACEs than white children—particularly in the U.S. (Slopen et al., 2016). And over the past few decades, the list of health problems linked to ACEs has expanded, as summarized in Table 6.2.

Table 6.2 Health outcomes associated with adverse childhood experiences

Outcome	Adults	Children and adolescents
Mental/ behavioral health	<ul><li>Alcoholism</li><li>Anger problems</li><li>Anxiety</li><li>Bipolar disorder</li><li>Criminal behavior</li><li>Depression</li><li>Drug abuse</li><li>Eating disorder</li><li>Hallucinations</li><li>High stress</li><li>Panic reactions</li><li>Posttraumatic stress disorder</li><li>Smoking</li><li>Suicide</li><li>Victimization</li><li>Violent behavior</li></ul>	<ul><li>Bullying</li><li>Dating violence</li><li>Delinquent behavior</li><li>Depressive symptoms</li><li>Eating disorder</li><li>Internalizing problems</li><li>Learning difficulties</li><li>Low self-esteem</li><li>Physical fighting</li><li>Risky sexual behavior</li><li>Self-harm</li><li>Suicide ideation</li><li>Social isolation</li><li>Smoking</li><li>Substance use</li><li>Victimization</li><li>Weapon-carrying</li></ul>
Physical health	<ul><li>Cancer</li><li>Autoimmune disease</li><li>Cardiovascular disease</li><li>Chronic lung disease</li><li>Diabetes</li><li>Early death</li><li>Emphysema</li><li>General poor health</li><li>Headaches</li><li>Hepatitis or jaundice</li><li>Ischemic heart disease</li><li>Obesity</li><li>Sexually transmitted infections</li><li>Skeletal fracture</li><li>Stroke</li></ul>	<ul><li>Acute respiratory infections</li><li>Adolescent pregnancy</li><li>Attention deficit hyperactivity disorder</li><li>Asthma</li><li>Autism</li><li>Dermatitis</li><li>Eye and ear infections</li><li>Hives</li><li>Intestinal disease</li><li>Overweight or obese</li><li>Poor dental health</li><li>Poor general health</li><li>Pneumonia</li><li>Viral infections</li></ul>

Source: Bucci et al. (2016). Toxic stress in children and adolescents. *Advances in Pediatrics, 63*, 403–428.

Why is it that ACEs manifest in such serious health and behavioral problems across the lifespan? One explanation has to do with how repeated exposure to stress in childhood affects the workings of the brain and the central nervous system. Adverse childhood experiences are thought of as *traumas*–disturbing events that increase stress, or that the brain interprets as life threatening and that trigger a "fight-or-flight" response. It does not matter if the threat is real, perceived, or imagined, only that the brain interprets danger and reacts accordingly.

Our fight-or-flight system works like this. Imagine you are walking in a forest and you see a bear. Immediately, your amygdala (the part of the brain that contributes to emotional processing) sends a distress signal to your hypothalamus (the part of the brain that communicates with the rest of the body through the autonomic nervous system). The hypothalamus then tells your adrenal glands to release stress hormones (like adrenaline and cortisol) into the bloodstream. The heart starts to pound, the small airways in your lungs open wide, and your sight and hearing become sharper. Blood is pumped away from the digestive tract and into your muscles and limbs to give them more fuel for running and fighting; your sensory awareness heightens; your impulses quicken; and your perception of pain diminishes. You become prepared—physically and mentally—to either run from or fight the bear. This stress response happens subconsciously and instantly in the face of danger—even before your brain's visual centers can fully process what is in front of you.

This fight-or-flight response can be helpful if you are in sudden danger, like when you accidentally cross paths with a bear—something that hopefully doesn't happen too often. But serious problems arise when this stress response is activated repeatedly. This is unfortunately the case for many children who are regularly exposed to violence, abuse, or maltreatment in the home—a place where they are supposed to feel safe and secure. What happens when the "bear" is someone who you encounter each day?

According to Harris (2015), when the fight-or-flight system is activated over and over again, "it goes from being adaptive, or life-saving, to maladaptive, or health-damaging." Indeed, while our fight-or-flight system is activated, we tend to perceive everything in our environment as a possible threat to our survival. By its very nature, the fight-or-flight system bypasses the parts of the brain where rational and thoughtful decision making occurs. It is not easy to make careful behavioral choices while this stress response is activated. Because our fear is exaggerated and our thinking is distorted, it may only take an ambiguous look, comment, or gesture to send us into defense or attack mode—much like the woman who pepper sprayed Walmart.

Children are especially sensitive to the activation of the stress system because their brains and bodies are still developing. When children repeatedly go into a state of hyperarousal (or "fight-or-flight" mode) because of what they experience at home, at school, or in the community, their bodies become routinely flooded with stress hormones. At high doses, these chemicals not only affect how children's brains are structured and function, but they can take a toll on the immune system, affect hormonal development and sleep patterns, and even alter the way in which DNA is read and transcribed (Nakazawa, 2015; Weder et al., 2014). These serious physiological changes can lead to various health, behavioral, and emotional problems in the short and long term.

Depending on how old children are, these problems can show themselves in different ways. Children under the age of 6 may react to ACEs with frequent tantrums, irritability or fussiness, or resort to behaviors that were common when they were younger (e.g., thumb sucking, bed wetting, or fear of the dark). In elementary school-age children (6–12 years), fighting, getting into trouble at school, having difficulty paying attention, and being tearful, quiet, upset, and withdrawn are more common. Among teenagers, defiant behaviors (e.g., refusing to follow rules or talking back more often), over- or under-sleeping, substance use, running away from home, and aggressive behaviors typically occur. This is important to recognize, since people tend to blame youth for having a "bad attitude" or "behavior problems," even though these issues can be tied back to trauma and stress dysregulation. If these various behaviors are punished severely or not addressed effectively, they can manifest in worse outcomes over time. The influence of ACEs on health and well-being over the life course is shown in Figure 6.2.

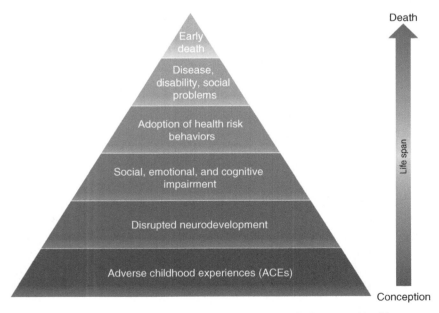

Figure 6.2 The influence of ACEs on health and well-being over the lifespan
Source: Adapted from Centers for Disease Control and Prevention (2016). Retrieved from www.cdc.gov/violenceprevention/acestudy/about.html.

The cycle of violence

Although ACEs encompass many forms of hardship, criminologists often fixate on one particular form of childhood adversity: physical abuse. This is partly due to the long-held belief that "abuse leads to abuse" or "violence begets violence"—the idea that people who are abused as children will grow up to abuse others and be violent adults. Today, we know that there is a link between childhood victimization and future violence, but for years scholars expressed strong opinions on this topic in the absence of rigorous empirical research.

For instance, in a 1963 clinical note entitled "Violence breeds violence—perhaps?," George C. Curtis, a psychiatrist, argued that abused children would "become tomorrow's murderers and perpetrators of other crimes of violence, if they survive" (Curtis, 1963: 386). Curtis put forth that, if children faced abuse, they would grow up harboring a lot of hostility toward their parents and the world in general. He predicted that, because children learn from and mimic their parents, they too would become aggressive and unleash their destructive behaviors on others—or, as he put it, "monkey see, monkey do" (Curtis, 1963: 386). While these assertions seemed to make sense, they were based on only three prior studies: one review published in the 1940s of "children and adolescents who kill" (Bender & Curran, 1940), a study of six male adult prisoners convicted of first-degree murder (Duncan et al., 1958), and a brief clinical account of eight boys who committed "murderous assaults" (Easson & Steinhilber, 1961). These studies, while interesting, were small and anecdotal—they did not exactly provide the type of ironclad science needed to establish that the "cycle of violence" was a real issue.

It was not until the late 1980s that the research started to catch up with what people assumed to be true about the effects of child abuse on future violent behavior. In 1989, Cathy Widom conducted one of the first rigorous empirical studies of the cycle of violence. The objective of her study was to determine the extent to which individuals who were abused approximately 20 years prior (as children) subsequently engaged in delinquent and adult criminal behavior. She relied exclusively on official records of substantiated and validated cases of child maltreatment (physical abuse, sexual abuse, and neglect), and of juvenile and adult arrests. Her research methods were an improvement over prior work in many ways, including the use of a large sample, a prospective research design, and a control group of non-maltreated individuals (matched as closely as possible to the maltreated cases on age, sex, race, and social class background). The study's findings confirmed that there was in fact a link between childhood maltreatment and criminal behavior later in life, and this work was published in *Science* (which is kind of a big deal).

Two important issues in Widom's (1989) work deserve special attention. The first is that this work used the terminology of the "cycle of violence" to refer to the effects of a particular form of maltreatment (physical abuse) on a particular form of adult behavior (violence), even though other forms of childhood maltreatment and delinquent and criminal behaviors were included in the study. The cycle of violence was limited to physical abuse because it was assumed that the key causal process linking early abuse to later violence was the adoption of antisocial attitudes and beliefs that condone violence as an acceptable way of solving adult problems. Second, Widom (1989) was quite clear in that most of the people in her data who were abused as children did not end up behaving violently as adults. Some, however, did—enough that the "cycle of violence" pattern was observed in her data. But it was unclear why this pattern existed for only some physically abused children.

Three decades later, a vast body of literature has been produced which confirms that the cycle of violence is a relatively consistent phenomenon, where the relationship between child abuse and later violent behavior has been found in many studies (Widom, 2017). But what is also readily apparent throughout the literature is that the cycle of violence is not inevitable. While childhood victimization has the potential to alter prosocial development in a number of ways, there are children who seem to be resilient—that is, they do not manifest any problem behaviors despite facing considerable adversity or trauma in childhood (McGloin & Widom, 2001). So what sets abused children who later perpetrate violence apart from those who do not?

One explanation may be found in the various protective factors some youth may have in their lives. Protective factors are elements of an abused or neglected child's life that reduce adversity following a challenging experience. Some studies have pointed to protective factors such as having strong connections to adults outside of the family (e.g., to a teacher, mentor, coach, or other role model), involvement in prosocial activities, attachments to school, positive school climate, close relationships with non-deviant peers, higher levels of self-control, and high verbal skills (Dubow et al., 2016; Lösel & Farrington, 2012; Wright et al., 2019).

Others argue that, in addition to protective factors, the frequency and duration of abuse, and whether multiple types of abuse were experienced (e.g., physical *and* sexual abuse), should have important implications for whether people become violent later in life. Experiencing more abuse, and more types of abuse (also referred to as "polyvictimization"), is thought to increase the likelihood of violence (Finkelhor, Ormrod, & Turner, 2007).

Scholars have also found that the social contexts in which child abuse happens can affect its impact on later violence, but not always in the way we would expect. For example, in their study of youth in Chicago, Wright and Fagan

(2013) found that the effects of child abuse on later violence were weaker in more structurally disadvantaged neighborhoods. The authors explained that because these are areas where violent behaviors are more abundant, "violence is more likely to be seen as a somewhat common, legitimate, or necessary way of interacting with others" (Wright & Fagan, 2013: 239). When experiences with violence are commonplace, child physical abuse may not "be viewed as particularly aberrant or 'abusive'" (Wright & Fagan, 2013: 240). This is not to say that children from such communities are more resilient or better off despite their life circumstances, but rather that, when compared to other structural disadvantages and enduring hardships in these children's lives, child abuse does not seem to hold up as a substantial risk factor for violence.

So, while it is apparent that we have learned a great deal about childhood maltreatment over the past few decades, important questions remain about how the cycle of violence is affected by the timing and intensity of maltreatment, as well as how the social contexts in which abuse occurs during childhood can either lead to or buffer against harmful consequences. One of the biggest challenges facing this literature is that studies can rarely take into account all of the genetic and environmental factors that may actually be responsible for the link between child victimization and adult violence (Forsman & Langström, 2012). In addition, there is not one single agreed-upon theory that is used to explain the cycle of violence. Outside of the social learning model put forth in earlier work (Bandura, 1973), other explanations have been offered. To be sure, social control theory proposes that child maltreatment disrupts the kinds of social bonds and attachments to parents that are necessary for avoiding crime and violence (Hirschi, 1969); general strain theory argues that delinquency and crime are caused by the inability to cope in prosocial ways with child abuse and neglect (Agnew, 1992); and other theories focus on the interaction between genetic and environmental effects (Caspi et al., 2002). The point here is that there is still a lot more to figure out about how abuse increases future violent behavior, and why many abused children never become violent.

What about childhood neglect?

Neglect is often overlooked in research on child abuse, given that it has not traditionally fitted into the narrative concerning the "cycle of violence." Indeed, while physical abuse is something that has been done to a child—a type of behavior that can be learned and modeled over time—neglect is the absence of action. Neglect is the failure of a parent, guardian, or other caregiver to provide for a child's basic needs. Neglect may be physical (e.g., failure to provide necessary food or shelter, or lack of appropriate supervision), medical (e.g., failure to provide necessary medical or mental health treatment), educational (e.g., failure to educate a child or attend to special education needs), or emotional (e.g., inattention to a child's emotional needs, failure to provide psychological care, or permitting the child to use alcohol or drugs). Sometimes religious or cultural values, the standards of care in the community, and poverty may contribute to neglect, indicating that the family is in need of information or assistance (Child Welfare Information Gateway, 2013).

Neglected children represent the majority of child maltreatment cases that come to the attention of authorities every year (U.S. Department of Health and Human Services, 2018); yet neglect is rarely focused on separately from other forms of maltreatment—a problem aptly referred to as "the neglect of neglect" (Widom, 2017). This omission is consequential given that some studies suggest that neglect may be an important predictor of crime and violence later in life. For example, using data on low-income minority children in Chicago, Mersky and Reynolds (2007) found that neglect prior to the age of 12 was associated with future violent delinquency; and in a study of juvenile offenders in Washington State, Ryan, Williams, and Courtney (2013) found that neglected youth were significantly more likely to continue offending compared to youth with no history of neglect, even after controlling for a large number of family, academic, mental health, peer, and substance abuse factors.

In fact, re-analyses of Widom's (1989) original data used in her famous "cycle of violence" study revealed that childhood neglect was actually a stronger predictor of violence in adulthood than physical abuse, and that the effects of physical abuse proved to be relatively unstable when the data were analyzed in different ways (see Myers et al., 2018). Widom (1989: 244) recognized in her original study that "being neglected as a child also showed a significant relation to later violent criminal behavior." But the fact that her core focus was devoted to the cycle of violence—one that honed in on the importance of violence experienced in childhood—may have actually contributed to childhood neglect taking a back seat in the literature. As the work moves forward in this area, neglect is certainly deserving of more focus.

Victimization and social relationships

Perhaps one of the most consequential harms of victimization we have yet to discuss is its impact on friendships and other relationships. Throughout childhood and adolescence in particular, meaningful friendships are an important part of life. Especially during the teen years, friendships take on deeper meaning as youth explore their independence and spend more time with peers outside of the home—often without their parents or other adults around to supervise them.

However, after being victimized, many youth have a hard time building and maintaining friendships, and they often find themselves stigmatized by their peers at school (Faris & Felmlee, 2014). In addition, depression, anxiety, detachment, and the other forms of negative emotionality that victims feel can put a strain on existing relationships. Peers may also avoid forming friendships with victims out of fear of being similarly targeted for victimization, or of being socially excluded by others (Goffman, 1963). Some youth may even break off existing friendships with victims as a means of preserving their standing in the social network (Bukowski & Sipploa, 2001). Studies on peer attitudes have revealed that adolescents often show little concern for their victimized peers, and they generally believe that victims bring their problems on themselves. Indeed, in their study of middle-school students, Graham and Juvonen (2001: 59) found that most youth believe that their peers cause their own victimization by engaging in provoking behaviors, such as being a "tattletale," a "show-off," or "badmouthing" someone else.

Research also shows that, in adolescence, victimization leads to the loss of existing friendships, and that non-victimized youth avoid forming friendships with victims (Turanovic & Young, 2016). With few other friendship options, victims are often left to form friendships with peers who have also been victimized. While these friendships may carry some benefits—where victims may have more compassion for one another because they have each "been there"—it can also be the case that hanging around with other victims may put them at an elevated risk for even more victimization. This is because friends who have been victimized may not be viewed as capable guardians against would-be perpetrators (because they have already been successfully targeted in the past). And because adolescent victims are more likely to engage in risky lifestyles, their friends might lead them into dangerous or hostile situations that could end up increasing their likelihood of being harmed (Schreck, Fisher, & Miller, 2004).

Victims may also not be the most capable and emotionally supportive friends, particularly if they are having a hard time dealing with their own victimization. Considering that strong friendships carry a range of social, emotional, and mental health benefits, young victims may lack an important source of support that can help them cope effectively (Agnew, 2006). Without such supports, the negative consequences of victimization may be magnified and continue to pile up into adulthood.

To be sure, victimization not only fractures friendships, but it can also lead in the future to other kinds of relationships that are also not very supportive or protective. For instance, a study by Kuhl, Warner, and Wilczak (2012) found that violent victimization during adolescence increased the likelihood of getting married or cohabitating with a romantic partner at the age of 17. And while unions such as marriage or cohabitation might be protective later in life, they are not known to be very healthy or beneficial during the teen years. A follow-up study even found that these victimized youth were more likely to experience intimate partner violence when they entered into these early unions (Kuhl, Warner, & Warner, 2015). It therefore seems that victimization can propel people into negative social ties that may lead to further harms.

These kinds of findings are troubling because meaningful social ties to others are the key to helping victims heal at any age. Even just one caring, safe relationship can give someone a better chance of overcoming their victimization in a healthy way. Regardless of whether these relationships are formed in the workplace, at school, with friends or family, or with a romantic partner, these ties often foster the perception of being loved and cared for by others, esteemed and valued, and part of a social network of mutual assistance and obligation. Supportive social ties can facilitate positive coping via access to emotional, social, and instrumental support, and can increase feelings of self-esteem and a sense of control over one's environment.

It is important to remember, however, that social ties are age-graded (Sampson & Laub, 1993)—meaning that over the life course, such ties can change along with age-specific social roles, and they can develop through a process of cumulative continuity (Laub & Sampson 2003). During childhood and adolescence, for example, social ties are primarily formed through family, school, and same-age peers, and thus they typically represent relationships with friends, teachers, and parents (Turanovic & Pratt, 2015). In emerging adulthood, these social ties change, and in addition to parents and friends, they may also come to reflect ties to higher education, a new job, or a romantic partner. And later on in adulthood, as people become more entrenched in their adult roles and responsibilities, social ties might represent a long-term career, a close relationship with a spouse, ties to children, and investment in the community (Umberson, Crosnoe, & Reczek, 2010). Meaningful relationships can also be fostered through mentorship programs and support groups (DuBois et al., 2011). The bottom line is that, regardless of where these ties are formed, if they are strong and prosocial, they can provide victims with the support and comfort they need to get back on track.

Gaps and challenges

Up until this point, we have talked a lot about the "bad"—the various ways in which victimization disrupts people's lives and leads to more problems over time. But we want to emphasize that victimization does not affect everyone in harmful ways, and not all victims are guaranteed to experience enduring, negative life consequences. On the one hand, it is certainly true that, when victimization is violent and unexpected, it can represent a *negative* turning point in the life course—one that sends people down a more troubled and disadvantaged life path (Macmillan, 2001). On the other hand, it is also true that, for some people, victimization has no real impact on their lives. And for others, victimization may even be a *positive* turning point that leads them to make prosocial changes to their behaviors (e.g., by reducing their involvement in risky lifestyles to avoid contact with potential offenders; see Turanovic & Pratt, 2014; Turanovic, Pratt, & Piquero, 2018). For example, qualitative interviews with offenders support the view that victimization can serve as a catalyst for desistance from crime (Farrall et al., 2014), especially when victimization is serious, and when offenders define the event as the result of their own criminal involvement (Jacques & Wright, 2008).

Furthermore, when it comes to the work produced on adverse childhood experiences, we want to point out that ACEs are not destiny. Most of us have had exposure to at least some adversities in childhood, and yet not all of us will end up facing the kinds of serious health, behavioral, or emotional problems that have been documented in the literature. Even if we do experience these problems, they can be targeted for change so that they do not have to be a permanent feature of our daily lives. With the appropriate treatment and support, stress responses can be reset, and people can heal from trauma. This also means that if you scored higher than 4 on the ACE quiz (see Table 6.1), don't despair—your fate is not sealed, and what is predictable is preventable.

Key readings

Felitti, V.J., Anda, R.F., Nordenberg, D., Williamson, D.F., Spitz, A.M., Edwards, V., & Marks, J.S. (1998). Relationship of childhood abuse and household dysfunction to many of the leading causes of death in adults: The Adverse Childhood Experiences (ACE) study. *American Journal of Preventive Medicine, 14*, 245-258.

Macmillan, R. (2001). Violence and the life course: The consequences of victimization for personal and social development. *Annual Review of Sociology, 27*, 1-22.

Turanovic, J.J. & Pratt, T.C. (2015). Longitudinal effects of violent victimization during adolescence on adverse outcomes in adulthood: A focus on prosocial attachments. *The Journal of Pediatrics, 166*, 1062-1069.

Widom, C.S. (1989). The cycle of violence. *Science, 244*, 160-166.

Wright, E.M. & Fagan, A.A. (2013). The cycle of violence in context: Exploring the moderating roles of neighborhood disadvantage and cultural norms. *Criminology, 51*, 217-249.

Discussion questions

1. How does victimization lead to so many behavioral, health, and psychological consequences over the life course?
2. Why is trauma most harmful when it happens earlier in life?

3. What are some possible reasons why most abused children will never go on to become violent adults?
4. How do social ties help victims overcome their experiences? And how can we strengthen social ties for victims of crime?

References

Agnew, R. (1992). Foundation for a general strain theory of crime and delinquency. *Criminology, 30*, 47–87.

Agnew, R. (2002). Experienced, vicarious, and anticipated strain: An exploratory study on physical victimization and delinquency. *Justice Quarterly, 19*, 603–632.

Agnew, R. (2006). *Pressured into crime: An overview of general strain theory*. Los Angeles, CA: Roxbury.

Anda, R.F., Butchart, A., Felitti, V.J., & Brown, D.W. (2010). Building a framework for global surveillance of the public health implications of adverse childhood experiences. *American Journal of Preventive Medicine, 39*(1), 93–98.

Bandura, A. (1973). *Aggression: A social learning analysis*. Englewood Cliffs, NJ: Prentice-Hall.

Bellis, M.A., Hughes, K., Leckenby, N., Jones, L., Baban, A., Kachaeva, M., & Raleva, M. (2014). Adverse childhood experiences and associations with health-harming behaviours in young adults: Surveys in eight eastern European countries. *Bulletin of the World Health Organization, 92*, 641–655.

Bender, L. & Curran, F.J. (1940). Children and adolescents who kill. *Criminal Psychopathology, 1*, 297–323.

Bucci, M., Marques, S.S., Oh, D., & Harris, N.B. (2016). Toxic stress in children and adolescents. *Advances in Pediatrics, 63*(1), 403–428.

Bukowski, W.M. & Sipploa, L.K. (2001). Groups, individuals, and victimization: A view of the peer system. In J. Juvonen & S. Graham (Eds.), *Peer harassment in school: The plight of the vulnerable and victimized* (pp. 355–377). New York: Guilford Press.

Caffo, E., Forresi, B., & Lievers, L.S. (2005). Impact, psychological sequelae and management of trauma affecting children and adolescents. *Current Opinion in Psychiatry, 18*, 422–428.

Caspi, A., McClay, J., Moffitt, T.E., Mill, J., Martin, J., Craig, I.W., Taylor, A., & Poulton, R. (2002). Role of genotype in the cycle of violence in maltreated children. *Science, 297*, 851–854.

Child Welfare Information Gateway (2013). *What is child abuse and neglect? Recognizing the signs and symptoms*. Washington, DC: Children's Bureau.

Cicchetti, D. & Toth, S.L. (2005). Child maltreatment. *Annual Review of Clinical Psychology, 1*, 409–438.

Curtis, G.C. (1963). Violence breeds violence–perhaps? *American Journal of Psychiatry, 120*, 386–387.

Danese, A., Moffitt, T.E., Harrington, H., Milne, B.J., Polanczyk, G., Pariante, C.M., & Caspi, A. (2009). Adverse childhood experiences and adult risk factors for age-related disease: Depression, inflammation, and clustering of metabolic risk markers. *Archives of Pediatrics & Adolescent Medicine, 163*(12), 1135–1143.

Dube, S.R., Anda, R.F., Felitti, V.J., Chapman, D.P., Williamson, D.F., & Giles, W.H. (2001). Childhood abuse, household dysfunction, and the risk of attempted suicide throughout the life span: Findings from the Adverse Childhood Experiences study. *Jama, 286*(24), 3089–3096.

DuBois, D.L., Portillo, N., Rhodes, J.E., Silverthorn, N., & Valentine, J.C. (2011). How effective are mentoring programs for youth? A systematic assessment of the evidence. *Psychological Science in the Public Interest, 12*, 57–91.

Dubow, E.F., Huesmann, L.R., Boxer, P., & Smith, C. (2016). Childhood and adolescent risk and protective factors for violence in adulthood. *Journal of Criminal Justice, 45,* 26-31.

Duncan, G.M., Frazier, S.H., Litin, E.M., Johnson, A.M., & Barron, A.J. (1958). Etiological factors in first-degree murder. *Journal of the American Medical Association, 168,* 1755-1758.

Easson, W.M. & Steinhilber, R.M. (1961). Murderous aggression by children and adolescents. *Archives of General Psychiatry, 4,* 27-35.

Faris, R. & Felmlee, D. (2014). Casualties of social combat: School networks of peer victimization and their consequences. *American Sociological Review, 79,* 228-257.

Farrall, S., Hunter, B., Sharpe, G., & Calverley, A. (2014). *Criminal careers in transition: The social context of desistance from crime.* Oxford: Oxford University Press.

Felitti, V.J., Anda, R.F., Nordenberg, D., Williamson, D.F., Spitz, A.M., Edwards, V., & Marks, J.S. (1998). Relationship of childhood abuse and household dysfunction to many of the leading causes of death in adults: The Adverse Childhood Experiences (ACE) study. *American Journal of Preventive Medicine, 14*(4), 245-258.

Finkelhor, D. (2008). *Childhood victimization: Violence, crime, and abuse in the lives of young people.* New York: Oxford University Press.

Finkelhor, D., Ormrod, R.K., & Turner, H.A. (2007). Poly-victimization: A neglected component in child victimization. *Child Abuse and Neglect, 31,* 7-26.

Forsman, M. & Långström, N. (2012). Child maltreatment and adult violent offending: Population-based twin study addressing the "cycle of violence" hypothesis. *Psychological Medicine, 42,* 1977-1983.

Goffman, E. (1963). *Stigma: Notes on the management of a spoiled identity.* Englewood Cliffs, NJ: Prentice-Hall.

Graham, S. & Juvonen, J. (2001). An attributional approach to peer victimization. In J. Juvonen & S. Graham (Eds.), *Peer harassment in school: The plight of the vulnerable and victimized* (pp. 49-72). New York: Guilford Press.

Halfon, N., Larson, K., Son, J., Lu, M., & Bethell, C. (2017). Income inequality and the differential effect of adverse childhood experiences in US children. *Academic Pediatrics, 17*(7), S70-S78.

Harris, N.B. (2015). *How childhood trauma affects health across a lifetime* [Video file, February]. Retrieved from www.ted.com/speakers/nadine_burke_harris_1.

Hart, H. & Rubia, K. (2012). Neuroimaging of child abuse: A critical review. *Frontiers in Human Neuroscience, 6*(52), 1-24.

Heim, C., Shugart, M., Craighead, W.E., & Nemeroff, C.B. (2010). Neurobiological and psychiatric consequences of child abuse and neglect. *Developmental Psychobiology, 52,* 671-690.

Hirschi, T. (1969). *Causes of delinquency.* Berkeley, CA: University of California Press.

Jacques, S. & Wright, R. (2008). The victimization–termination link. *Criminology, 46,* 1009-1038.

Kuhl, D.C., Warner, D.F., & Warner, T.D. (2015). Intimate partner violence risk among victims of youth violence: Are early unions bad, beneficial, or benign? *Criminology, 53,* 427-456.

Kuhl, D.C., Warner, D. F., & Wilczak, A. (2012). Adolescent violent victimization and precocious union formation. *Criminology, 50,* 1089-1127.

Langton, L. & Truman, J.L. (2014). *Socio-emotional impact of violent crime.* Washington, DC: U.S. Department of Justice, Office of Justice Programs, Bureau of Justice Statistics.

Laub, J.H. & Sampson, R.J. (2003). *Shared beginnings, divergent lives: Delinquent boys to age 70.* Cambridge, MA: Harvard University Press.

Lösel, F. & Farrington, D.P. (2012). Direct protective and buffering protective factors in the development of youth violence. *American Journal of Preventive Medicine, 43,* S8-S23.

Macmillan, R. (2001). Violence and the life course: The consequences of victimization for personal and social development. *Annual Review of Sociology, 27,* 1-22.

McGloin, J.M. & Widom, C.S. (2001). Resilience among abused and neglected children grown up. *Development and Psychopathology, 13,* 1021-1038.

Mersky, J.P. & Reynolds, A.J. (2007). Child maltreatment and violent delinquency: Disentangling main effects and subgroup effects. *Child Maltreatment, 12,* 246-258.

Myers, W., Lloyd, K., Turanovic, J.J., & Pratt, T.C. (2018). Revisiting a criminological classic: The cycle of violence. *Journal of Contemporary Criminal Justice, 34,* 266-286.

Nakazawa, D.J. (2015). *Childhood disrupted: How your biography becomes your biology, and how you can heal.* New York: Simon & Schuster.

Ong, A.D., Bergeman, C.S., Bisconti, T.L., & Wallace, K.A. (2006). Psychological resilience, positive emotions, and successful adaptation to stress in later life. *Journal of Personality and Social Psychology, 91,* 730-749.

Pharo, H., Sim, C., Graham, M., Gross, J., & Hayne, H. (2011). Risky business: Executive function, personality, and reckless behavior during adolescence and emerging adulthood. *Behavioral Neuroscience, 125,* 970-978.

Pratt, T.C. (2016). A self-control/life-course theory of criminal behavior. *European Journal of Criminology, 13,* 129-146.

Romeo, R.D. & McEwen, B.S. (2006). Stress and the adolescent brain. *Annals of the New York Academy of Sciences, 1094,* 202-214.

Romer, D. (2010). Adolescent risk taking, impulsivity, and brain development: Implications for prevention. *Developmental Psychobiology: The Journal of the International Society for Developmental Psychobiology, 52,* 263-276.

Russell, M.A., Vasilenko, S.A., & Lanza, S.T. (2016). Age-varying links between violence exposure and behavioral, mental, and physical health. *Journal of Adolescent Health, 59,* 189-196.

Ryan, J.P., Williams, A.B., & Courtney, M.E. (2013). Adolescent neglect, juvenile delinquency and the risk of recidivism. *Journal of Youth and Adolescence, 42,* 454-465.

Sacks, V., Murphey, D., & Moore, K. (2014). *Adverse childhood experiences: National and state-level prevalence.* Research Brief. Child Trends. Publ. No. 2014-28, Bethesda.

Sampson, R.J. & Laub, J.H. (1993). *Crime in the making: Pathways and turning points through life.* Cambridge, MA: Harvard University Press.

Schreck, C.J., Fisher, B.S., & Miller, J.M. (2004). The social context of violent victimization: A study of the delinquent peer effect. *Justice Quarterly, 21,* 23-47.

Sincerely, X. (2017). *Episode 2: Pepper spray* [Audio file]. Retrieved from www.ted.com/read/ted-podcasts/sincerely-x.

Slopen, N., Shonkoff, J.P., Albert, M.A., Yoshikawa, H., Jacobs, A., Stoltz, R., & Williams, D.R. (2016). Racial disparities in child adversity in the US: Interactions with family immigration history and income. *American Journal of Preventive Medicine, 50*(1), 47-56.

Smith, A.R., Steinberg, L., & Chein, J. (2014). The role of the anterior insula in adolescent decision making. *Developmental NEUROSCIENCE, 36,* 196-209.

Staff Reports. (2016). Woman arrested after unleashing mace in Walmart. *The Record-Courier,* February 13. Retrieved from www.recordcourier.com/news/local/woman-arrested-after-unleashing-mace-in-walmart/.

Topitzes, J., Mersky, J.P., & Reynolds, A.J. (2012). From child maltreatment to violent offending: An examination of mixed-gender and gender-specific models. *Journal of Interpersonal Violence, 27,* 2322-2347.

Turanovic, J.J. (2015). *The age-graded consequences of victimization.* Doctoral dissertation, Arizona State University.

Turanovic, J.J., & Pratt, T.C. (2013). The consequences of maladaptive coping: Integrating general strain and self-control theories to specify a causal pathway between victimization and offending. *Journal of Quantitative Criminology, 29,* 321-345.

Turanovic, J.J. & Pratt, T.C. (2014). "Can't stop, won't stop": Self-control, risky lifestyles, and repeat victimization. *Journal of Quantitative Criminology, 30,* 29-56.

Turanovic, J.J. & Pratt, T.C. (2015). Longitudinal effects of violent victimization during adolescence on adverse outcomes in adulthood: A focus on prosocial attachments. *The Journal of Pediatrics, 166,* 1062-1069.

Turanovic, J.J. & Young, J.T.N. (2016). Violent offending and victimization in adolescence: Social network mechanisms and homophily. *Criminology, 54,* 487-519.

Turanovic, J.J., Pratt, T.C., & Piquero, A.R. (2018). Structural constraints, risky lifestyles, and repeat victimization. *Journal of Quantitative Criminology, 34,* 251-274.

Umberson, D., Crosnoe, R., & Reczek, C. (2010). Social relationships and health behavior across the life course. *Annual Review of Sociology, 36,* 139-157.

U.S. Department of Health and Human Services. (2018). *Child maltreatment 2016.* Washington, DC: Administration on Children, Youth and Families, Children's Bureau.

Weder, N., Zhang, H., Jensen, K., Yang, B.Z., Simen, A., Jackowski, A., & O'Loughlin, K. (2014). Child abuse, depression, and methylation in genes involved with stress, neural plasticity, and brain circuitry. *Journal of the American Academy of Child & Adolescent Psychiatry, 53*(4), 417-424.

Widom, C.S. (1989). The cycle of violence. *Science, 244,* 160-166.

Widom, C.S. (2017). Long-term impact of childhood abuse and neglect on crime and violence. *Clinical Psychology: Science and Practice, 24,* 186-202.

Wright, E.M. & Fagan, A.A. (2013). The cycle of violence in context: Exploring the moderating roles of neighborhood disadvantage and cultural norms. *Criminology, 51,* 217-249.

Wright, K.A., Turanovic, J.J., O'Neal, E.N., Morse, S.J., & Booth, E.T. (2016). The cycle of violence revisited: Childhood victimization, resilience, and future violence. *Journal of Interpersonal Violence, 34,* 1261-1286.

al consequences of
imization

Over nine long winter days in January 2018, across two Michigan counties, 204 victims of Larry Nassar's abuse had their victim impact statements read aloud in court (Rahal & Kozlowski, 2018). These women were victims of arguably the worst sexual abuse scandal in the history of sports—one that Larry Nassar carried out for over two decades. During his time as the national team doctor for U.S.A. Gymnastics, and through his clinic and gymnastics club at Michigan State University, Nassar sexually abused hundreds of young women and girls. This abuse was often carried out under the guise of a medical treatment—invasive massage—that entailed touching girls around their pelvic areas and vaginas (Park, 2017). Regardless of the type of pain or injury that these young athletes sought treatment for—a torn hamstring, sore heels, an aching back, or an injured shoulder—"pelvic massage" was the treatment that Nassar prescribed. He rarely used gloves, and would touch his patients with his bare hands and penetrate them with his fingers (Hauser & Astor, 2018). He also groomed and manipulated these young athletes into believing he was their friend and protector, and bestowed gifts, candy, and words of encouragement upon them. At the time, many of Nassar's victims were unaware that they were even being molested, and instead believed that they were receiving medical treatments from a trusted doctor who would help them succeed in their sport (Park, 2017). Nassar operated this way for years in the elite gymnastics and sports medicine world—one in which he had an almost celebrity-like status, and where he upheld the image of himself as a hard-working, caring doctor.

After Nassar was convicted on multiple counts of sexual assault, those affected by his actions were given the opportunity to appear in court at the sentencing hearing and deliver victim impact statements. They were to let the court know how Nassar's abuse impacted their lives, in hopes that the judge would take these issues into account at sentencing. The number of women who stepped forward to speak was remarkable. They came from around the nation to face Nassar in person, virtually, or through letters. Many brought photos of themselves at the age when they were first abused by Nassar. One of the most powerful statements came from Aly Raisman, an American gymnast and six-time Olympic medalist. Standing up in front of the court, and looking directly at Nassar at times during her testimony, she recounted his abuse and the lasting effects it had on her and on so many other women. Here are some words from her 13-minute statement:

I didn't think I would be here today. I was scared and nervous. It wasn't until I started watching the impact statements from the other brave survivors that I realized I, too, needed to be here. Larry, you do realize now that we, this group of women you so heartlessly abused over such a long period of time, are now a force and you are nothing. The tables have turned, Larry. We are here. We have our voices, and we are not going anywhere. And now, Larry, it's your turn to listen to me.

There is no map that shows you the pathway to healing. Realizing that you are a survivor of sexual abuse is really hard to put into words. I cannot adequately capture the level of disgust I feel when I think about how this happened. Larry, you abused the power and trust I and so many others placed in you, and I am not sure I will ever come to terms with how horribly you manipulated and violated me. You were the U.S.A. Gymnastics national team doctor, the Michigan [State team] doctor and the United States Olympic team doctor. You were trusted by so many and took advantage of countless athletes and their families.

The effects of your actions are far-reaching. Abuse goes way beyond the moment, often haunting survivors for the rest of their lives, making it difficult to trust and impacting their relationships. It is all the more devastating when such abuse comes at the hand of such a highly regarded doctor, since it leaves survivors questioning the organizations and even the medical profession itself upon which so many rely. I am here to face you, Larry, so you can see I've regained my strength, that I am no longer a victim, I am a survivor.

. . . You are so sick I can't even comprehend how angry I feel when I think of you. You lied to me and manipulated me to think that when you treated me, you were closing your eyes because you had been working hard when you were really touching me, an innocent child, to pleasure yourself. Imagine feeling like you have no power and no voice. Well you know what, Larry? I have both power and voice and I am only beginning to just use them. All these brave women have power and we will use our voices to make sure you get what you deserve—a life of suffering spent replaying the words delivered by this powerful army of survivors.

. . . Your Honor, I ask you to give Larry the strongest possible sentence, which his actions deserve. For by doing so, you will send a message to him

and to other abusers that they cannot get away with their horrible crimes. They will be exposed for the evil they are and they will be punished to the maximum extent of the law. Let this sentence strike fear in anyone who thinks it is OK to hurt another person. Abusers, your time is up. The survivors are here, standing tall, and we are not going anywhere.

The New York Times published the full text of Aly Raisman's statement the following day (January 20, 2018).

In Ingham County Larry Nassar was sentenced up to 175 years in prison, and in Eaton County up to 125 years. He was also sentenced up to 60 years in federal prison on charges of child pornography.

Victims of crime did not always have the opportunity to do what Aly Raisman and the hundreds of other women in Larry Nassar's case got to do: appear in court, confront their abuser, and speak about how their lives were impacted. Indeed, it is still relatively new that victims are allowed to prepare statements that will be considered during sentencing. Even though not all judges will agree to let victims make their statements in person, at the very least, the act of submitting them is thought to help victims heal, find closure, and feel as though they are participating in the judicial process. In general, victims of crime have limited roles to play in the administration of justice.

But not everyone views victim impact statements as a good thing, with opponents concerned that they may undermine offenders' due process rights, draw attention away from the facts of the case, or lead to harsher prison sentences (Erez, 1999). In a system built with offenders' rights (rather than victims' rights) in mind, victims have a hard time finding their place. Crimes are technically considered offenses against the *state*, which means that victims are rarely treated as more than witnesses to a case. Navigating the criminal justice process can therefore be intimidating, confusing, and frustrating for many victims of crime.

With these issues in mind, this chapter focuses on victims' experiences with the criminal justice system—namely how victims are treated during the arrest, prosecution, and punishment of offenders. An important theme in this chapter concerns how some victims have more positive experiences than others, and how some experience a form of secondary victimization with respect to how they are treated throughout the legal process. We will also discuss the impact of victimization on legal reforms, including victim impact statements, and victim compensation. Overall, the broader purpose of this chapter is to better understand the consequences—both positive and negative—victims experience as a result of their contact with the criminal legal system.

Victims and the criminal justice system

Way back in the day, before societies formed their own formal criminal justice systems, victims were fully in charge of punishing offenders and seeking their own justice. Societies operated under the principle of *lex talionis*—meaning an eye for an eye, a tooth for a tooth—where victims (or their relatives) took it upon themselves to pursue retribution, fines, or other punishments from wrongdoers that were meant to equal the harms inflicted. This sort of victim-initiated justice system was in place for a long time, and remained intact throughout the Middle Ages. It was not until greedy feudal barons decided that they wanted to claim the compensation paid to victims that criminal acts were redefined as violations against the state (Schafer, 1968). As modern criminal justice systems were established, victims were virtually left out of the equation. While things are certainly improving, victims still face many challenges in their contact with the criminal justice system—particularly in their interactions with law enforcement and the courts.

Victims and law enforcement

More likely than not, a victim's first (and sometimes only) contact with the criminal justice system is with law enforcement. The ways in which police interact with victims can thus profoundly shape victims' perceptions of the legal system. Many victims are intimidated by the thought of opening up to police officers, and for some, even just the decision to call the police can be nerve-racking. As we discussed in Chapter 2, slightly fewer than half of all violent crime victims and just over one-third of property crime victims report their victimization to the police (Morgan & Kena, 2017). Reluctant victims often fear that they will be shamed or disbelieved, or they anticipate that involvement with the legal system will bring further troubles and psychological harm (Patterson, Greeson, & Campbell, 2009). Either way, if a crime becomes known to law enforcement, victims will likely be interviewed by police officers.

As the initial gatekeepers of the criminal justice system, police officers hold considerable discretion in the investigation of offenses and in the decision to make an arrest. Traditionally, the police have not been viewed as highly sympathetic toward victims—especially victims of intimate partner violence or sexual assault. Studies suggest that almost half of rape victims who make a police report are treated by law enforcement in ways that are upsetting (Monroe et al., 2005). Victims often report that police are cold and unsupportive, and in some cases police officers have threatened to charge victims with a crime if they did not provide an accurate story (Logan et al., 2005). These sorts of negative interactions are referred to as "secondary victimization" because they can make it feel like one is being victimized all over again. Insensitive and inappropriate questions that put pressure on victims to expose any inconsistencies in their statements can change the emphasis of the case from what the accused did to what the victim did or did not do. Some victims note that they would not have even reported the offense if they had known what the subsequent experience would be like (Campbell, 2008).

Patterson (2011), for example, conducted in-depth interviews with female victims of rape in a single U.S. county to examine their experiences with law enforcement. Many victims did not feel they were treated well, such as one victim who described her encounter with a detective:

> He was just so mean to me, kept questioning everything that I said, he made me so uncomfortable. . . . He used this huge word. I can't remember what it was, and I asked him what that meant, and what do you mean by that, and he said, "What, you don't know? Why don't you look it up?" I said, "Okay, thanks." I felt stupid. . . . You would think that they would care about people, but they didn't. I just wanted them to be there for me, to help me, to tell me what was going on, to understand, to help me out, rather than push me away.
>
> (Patterson, 2011: 338)

Even though studies have routinely shown that secondary victimization occurs, this does not happen to all victims who interact with the police, and less is known about why some victims have more positive experiences with law enforcement than others. There is some evidence to suggest that victims may fare better when detectives display a caring demeanor, when they show concern for victims' safety and well-being, when they listen intently to their stories and concerns, and when they offer victims additional help and information (Heydon & Powell, 2018). Another victim in the study by Patterson (2011) relayed the following about her positive experience:

> He [the detective] made it very clear to me that if I ever needed someone to talk to, he would be there. He gave me his, along with his card, he wrote his personal number on the back so I could leave a message for him. I was very thankful for that. He said if I remembered anything or if I had any questions or if there was just anything whatsoever that he could help me with, he made me feel that he took me seriously.
>
> (Patterson, 2011: 335)

It therefore seems that with increased sensitivity training and empathetic interviewing techniques police may be better able to respond to victims of crime in positive ways (Maddox, Lee, & Barker, 2011). Because the amount and quality of training for law enforcement varies greatly across communities, some officers may receive minimal training on how to interact with victims of crime (Lonsway, Welch, & Fitzgerald, 2001). With more in-depth, specialized training on how to respond sensitively to victims, issues of secondary victimization by law enforcement might be improved.

Victims and the courts

If police make an arrest, the case is forwarded to the prosecutor who will decide whether or not to file charges against the suspect. Prosecutors have virtually unfettered discretion in making this key decision, and they tend to reject a significant percentage of cases at screening. In attempts to avoid uncertainty, prosecutors will typically only file charges in cases where the odds of conviction are high and reject filing charges in cases where getting a conviction seems unlikely (Albonetti, 1987). This concern with convictability creates a "downstream orientation" in prosecutorial decision making—that is, an anticipation and consideration of how others (i.e., the jury and defense) will interpret and respond to a case as it moves forward (Pattavina, Morabito, & Williams, 2016). Accordingly, prosecutors are more likely to file charges when the offense is serious, when it is clear that the victim has suffered real harm, and when the evidence against the suspect is strong.

In making judgments about which cases are most likely to result in conviction, prosecutors develop a perceptual shorthand that incorporates stereotypes of "real crimes" and "genuine victims." A "genuine victim" is an essential element of a strong case (Frohmann, 1991). These are individuals whom jurors would be most likely to perceive as credible, innocent, and undeserving of victimization—namely upstanding citizens who did little to encourage the crime against them. Consequently, prosecutors consider not only the legally relevant indicators of case seriousness and offender culpability, but also the background, character, and behavior of the victim, the relationship between the suspect and the victim, and the willingness of the victim to cooperate as the case moves forward (Beichner, & Spohn, 2012).

Frohmann's (1991) qualitative interviews with district attorneys shed light on this issue. In particular, her findings suggested that prosecutors actively look for " 'holes' or problems that will make the victim's version of 'what happened' unbelievable or not convincing beyond a reasonable doubt" (Frohmann, 1991: 214). Other studies have also confirmed these patterns. When Spohn, Beichner, and Davis-Frenzel (2001) asked prosecutors in Miami, Florida to identify the factors that influenced their decision to file charges, all of them mentioned the strength of evidence in the case and the credibility of the victim. One prosecutor explained:

You have to look at the victim, her demeanor and her behavior. You have to look closely at the allegations that have been made. If there is other evidence or testimony that conflicts with what she's saying—if, for example, the suspect has an entirely different account of the encounter and there are witnesses who corroborate his story—then you have to determine what set of circumstances you accept and what you don't find credible.

(Spohn et al., 2001: 229)

The ability of prosecutors to construct a credible narrative for the jury—one in which they will buy into the victim's account of what happened—is essential to the decision to file charges in a case. In this regard, numerous extralegal factors, such as the victim's age, moral character, and involvement in risky lifestyles (e.g., using or selling drugs, engaging in crime, and being out on the streets late at night) have been found to influence prosecutors' decisions (Frohmann, 1997). These issues are heightened when it comes to the prosecution of sexual assault cases, which is why a lot of these cases ultimately do not result in charges being filed. In their study of a Midwestern Police Department, for instance, Alderden and Ullman (2012) found that only 9.7 percent of sexual assault cases reported to police ultimately result in charges being filed, despite arrests being made in 31.8 percent of cases, as shown in Figure 7.1. Other studies indicate that fewer than half of sexual assault cases that result in arrest will ultimately result in charges being filed by prosecutors (Spohn & Tellis, 2018).

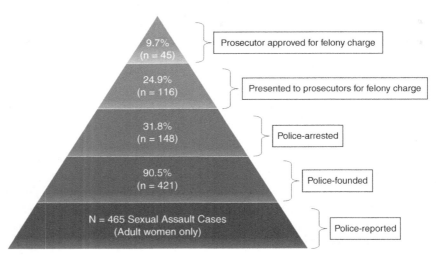

Figure 7.1 Patterns of attrition in sexual assault cases reported to a Midwestern police department

Source: Alderden & Ullman (2012).

Being under scrutiny by prosecutors or having charges dropped can be tough for victims. However, if charges are ultimately filed in a case, then one of two things will probably happen. Either the accused will be offered and agree to a plea deal made by the prosecutor, or the case will go to trial. If it goes to trial, the victim may be called as a witness to provide sworn testimony against the defendant. For victims, the prospect of serving as a witness can be intimidating for a number of reasons, such as having to face their offender, or having to once again recount in detail what happened to them. But as several critics have recognized, the inefficiency and unpredictability of the court system itself can also add to victims' stress and confusion. Ash (1972: 390) described this process as follows:

> In the typical situation the witness will several times be ordered to appear at some designated place, usually a courtroom, but sometimes a prosecutor's office or grand jury room. Several times he will be made to wait tedious, unconscionably long intervals in dingy courthouse corridors or in other grim surroundings. Several times he will suffer the discomfort of being ignored by busy officials and the bewilderment and painful anxiety of not knowing what is going on around him or what is going to happen to him. On most of these occasions he will never be asked to testify or give anyone any information, often because of a last-minute adjournment granted in a huddled conference at the judge's bench. He will miss many hours from work (or school) and consequently will lose many hours of wages. In most jurisdictions he will receive at best only token payment in the form of ridiculously low witness fees for his time and trouble. . . . Through the long months of waiting for the end of a criminal case, he must remain ever on call, reminded of his continuing attachment to the court by sporadic subpoenas. For some, each subpoena and each appearance at court is accompanied by tension and terror prompted by fear of the lawyers, fear of the defendant or his friends, and fear of the unknown. In sum, the experience is dreary, time-wasting, depressing, exhausting, confusing, frustrating, numbing, and seemingly endless.

Even though this criticism was levied nearly 50 years ago, much of these concerns still ring true today.

Victim-witness programs

To try to remedy some of these problems and help victims navigate the court process, victim-witness programs have been established. These programs are staffed by victim advocates who are trained to help victims prepare for their testimony by performing mock trials, by accompanying them to court, and by providing them the support and guidance they need as their case proceeds (or not) through the legal system. These programs are often established through law enforcement or prosecutor's offices, and generally offer the following services to victims:

- Inform victims if the status of their case changes
- Notify victims of case events
- Educate victims about the criminal justice system
- Provide referrals to community-based treatment providers
- Assist victims in applying for victim compensation
- Accompany victims to court proceedings
- Assist with the preparation of victim-impact statements.

In the U.S., there are over 9,000 local, state, and national organizations that provide assistance and support to victims of crime (U.S. Department of Justice, 2018).

Despite the availability of programming, these services are not often used by victims. Recent estimates from the NCVS suggest that only 10 percent of victims of violent crime receive victim services (Morgan & Kena, 2017). Similarly, Sims, Yost, and Abbott (2005) found that, in their survey of victims in Pennsylvania, only 1 in 25 (3%) reported ever using victim services or a victim-witness program. This was likely because the majority of the victims surveyed (57%) had not been notified that these programs exist. Other victims reported not using these services because they thought it would be a hassle, and others noted that they could receive assistance from friends or family members instead. Sims and colleagues (2005) therefore recommended that, to increase the use of services by crime victims, the following things need to happen: (1) a greater emphasis needs to be placed on educating the public about such services, (2) these programs need to be staffed by well-trained individuals who can meet the needs of crime victims, and (3) the services provided to victims need to be broadened.

Legal reforms for victims of crime

Having recognized that victims face many difficulties after coming into contact with the criminal justice system, governments around the world have enacted reforms to provide services, rights, and compensation to victims of crime (Maguire, 1991). While the nature and substance of these reforms vary from place to place, the push to improve victims' experiences with the criminal justice system has gained a lot of momentum. In the U.S., all 50 states and the federal government have passed legislation to guarantee certain rights to victims throughout the criminal justice process. These include making sure that victims are treated well and kept informed throughout case proceedings, that they have the right to prepare a victim impact statement, and that they have the right to apply for compensation. Here we will focus on two of the most important legislative developments for victims: victim impact statements, and victim compensation.

Victim impact statements

One of the most far-reaching legal reforms accomplished by the victims' rights movement has been the allowance of victim impact statements in court proceedings. Victim impact statements, such as the one delivered by Aly Raisman (that we discussed at the start of this chapter), are either written or oral statements that detail the impact of the defendant's crime on the victim or the victim's surviving family. These statements can be highly emotional, and usually describe how crime took a toll on the person's well-being—physically, psychologically, and financially. Since the U.S. Supreme Court held that such statements were constitutional (*Payne v. Tennessee*, 1991), the right to give a victim impact statement has been recognized in every U.S. state and by the federal government, as well as in the United Kingdom, Canada, Australia, and New Zealand.

Victim impact information is typically included in the pre-sentencing report provided to judges, although some U.S. states will even allow victim impact information to be introduced during bail, pretrial release, plea bargain, and parole hearings (National Center for Victims of Crime, 2018a). Out of the 31 U.S. states that enforce the death penalty, 26 allow for victim impact statements during the penalty phase of the trial (Death Penalty Information Center, 2018). For many victims of crime, the victim impact statement is the only opportunity to participate in the criminal justice process and to speak out against the offender who harmed them. Scholars argue that it is important for victims to feel that they have a say in the process. Erez (1999: 553) stated that "a major source of satisfaction for victims is when judges pay attention to their input by citing victims' own phrases from impact statements in judicial sentencing comments."

But as we mentioned earlier, the integration of victim impact statements into the court process has not been without controversy. Proponents argue that victim impact statements can bias decisions against the accused—namely by arousing strong emotions in jurors and skewing them in favor of harsher sentences, particularly in capital cases (i.e., those where the death penalty is an option). There seems to be some truth behind this criticism. Although the evidence is mixed, some research shows that victim impact statements incite or amplify jurors' anger toward the defendant, which can interfere with care-ful decision making. As Nadler and Rose (2003) argued, victim impact state-ments can make jurors so eager to punish that they search for evidence to validate their anger and ignore evidence in the defendant's favor. Experimental research conducted by Paternoster and Deise (2011), for example, found that mock jurors who heard victim impact statements during the penalty phase of a trial had more sympathy and empathy toward the victim, and more anger, hos-tility, and vengeance toward the offender. Jurors in this study were also more likely to impose a death sentence if they heard a victim impact statement, and this relationship was explained by increased feelings of sympathy and empathy for the victim and the victim's family (Paternoster & Diese, 2011).

Other critics of victim impact statements suggest that the statements reinforce harmful stereotypes and encourage judgments about "worthy" and "unworthy" victims (Bandes, 2016), especially since jurors may feel more sym-pathetic toward some victims than toward others. To be sure, the impact state-ment of a victim who met her assailant while out late at night trying to buy drugs will probably be valued less than a victim attacked while hiking with her dog on a Saturday afternoon. These judgments can also be highly racialized and class-based. More recent research even suggests that the kinds of emo-tions conveyed in victim impact statements influence mock jurors' decisions, where angry victim impact statements have been shown to lead to harsher sentencing recommendations than sad ones (Nuñez et al., 2017).

Furthermore, the effectiveness of impact statements in facilitating victims' recovery is still a hot topic of debate. Whereas some argue that they are thera-peutic and central to the healing process (Chalmers, Duff, & Leverick, 2007), others suggest that they may be counter-productive and re-traumatize victims–especially if victims have to recount and relive all of their painful feelings and memories. A recent study by Lens and colleagues (2015) found that deliver-ing impact statements had no direct therapeutic effects on victims' levels of anger or anxiety, or on how much control victims' felt they had over their own recovery process. Although, in general, scholars suggest that victims are more satisfied with the criminal justice process if they present an impact statement (Roberts & Erez, 2004), more research is certainly needed to determine the conditions under which impact statements can be helpful (or harmful) to vic-tims of crime (Lens et al., 2015). It also remains unclear how much these state-ments actually influence judges' sentencing decisions (Roberts, 2009).

Victim compensation

Another important legal reform intended to help victims is the establishment of *victim compensation*–state payments made to victims of crime. New Zealand passed the first compensation legislation in 1963, followed closely by England in

1964. In the U.S., victim compensation started in California in 1965, and today, compensation programs operate in every state. Money for compensation can be drawn from a variety of places, but a popular funding source is from the fees and fines collected from offenders.

In 1984, the United States "Victims of Crime Act" (VOCA) was passed, which initiated a process whereby the federal government would provide victim compensation for federal offenses and federal funds for state compensation programs. These VOCA funds were drawn exclusively from fines, bond forfeitures, and special assessments levied on convicted criminals and businesses. Today, VOCA funds provide more than $700 million annually to states to assist victims of crime–representing about one-third of each state's program funding–and the Crime Victims Fund has received more than $20 billion in deposits since it began in 1984 (National Association of VOCA Assistance Administrators, 2018). U.S. crime victim compensation programs have a maximum that will be paid for each claim, which varies from state to state, and can range from $10,000 to $100,000 (National Center for Victims of Crime, 2018b). Because it may take several weeks or months to process a claim for victim compensation, many states offer emergency awards, which are compensation payments of $500 to $1,000 to cover emergency expenses such as those for medications, food, or shelter.

However, not all victims are eligible for compensation from the Crime Victims Fund. Compensation typically serves a narrow class of victims–usually only victims of violence (e.g., homicide, rape, domestic violence, assault, child sexual abuse, and drunk driving)–given that these crimes are thought to be the most traumatic and financially taxing. Some states even require that victims be physically injured (not only emotionally traumatized) in order to receive compensation. In fact, some states have extremely strict eligibility requirements that make it difficult for a lot of victims to receive compensation. In Florida, for instance, victims are only eligible for compensation if:

- They reported their crime to law enforcement within 72 hours
- They cooperate fully with law enforcement, the State Attorney's Office, and the Attorney General's Office
- They were not engaged in an unlawful activity at the time of the crime
- Their conduct did not contribute to the situation that brought about their own injuries
- They have never been confined or in custody in a county or municipal facility, a state or federal correctional facility, or a juvenile detention, commitment, or assessment facility
- They have never been adjudicated as a habitual felony offender, habitual violent offender, or violent career criminal
- They have never been adjudicated guilty of a forcible felony offense (Florida Office of the Attorney General, 2018).

These stringent criteria render many victims ineligible for compensation, and penalize victims who have a criminal history or who may have needed to take a few extra days to report their crime to police. What is more, these criteria also affect the surviving family members of victims who are killed or seriously injured. This means that if the victim had a criminal history or was doing something unlawful at the time of the attack, the surviving family members would not be eligible for compensation. This is problematic, considering that compensation can be used to help cover the loss of household income, as well as medical expenses, mental health counseling, and funeral/burial costs.

These rigid compensation criteria are in contrast to the requirements put forth in other places, like England, where you can claim compensation for a crime that happened up to two years ago (Government Digital Service, 2018); or in Canada, where victims have one to two years to file a claim (depending on the province). Even then, many exceptions can be made for victims who wait longer to notify law enforcement (Canadian Resource Centre for Victims of Crime, 2018).

In practice, few victims appear to receive compensation—either because they choose not to apply, they have their claims denied, or they are unaware that these funds exist (Rutledge, 2011). One reason may be that police officers sometimes forget to provide victims with information about compensation when responding to a crime. For example, in their survey of police in Texas, Fritsch et al. (2004) found that the majority of officers (75%) did not frequently advise crime victims about compensation, and that 24 percent of officers were unaware that a victim compensation fund existed (despite it being in place for almost 20 years). This was concerning for a couple reasons: (1) police officers in Texas were statutorily required to disseminate information to crime victims regarding how to obtain compensation; and (2) at around the time that the study was conducted, the Texas victim compensation fund had a balance surplus in excess of $140 million (Fritsch et al., 2004). In fact, in the U.S., many states end up with cash surpluses in their victim compensation funds each year (Newmark et al., 2003). Because police officers typically have the criminal justice system's initial (and sometimes only) contact with victims, it is important that they—or the victim advocates who work alongside them—provide information regarding victim compensation.

Gaps and challenges

The legal reforms discussed here are certainly not exhaustive, and we wish to point out that victims also have a right to restitution in addition to compensation. Restitution differs from compensation in that it is a court-ordered payment *made by offenders* to victims, and it is imposed upon an offender at the time of sentencing. There are not many studies examining how victims find out about restitution or about which victims apply for and are awarded restitution, and these are important avenues for future research (Haynes, Cares, & Ruback, 2015).

Furthermore, the consequences–both positive and negative–of victims' contact with the criminal justice system need to be explored further. Some research suggests that when victims are treated poorly by law enforcement, they may be less likely to seek help from other systems–such as for medical care and mental health services–which can have long-lasting negative consequences for their well-being (Campbell, 2005). Other studies suggest that unfavorable experiences with the criminal justice system can have implications for future behaviors, and even subsequent victimization. In one U.S. study, Wolfe and McLean (2017) found that adolescents who viewed the police as procedurally unfair were more likely to engage in criminal behaviors and other risky activities that, in turn, increased their risk of victimization.

Finally, one part of our criminal justice system has not been discussed here: corrections. With respect to offender re-entry, there are current debates about when victims can and should have a voice in the process. On the one hand, advocates believe that increased victim involvement in the planning, management, and implementation of re-entry policies and programs can result in better informed decisions and the achievement of re-entry goals (Herman & Wasserman, 2001). On the other hand, opponents argue that victims seldom possess information relevant to parole and re-entry decisions. According to Roberts (2009), victim input at corrections is an example of "punitive victim rights" that is inconsistent with the principles of our justice system. Indeed, there is a lot left to explore as we figure out where victims belong and what their roles should be within an offender-focused criminal justice system.

Key readings

Frohmann, L. (1991). Discrediting victims' allegations of sexual assault: Prosecutorial accounts of case rejections. *Social Problems, 38*, 213–226.

Paternoster, R. & Deise, J. (2011). A heavy thumb on the scale: The effect of victim impact evidence on capital decision making. *Criminology, 49*, 129–161.

Patterson, D. (2011). The linkage between secondary victimization by law enforcement and rape case outcomes. *Journal of Interpersonal Violence, 26*, 328–347.

Roberts, J.V. (2009). Listening to the crime victim: Evaluating victim input at sentencing and parole. *Crime and Justice, 38*, 347–412.

Rutledge, N.M. (2011). Looking a gift horse in the mouth: The underutilization of crime victim compensation funds by domestic violence victims. *Duke Journal of Gender Law and Policy, 19*, 223–273.

Discussion questions

1. What can police officers do to better respond to victims of crime?
2. What does it mean to say that prosecutors have a "downstream orientation?" How does this orientation affect victims of crime?
3. Why are victims permitted to present their impact statements during sentencing hearings, but not earlier on in the trial process?
4. What are some ways to improve participation in victim–witness programs?

References

Albonetti, C. (1987). Prosecutorial discretion: The effects of uncertainty. *Law and Society Review, 21*, 291–314.

Alderden, M.A. & Ullman, S.E. (2012). Creating a more complete and current picture: Examining police and prosecutor decision-making when processing sexual assault cases. *Violence against Women, 18*, 525–551.

Ash, M. (1972). On witnesses: A radical critique of criminal court procedures. *Notre Dame Law Review, 48*, 386–425.

Bandes, S.A. (July 23, 2016). What are victim-impact statements for? *The Atlantic*, July 23. Retrieved from www.theatlantic.com/politics/archive/2016/07/what-are-victim-impact-statements-for/492443/.

Beichner, D. & Spohn, C. (2012). Modeling the effects of victim behavior and moral character on prosecutors' charging decisions in sexual assault cases. *Violence and Victims, 27*, 3–24.

Campbell, R. (2005). What really happened? A validation study of rape survivors' help-seeking experiences with the legal and medical systems. *Violence & Victims, 20*, 55–68.

Campbell, R. (2008). The psychological impact of rape victims. *American Psychologist, 63*, 702.

Canadian Resource Centre for Victims of Crime. (2018). *Financial assistance*. Retrieved from: https://crcvc.ca/for-victims/financial-assistance/.

Chalmers, J., Duff, P., & Leverick, F. (2007, May). Victim impact statements: Can work, do work (for those who bother to make them). *Criminal Law Review*, 360–379.

Death Penalty Information Center. (2018). *Legal issues: States that allow victim impact statements*. Retrieved from https://deathpenaltyinfo.org/legal-issues-states-allow-victim-impact-statements.

Erez, E. (1999). Who's afraid of the big bad victim? Victim impact statements as victim empowerment *and* enhancement of justice. *Criminal Law Review, July*, 545–556.

Florida Office of the Attorney General. (2018). *Victim compensation brochure*. Retrieved from http://myfloridalegal.com/webfiles.nsf/WF/MRAY-8CVP5T/$file/BVCVictimCompensationBrochure.pdf.

Fritsch, E.J., Caeti, T.J., Tobolowsky, P.M., & Taylor, R.W. (2004). Police referrals of crime victims to compensation sources: An empirical analysis of attitudinal and structural impediments. *Police Quarterly, 7*, 372–393.

Frohmann, L. (1991). Discrediting victims' allegations of sexual assault: Prosecutorial accounts of case rejections. *Social Problems, 38*, 213–226.

Frohmann, L. (1997). Convictability and discordant locales: Reproducing race, class, and gender ideologies in prosecutorial decisionmaking. *Law and Society Review*, 531–556.

Government Digital Service. (2018). *Claim compensation if you were a victim of a violent crime*. Retrieved from www.gov.uk/claim-compensation-criminal-injury/eligibility.

Hauser, C. & Astor, M. (2018). The Larry Nassar case: What happened and how the fallout is spreading. *New York Times*, January 25.

Haynes, S.H., Cares, A.C., & Ruback, R.B. (2015). Reducing the harm of criminal victimization: The role of restitution. *Violence and Victims, 30*, 450–469.

Herman, S. & Wasserman, C. (2001). A role for victims in offender reentry. *Crime & Delinquency, 47*(3), 428–445.

Heydon, G. & Powell, A. (2018). Written-response interview protocols: An innovative approach to confidential reporting and victim interviewing in sexual assault investigations. *Policing and Society, 28*, 631–646.

Lens, K.M., Pemberton, A., Brans, K., Braeken, J., Bogaerts, S., & Lahlah, E. (2015). Delivering a Victim Impact Statement: Emotionally effective or counter-productive? *European Journal of Criminology, 12*(1), 17–34.

Logan, T.K., Evans, L., Stevenson, E., & Jordan, C.E. (2005). Barriers to services for rural and urban survivors of rape. *Journal of Interpersonal Violence, 20*, 591–616.

Lonsway, L., Welch, S., & Fitzgerald, L. (2001). Police training in sexual assault response. *Criminal Justice and Behavior, 28*, 695–730.

Maddox, L., Lee, D., & Barker, C. (2011). Police empathy and victim PTSD as potential factors in rape case attrition. *Journal of Police and Criminal Psychology, 26*, 112–117.

Maguire, M. (1991). The needs and rights of victims of crime. *Crime and Justice, 14*, 363–433.

Monroe, L.M., Kinney, L.M., Weist, M.D., Dafeamekpor, D.S., Dantzler, J., & Reynolds, M.W. (2005). The experience of sexual assault: Findings from a statewide victim needs assessment. *Journal of Interpersonal Violence, 20*, 767–777.

Morgan, R.E. & Kena, G. (2017). *Criminal victimization, 2016*. Washington, DC: U.S. Department of Justice, Bureau of Justice Statistics.

Nadler, J. & Rose, M.R. (2003). Victim impact testimony and the psychology of punishment. *Cornell Law Review, 88*, 419–456.

National Association of VOCA Assistance Administrators. (2018). *VOCA funding*. Retrieved from www.navaa.org/budget/.

National Center for Victims of Crime. (2018a). *Victim impact statements*. Retrieved from http://victimsofcrime.org/help-for-crime-victims/get-help-bulletins-for-crime-victims/victim-impact-statements.

National Center for Victims of Crime. (2018b). *Crime victim compensation*. Retrieved from http://victimsofcrime.org/help-for-crime-victims/get-help-bulletins-for-crime-victims/crime-victim-compensation.

Newmark, L., Bonderman, J., Smith, B., & Liner, B. (2003). *The national evaluation of state Victims of Crime Act compensation and assistance programs: Trends and strategies for the future*. Washington, DC: Urban Institute.

Nuñez, N., Myers, B., Wilkowski, B.M., & Schweitzer, K. (2017). The impact of angry versus sad victim impact statements on mock jurors' sentencing decisions in a capital trial. *Criminal Justice and Behavior, 44*(6), 862–886.

Park, A. (2017). Aly Raisman opens up about sexual abuse by USA gymnastics doctor Larry Nassar. *Time*, November 13.

Paternoster, R. & Deise, J. (2011). A heavy thumb on the scale: The effect of victim impact evidence on capital decision making. *Criminology, 49*, 129–161.

Pattavina, A., Morabito, M., & Williams, L.M. (2016). Examining connections between the police and prosecution in sexual assault case processing: Does the use of exceptional clearance facilitate a downstream orientation? *Victims and Offenders, 11*, 315–334.

Patterson, D. (2011). The linkage between secondary victimization by law enforcement and rape case outcomes. *Journal of Interpersonal Violence, 26*, 328–347.

Patterson, D., Greeson, M., & Campbell, R. (2009). Understanding rape survivors' decisions not to seek help from formal systems. *Health and Social Work, 34*, 127–136.

Payne v. Tennessee, 111, S. Ct., 2597 (1991).

zlowski, K. (2018). 204 impact statements, 9 days, 2 counties, and a life r Larry Nassar. *Detroit News*, February 8.

2009). Listening to the crime victim: Evaluating victim input at sentencing *Crime and Justice, 38*, 347–412.

Roberts, J.V. and Erez, E. (2004) Communication in sentencing: Exploring the expressive function of victim impact statements. *International Review of Victimology, 10*, 223–244.

Rutledge, N.M. (2011). Looking a gift horse in the mouth: The underutilization of crime victim compensation funds by domestic violence victims. *Duke Journal of Gender Law and Policy, 19*, 223–273.

Schafer, S. (1968). *The victim and his criminal: A study in functional responsibility*. New York: Random House.

Sims, B., Yost, B., & Abbott, C. (2005). Use and nonuse of victim services programs: Implications from a statewide survey of crime victims. *Criminology and Public Policy, 4*, 361–384.

Spohn, C. & Tellis, K. (2018). Sexual assault case outcomes: Disentangling the overlapping decisions of police and prosecutors. *Justice Quarterly*, 1–29.

Spohn, C., Beichner, D., & Davis-Frenzel, E. (2001). Prosecutorial justifications for sexual assault case rejection: Guarding the "gateway to justice". *Social Problems, 48*, 206–235.

U.S. Department of Justice. (2018). *Victim witness program*. Retrieved from www.justice.gov/uspc/victim-witness-program.

Wolfe, S.E. & McLean, K. (2017). Procedural injustice, risky lifestyles, and violent victimization. *Crime and Delinquency, 63*, 1383–1409.

8 Social and political consequences of victimization

In both criminological and political circles, Willie Horton is famous (or perhaps infamous). He was doing life without parole in a Massachusetts prison for the murder of a 17-year-old gas station attendant in what started out as a robbery in 1974. Horton stabbed the kid 19 times after the boy had already handed over the money and then stuffed the dead body into a nearby trash can.

It is therefore safe to say that Willie was a poster boy for James Q. Wilson's famous quote that "Wicked people exist. Nothing avails but to set them apart from innocent people" (Wilson, 1975: 209). But he was let out of prison as part of a weekend work furlough program in 1986. He left the prison that day and didn't come back. On April 3, 1987, while in Oxon Hill, Maryland, he raped a woman twice after pistol whipping her fiancé and making sure he was bound and gagged. As horrific as this crime was, under normal circumstances such an offense would likely not make national news. But these were not normal circumstances: there was a major Presidential election brewing at the time.

The 1988 United States Presidential election—like virtually all of those before it and those that came after it—got a little dirty. On the Republican ticket was George Herbert Walker Bush, a former Director of the Central Intelligence Agency and Vice President under Ronald Reagan. On the Democratic side was Michael Dukakis, the longest-serving Governor of the State of Massachusetts. Things were heating up on both campaigns and even the Vice Presidential debates were making for some really juicy political theater. Lloyd Bensten—the crusty Texas Senator (and former World War II Air Force pilot) who was Dukakis' running mate—had just told Dan Quayle "You're no Jack Kennedy" in a televised debate. Oh it was on![1]

---

1 We recognize that we are living in a political era when the President of the United States can publicly refer to political opponents as "Lyin' Ted" (for Ted Cruz),

It was at this time that folks in the Bush campaign got word of Willie Horton. Despite Mr. Bush's gentle demeanor and call for "compassionate conservatism" (McAdams, 2011), the Bush team made the explicit decision to "go negative" and run with the Willie Horton angle, namely that a dangerous offender who should never have taken a breath outside of prison was let out to victimize a woman because of a policy endorsed by a liberal Massachusetts Governor (Simon, 2015). Adding to the drama was the fact that Horton was black and his female victim was white. The message was that Dukakis was the worst thing a policy maker could be: soft on crime.

It turned out that, for Michael Dukakis, Willie Horton was political Kryptonite. The Bush camp did a masterful job of linking Dukakis to this one particular crime. As Lee Atwater—Bush's campaign manager—said: "By the time we're finished, they're going to wonder whether Willie Horton is Dukakis' running mate" (Simon, 1990). The damage was done, and Dukakis found it exceedingly difficult to shed his label as a coddler of criminals. That he went on television in a debate with Bush and told the world that he would not support the death penalty even if his wife Kitty Dukakis were raped and murdered certainly did not help his cause (McNulty, 1988).

The consequence was that Dukakis' popularity slipped hard in the polls. He tried to rebound and combat the image that he was "soft" with a television ad that featured him riding in a tank—a visual that had him sporting a goofy grin while wearing a helmet that was clearly a size too big. The ad was a disaster, so much so that the Bush camp used the tank picture in tandem with the Willie Horton story. Things got so laughably bad for Dukakis that *Saturday Night Live* even got in on the act with a series of fake commercials that not only made fun of his weak stance on crime, but even his rather diminutive stature—the commercial ended with the phrase: "George Bush, he's taller." The game had changed in a fundamental way, and the political lesson was clear: coming off as soft on crime—where offenders would be left free to victimize the public with impunity—would no longer be at all acceptable for any political candidate. Getting tough—or at least appearing to have the willingness to do so—was now mandatory.

The point of the Willie Horton story—beyond the lessons it carries about political strategy—is to show how powerful victimization can be both socially and politically. We therefore close Part III of the book with a chapter that

---

"Crooked Hillary" (for Hillary Clinton), and "Little Marco" (for Marco Rubio) and still remain popular with over 60 million voters. He can even refer to women as "dogs" and suffer little in the way of consequences (Graham, 2018). So hearing that a candidate for the second-highest office in the country said "You're no Jack Kennedy" likely seems incredibly G-rated. But at the time it was a really big deal.

focuses more generally on the broader social and political consequences of victimization. These include how victimization can result in elevated levels of fear of crime, which can in turn be a source of community change (e.g., residents withdrawing from neighborhood life or moving away to a different community). The chapter also covers how the fear of victimization has been used by policy makers to generate support for a wide array of punitive policies that have done little to enhance public safety or to reduce levels of victimization.

The social consequences of victimization

One of the most popular and compelling ideas to hit criminology in the past few decades is the "broken windows" perspective. Developed by James Q. Wilson and George Kelling in 1982, the gist of the idea is that when public spaces are left unattended and appear to be neglected, it sends a signal to community residents that no one really cares about the place. Once that happens, things just seem to spiral downhill, where additional signs of physical and social disorder— even if rather modest (e.g., the proverbial "broken window")—elicit fear on the part of those in the neighborhood because they are a harbinger of worse things to come. Today's litter on the street is tomorrow's gun-toting and drug-peddling gang on the street corner. And because of that fear, citizens will withdraw from public places, which will send the message to the criminal element that the community is theirs for the taking.

This perspective immediately became wildly popular, particularly in policy circles. New York City famously put the plan into action, where the police took an aggressive stance toward non-serious forms of offending (e.g., panhandling; loitering; the guys who try to squeegee your car windows when you are stopped at a light). The problem, however, is that despite its intuitive appeal (and backing among certain political elites), much of the idea turned out to be problematic when the research started coming in. As it turns out, people are not really afraid of small signs of disorder (they know the difference between trash and drug dealing; Gau & Pratt, 2008); criminals tend not to travel too far to commit their offenses (they are more likely to stay close to home for such opportunities, so no "influx" of new criminals is necessary; see Wright & Decker, 1994); and community residents are not always happy with police when they target minor forms of misbehavior (Harcourt, 2009).

But the idea of broken windows did get one thing right: it highlighted the fact that crime and violence can have rather dramatic effects on the social and physical functioning of a community. In particular, it focused our attention on how victimization can cause entire communities to change in a couple of important ways: through increased residential turnover and by weakening levels of community collective efficacy.

Residential turnover

It has long been noted in the criminological literature that certain community characteristics lead to higher levels of violence and victimization. Dating back to the 1920s, scholars have recognized that communities that have a more stable population–where residents move in and stay there for a while–tend to have lower rates of crime and victimization (Pratt & Cullen, 2005). The reasons why are varied, but the general idea is an old one: that members of stable communities are better able to exert informal social control over residents, particularly young people (Shaw & McKay, 1942). Put simply, when people in a neighborhood know everybody–they know the kids and their parents–they are in a better position to keep misbehavior in check (Sampson & Groves, 1989).

Victimization, however, can end up throwing a wrench into the works. Indeed, recent research using data from the NCVS indicates that victimization can be both a consequence and a source of residential instability. For example, Xie and McDowall (2008a) found that residents who are new to a neighborhood–where they may not have fully figured out what kinds of personal precautions they should be taking–are most likely to be victimized. In addition, Xie and McDowall (2008b) also found that being victimized is a primary reason for people wanting to move out of a community into what they hope will be a safer environment. Victimization is therefore a critically important component of community change–one that has the potential to disrupt social relationships and to undermine neighborhood stability.

Weakened collective efficacy

Closely related to the idea of community stability and informal social control is another concept that is well-known in criminology: collective efficacy. Collective efficacy is generally defined as the ability of community residents to come together and accomplish common goals (Sampson, Raudenbush, & Earls, 1997). It therefore entails elements of social capital, trust between members of the community, a willingness to step in and help others out, and a belief that doing so will actually bring about positive change (Morenoff, Sampson, & Raudenbush, 2001; see also Hipp, 2016). There is evidence from a long list of empirical studies demonstrating that collective efficacy is one of the strongest predictors of community crime rates, where neighborhoods characterized by high collective efficacy enjoy much lower levels of victimization (Pratt & Cullen, 2005).

Yet, once again, victimization can get in the way if these important community processes. In communities with high rates of victimization, residents are more likely to withdraw socially and to avoid public spaces; they are less likely to intervene in situations that might end up with a crime being committed; they are less likely to come to the aid of a fellow community resident; and they may be less likely to trust calling the police if a crime has occurred (Nix et al., 2015). The bottom line is that there is a reciprocal relationship between victimization and collective efficacy, where low levels of collective efficacy tend to breed higher rates of victimization, and where higher rates of victimization end up eroding collective efficacy even further (Sampson, 2012).

The political consequences of victimization

During the 2016 U.S. Presidential campaign season and election, it became abundantly clear that a sizable portion of the American electorate was really scared of Hillary Clinton. The fear did not appear to be specific to a given policy position that she held. Sure, there were concerns that she was hell-bent on taking away everyone's guns and therefore leaving the entire country unprotected (NRA-ILA, 2016). But the fear was more "general" than that, particularly among older white men who seemed scared that the changing demographics of the nation would mean that their hold on the country was slipping, and it seemed as though Hillary's popularity was further evidence of their social and cultural victimization (Hochschild, 2016).

Thus, when fear runs this high, people become willing to believe a lot of crazy things. One of them was a fake story that came out in 2016 peddled online by alt-right hucksters like Alex Jones of "Infowars." The story was that, after Hillary Clinton's emails were hacked (as well as others in the Democratic Party), there was "coded" evidence embedded in the emails that Clinton was running an international human trafficking sex ring in the basement of a Washington, DC pizza joint (Wending, 2016). Believing this to be true, 28-year-old Edgar Maddison Welch left his home in Salisbury, North Carolina armed with an assault rifle, and headed up to DC to rescue Hillary's sex slaves. He even tried to recruit a few buddies to join him, urging them to watch a YouTube video that Welch felt contained incontrovertible evidence of the sex ring (which was possibly Satanic as well). The others did not join him, but that did not stop Welch firing three shots into the restaurant (Hsu, 2017).

Of course, there was no human smuggling operation going on. And Welch's falling for the story cannot be dismissed as the consequence of some form of mental illness on his part; he was not mentally ill, but was instead thoroughly convinced that all of it was real. So what this really shows is how harmful it can be when victimization—even if it is not happening directly to us—mixes with the politics of fear.

Victimization and the fear of crime

To understand how powerful a political force victimization can be, we need look no further than the "get-tough" movement in the United States. Prior to the 1960s, crime was not cited by the American public as a major issue of concern. Even when President Reagan launched his "War on Drugs" in 1982—which essentially tied the issues of crime and drugs together for years to come—less than 2 percent of American citizens cited drugs as the nation's most pressing problem (Beckett, 1997). Even as late as 1993—under the leadership of President Bill Clinton this time, immediately before Congress began its debate over his "crime bill" proposal—only 7 percent of Americans cited crime as the nation's most important problem. But just six months later, and largely as a result of the intense publicity these legislative sessions received, that number had increased to 30 percent (Braun & Pasternak, 1994). By August 1994, that figure had reached 52 percent, which public opinion pollsters attributed to Clinton's discussion of the crime bill in the State of the Union Address, and to the extensive media coverage of how Congress was considering the bill (Moore, 1994).

But what is critically important is that citizens tend to suffer from a case of what has been termed "categorical contagion." According to Zimring and Hawkins (1997: 13), categorical contagion refers to "the agency whereby citizens come to fear many forms of criminal behaviour because they imagine them all committed by extremely violent protagonists." What this means is that when people have a particular experience with victimization—or even a vicarious one—regardless of what kind of crime it was, it can result in a more "general" fear of all crime (Ruhs, Greve, & Kappes, 2017). The result is a spreading assumption that today's low-level drug dealer (or thief or trespasser or vagrant) is tomorrow's murderer, and that it is therefore perfectly rational to be concerned about all types of crime and victimization (Jackson, 2015; see also Singer et al., 2018).

It is not just being concerned about crime and victimization that really matters. What is equally important with respect to public opinion is whether or not people think the problem is getting worse, because the idea that crime is getting worse is a primary driver of the fear of being victimized (Bolger & Bolger, 2018). On that front, there seemed to be at least a reasonable association between public perception and reality during the Clinton years. As may be seen in Figure 8.1, since crime was dropping during the 1990s, the percentage of U.S. residents who thought that the crime problem was worse than it was

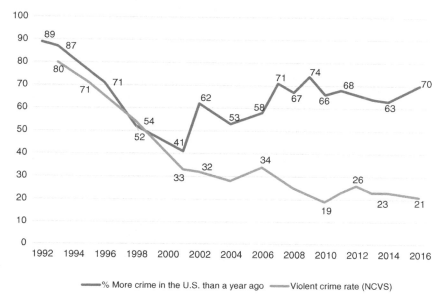

Figure 8.1 U.S. violent crime rate and Americans' perceptions of crime rate vs. a year ago*

Note: * Violent crime rate is number of victimizations per 1,000 persons that occurred during the year.

Sources: Bureau of Justice Statistics, National Crime Victimization Survey, 1993-2017; Gallup Annual Crime Poll (2016).

the year before dropped accordingly. But as we entered the era of President George W. Bush—one that saw the terrorist attacks on September 11, 2001—there was a sharp upswing in the public's perception that the crime problem was getting worse, even though it clearly was not. And the disconnect between perception and reality never really got much better after that under the Obama years, with a steady increase in the public's perception that crime was continuing to get worse, all while actual rates of violent victimization continued to plummet.

Things seem relatively similar when we look at trends in fear of crime over time. In Figure 8.2, for example, fear of crime dropped in the early 2000s, which is when media attention over the crime drop of the 1990s was arguably at its peak. But even as actual rates of victimization continued to go down, fear of crime remained steady, with nearly half of U.S. citizens expressing concern over the crime problem. And after 2014, when both crime and the fear of it were at an historical low, the fear of crime once again took a sharp jump upward to a 15-year high (despite the absence of an upturn in violence that would justify such a spike). In short, it turns out that the reality of criminal victimization bears a surprisingly inconsistent relationship with the perception of victimization.

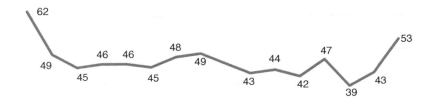

Figure 8.2 Percent of Americans who report worrying about crime and violence "a great deal," 2001-2016.
Source: Gallup Annual Crime Poll (2016).

In addition, policy makers—abetted and enabled by a willing news media—have discovered that they can cultivate the public's fear of crime and gain political capital in the process. But to do that, policy makers needed to frame the apparent crime problem—and the victimization that we all fear—as a consequence of excessive leniency on the part of the criminal justice system—the techniques for which have been honed to perfection by political elites over the past 40 years (Pratt, 2019). It is clear, however, that their ability to do so has been predicated on misinformation about the degree to which citizens' fears about being victimized are driven by their own experiences versus the lurid images of crime and victimization with which they are flooded on a regular basis.

Fear-based policy and its consequences

In an effort to address this apparent leniency on the part of the American criminal justice system, and to assuage citizens' fears about being victimized, policy makers went on a decades-long binge of "getting tough" (Pratt, 2019). There were "Scared Straight!" programs that took juvenile offenders into maximum security prisons and had inmates with life sentences yell at them and threaten them with physical and sexual violation in the hope that it would scare them enough that they would correct their own misbehavior (Maahs & Pratt, 2017); then there were military-style "boot camps" (again, mostly for juveniles) which seemed to assume that criminal behavior could be cured by push-ups and making one's bed correctly (Lutze & Brody, 1999); and there was also all manner of sentencing enhancements, with mandatory minimum sentences, additional sentences for aggravating circumstances, and the widespread popularity of "three-strikes" sentencing laws (Karch & Cravens, 2014; Spohn, 2015). All of this was done with the support of the American public, who were convinced that such efforts would keep them from being victimized.

So did these get-tough policy efforts "work" to keep the American public safe from victimization? The short answer is "no." Research indicates that programs like Scared Straight! and boot camps have no appreciable effect on recidivism (MacKenzie et al., 1995), and sentence enhancements do not appear to have any discernible deterrent effect on crime (Pratt & Cullen, 2005). But, in a way, that may have never been the point, at least not politically. The point is that the fear of victimization was used by policy makers in incredibly effective ways. It was the political hijacking of American citizens' fear of being victimized that literally transformed the entire criminal justice system.

Nowhere is that transformation more visible than in the current state of incarceration in America. Beginning in the early 1980s, incarceration rates in the United States rose dramatically (see Figure 8.3). American prisons and jails currently hold just under 2.2 million people behind bars (Kaeble & Cowhig, 2018)—a figure that places the United States as the world's leader in incarceration (Russia used to top the mark, but they let a bunch of people out over health concerns in some of their prisons). Just to put this figure into perspective, this

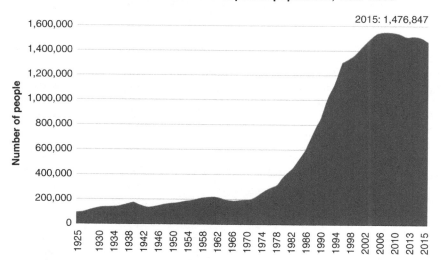

Figure 8.3 Trends in U.S. correctional population over time
Source: Bureau of Justice Statistics *Prisoners Series*.

is approximately the same number of people who populate the Canadian cities of Edmonton Alberta, Ottawa Ontario, and Halifax Nova Scotia—combined (Pratt, 2018). This group of incarcerated citizens would also fill the seats of the largest U.S. college football stadium at the University of Michigan 20 times over. It is now the case that the American prison industry currently does $74 billion a year in business. In the State of California, one out of every six state employees works for the Department of Corrections. As prison expenditures have assumed a larger proportion of state budgets, a few states (most notably California and New York) are currently spending more on incarceration than they are on higher education (Pratt, 2019).

It is not just incarceration that has been dramatically affected by the effort to get tough on crime. The sheer volume of offenders entering the criminal justice system has clogged the courts. There is now a whole roster of "specialty courts" (e.g., drug courts, domestic violence courts) that have been put into place to help deal with the added bottleneck of cases (Gover, Brank, & MacDonald, 2007; Lowenkamp, Holsinger, & Latessa, 2005). Police organizations have also been affected, particularly with respect to the war on drugs. Research indicates, for example, that some police departments depend on funds raised from drug-related property seizures for nearly all of their annual budget (Worrall, 2001).

All of this happened because policy makers found out that people are really afraid of being victimized. And when people are scared, they tend not to make the best decisions (recall the discussion in Chapter 6 about the psycho-emotional consequences of victimization). For better or for worse, there is no denying that victimization—and the fear that it engenders—has had an enormous impact in the political arena. But what does all of this mean for victims of crime? Getting tough was done in their name (after all, we need to get tough to protect people), but victims really do not have much of a place or a voice in any of this. The criminal justice system—at least in the United States—is almost completely offender-centered, and whether it was intended or unintended, victims are largely marginalized politically.

Gaps and challenges

There is still a lot of work to be done if we are to fully understand the social and political consequences of victimization—particularly if we want to be in a position to help those communities most affected by crime and violence. One of the key factors lying ahead will be to recognize that victimization is but one problem—one that is difficult to disentangle from other social and structural issues—that plagues high-risk communities (Ulmer, Harris, & Steffensmeier, 2012). To be sure, such communities suffer from structural and economic disadvantages (McNulty & Bellair, 2003), weakened social institutions (e.g., schools;

health care; see Kirby & Kaneda, 2005), scant prospects for legitimate employ-ment (Wilson, 1996), and a wide array of health problems (e.g., elevated risks for heart disease and early mortality; see Browning & Cagney, 2002).

It is important to acknowledge that complex problems like these cannot be meaningfully addressed solely with a criminal justice response. Adding more police, for instance, or encouraging them to be more proactive in certain parts of the community may be all well and good, but on its own it is a response that ignores all of the other problems that high-risk communities have to contend with on a daily basis (Weisburd, Davis, & Gill, 2015; see also Reisig & Parks, 2004). There is also an added risk that more aggressive police presence in such com-munities can end up exacerbating what may already be tense community–police relations, which may serve to compromise the sense of legitimacy that the police may be trying to effect (Kane, 2005). The challenge, then, is to accept the reality that multifaceted problems require multifaceted solutions; one that addresses victimization, yes, but the myriad other problems facing communities as well.

With respect to the political consequences of victimization, we need to do a better job in moving forward to narrow the gap between perception and reality when it comes to crime and victimization. Things were not always this bad—they have got worse in recent years in a political context where respect for "facts" seems to be at an all-time low (Pratt, 2019). It is important for researchers to stay engaged and to communicate the reality of their work, and to push back against "fake news" or "alternative facts" about victimization. Indeed, we can-not meaningfully address the reality of victimization until we have a shared understanding of what that reality is.

Key readings

Karch, A. & Cravens, M. (2014). Rapid diffusion and policy reform: The adoption and modi-fication of three strikes laws. *State Politics and Policy Quarterly, 14*, 461–491.
Sampson, R.J. (2012). *Great American city*. Chicago, IL: University of Chicago Press.
Spohn, C. (2015). Race, crime, and punishment in the twentieth and twenty-first centuries. *Crime and Justice: A Review of Research, 44*, 49–97.
Xie, M. & McDowall, D. (2008). Escaping crime: The effects of direct and indirect victimiza-tion on moving. *Criminology, 46*, 809–840.
Zimring, F.E. & Hawkins, G. (1997). *Crime is not the problem: Lethal violence in America*. New York: Oxford University Press.

Discussion questions

1. How did Willie Horton change the relationship between victimization and politics?
2. How can high rates of victimization cause communities to change with respect to residential stability and collective efficacy?

3. How well do citizens' perceptions of the crime problem "match up" with the reality of victimization? How has this changed over time?
4. What is "categorical contagion"? And how has that phenomenon been used by policy makers to justify a wide array of "get-tough" policies with respect to crime?

References

Beckett, K. (1997). *Making crime pay: Law and order in contemporary American politics.* New York: Oxford University Press.

Bolger, M.A. & Bolger, C. (2018). Predicting fear of crime: Results from a community survey of a small city. *American Journal of Criminal Justice,* in press.

Braun, S. & Pasternak, J. (1994). A nation with peril on its mind. *Los Angeles Times,* February 19: A1, A16.

Browning, C.R. & Cagney, K.A. (2002). Neighborhood structural disadvantage, collective efficacy, and self-rated physical health in an urban setting. *Journal of Health and Social Behavior, 43,* 383–399.

Gau, J.M. & Pratt, T.C. (2008). Broken windows or window dressing? Citizens' (in)ability to tell the difference between disorder and crime. *Criminology and Public Policy, 7,* 163–194.

Gover, A.R., Brank, E.M., & MacDonald, J.M. (2007). A specialized domestic violence court in South Carolina: An example of procedural justice for victims and defendants. *Violence Against Women, 13,* 603–626.

Graham, M. (2018). Commentary: Here's one reason Trump's average approval rating is going up. *Cbsnews.com,* September 3.

Harcourt, B.E. (2009). *Illusion of order: The false promise of broken windows policing.* Cambridge, MA: Harvard University Press.

Hipp, J.R. (2016). Collective efficacy: How is it conceptualized, how is it measured, and does it really matter for understanding perceived neighborhood crime and disorder. *Journal of Criminal Justice, 46,* 32–44.

Hochschild, A.R. (2016). *Strangers in their own land: Anger and mourning on the American right.* New York: The New Press.

Hsu, S. (2017). Comet pizza gunman pleads guilty to federal and local charges. *The Washington Post,* December 9.

Jackson, J. (2015). Cognitive closure and risk sensitivity in the fear of crime. *Legal and Criminological Psychology, 20,* 222–240.

Kaeble, D. & Cowhig, M. (2018). *Correctional populations in the United States, 2016.* Washington, DC: Bureau of Justice Statistics Bulletin.

Kane, R.J. (2005). Compromised police legitimacy as a predictor of violent crime in structurally disadvantaged communities. *Criminology, 43,* 469–498.

Karch, A. & Cravens, M. (2014). Rapid diffusion and policy reform: The adoption and modification of three strikes laws. *State Politics and Policy Quarterly, 14,* 461–491.

Kirby, J.B. & Kaneda, T. (2005). Neighborhood socioeconomic disadvantage and access to health care. *Journal of Health and Social Behavior, 46,* 15–31.

Lowenkamp, C.T., Holsinger, A.M., & Latessa, E.J. (2005). Are drug courts effective: A meta- analytic review. *Journal of Community Corrections, Fall,* 5–10, 28.

Lutze, F.E. & Brody, D.C. (1999). Mental abuse as cruel and unusual punishment: Do boot camp prisons violate the Eighth Amendment? *Crime and Delinquency, 45,* 242–255.

Maahs, J. & Pratt, T.C. (2017). "I hate these little turds!": Science, entertainment, and the enduring popularity of Scared Straight programs. *Deviant Behavior, 38,* 47–60.

MacKenzie, D.L., Brame, R., McDowall, D., & Souryal, C. (1995). Boot camp prisons and recidivism in eight states. *Criminology, 33,* 327–358.

McAdams, D.P. (2011). *George W. Bush and the redemptive dream: A psychological portrait*. New York: Oxford University Press.

McNulty, T.J. (1988). "Outrageous" debate question angers Kitty Dukakis. *Chicago Tribune*, October 15.

McNulty, T.L. & Bellair, P.E. (2003). Explaining racial and ethnic differences in adolescent violence: Structural disadvantage, family well-being, and social capital. *Justice Quarterly, 20*, 1-31.

Moore, D.W. (1994). Public wants crime bill. *The Gallup Poll Monthly, 347*(August), 11.

Morenoff, J.D., Sampson, R.J., & Raudenbush, S.W. (2001). Neighborhood inequality, collective efficacy, and the spatial dynamics of urban violence. *Criminology, 39*, 517-558.

Nix, J., Wolfe, S.E., Rojek, J., & Kaminski, R.J. (2015). Trust in the police: The influence of procedural justice and perceived collective efficacy. *Crime and Delinquency, 61*, 610-640.

NRA-ILA. (2016). Leaked emails reveal Clinton's true gun control intentions. *Nraila.org*, October 14.

Pratt, T.C. (2018). Mass incarceration. In H.O. Griffin & V. Woodward (Eds.), *Handbook of corrections in the United States*. New York: Routledge.

Pratt, T.C. (2019). *Addicted to incarceration: Corrections policy and the politics of misinformation in the United States* (2nd edition). Thousand Oaks, CA: Sage.

Pratt, T.C. & Cullen, F.T. (2005). Assessing macro-level predictors and theories of crime: A meta-analysis. *Crime and Justice: A Review of Research, 32*, 373-450.

Reisig, M.D. & Parks, R.B. (2004). Can community policing help the truly disadvantaged? *Crime and Delinquency, 50*, 139-167.

Ruhs, F., Greve, W., & Kappes, C. (2017). Coping with criminal victimization and fear of crime: The protective role of accommodative self-regulation. *Legal and Criminological Psychology, 33*, 359-377.

Sampson, R.J. (2012). *Great American city*. Chicago, IL: University of Chicago Press.

Sampson, R.J. & Groves, W.B. (1989). Community structure and crime: Testing social-disorganization theory. *American Journal of Sociology, 94*, 774-802.

Sampson, R.J., Raudenbush, S.W., & Earls, F. (1997). Neighborhoods and violent crime: A multilevel study of collective efficacy. *Science, 277*, 918-924.

Shaw, C.R. & McKay, H.D. (1942). *Juvenile delinquency and urban areas*. Chicago, IL: University of Chicago Press.

Simon, R. (1990). How a murderer and rapist became the Bush campaign's most valuable player. *The Baltimore Sun*, November 11.

Simon, R. (2015). The GOP and Willie Horton: Together again. *Politico.com*, May 19.

Singer, A.J., Chouhy, C., Lehmann, P.S., Walzak, J.N., Gertz, M., & Biglin, S. (2018). Victimization, fear of crime, and trust in criminal justice institutions: A cross-national analysis. *Crime and Delinquency*, in press.

Spohn, C. (2015). Race, crime, and punishment in the twentieth and twenty-first centuries. *Crime and Justice: A Review of Research, 44*, 49-97.

Ulmer, J.T., Harris, C.T., & Steffensmeier, D. (2012). Racial and ethnic disparities in structural disadvantage and crime: White, black, and Hispanic comparisons. *Social Science Quarterly, 93*, 799-819.

Weisburd, D., Davis, M., & Gill, C. (2015). Increasing collective efficacy and social capital at crime hot spots: New crime control tools for police. *Policing: A Journal of Policy and Practice, 9*, 265-274.

Wending, M. (2016). The saga of "pizzagate": The fake story that shows how conspiracy theories spread. *BBCNews*, December 2.

Wilson, J.Q. (1975). *Thinking about crime*. New York: Basic Books.

Wilson, J.Q. & Kelling, G.L. (1982). Broken windows: The police and neighbourhood safety. *The Atlanticonline*, March.

Wilson, W.J. (1996). *When work disappears: The world of the new urban poor*. New York: Knopf.

Worrall, J.L. (2001). Addicted to the drug war: The role of civil asset forfeiture as a budgetary necessity in contemporary law enforcement. *Journal of Criminal Justice, 29*, 171-187.

Wright, R.T. & Decker, S.H. (1994). *Burglars on the job: Streetlife and residential break-ins*. Boston, MA: Northeastern University Press.

Xie, M. & McDowall, D. (2008a). The effects of residential turnover on household victimization. *Criminology, 46*, 539-575.

Xie, M. & McDowall, D. (2008b). Escaping crime: The effects of direct and indirect victimization on moving. *Criminology, 46*, 809-840.

Zimring, F.E. & Hawkins, G. (1997). *Crime is not the problem: Lethal violence in America*. New York: Oxford University Press.

PART IV

SPECIAL TOPICS IN VICTMIZATION

9 Violence against women

On January 17, 2015, a 22-year-old young woman was enjoying a quiet Saturday night at home. Her younger sister was home from college to visit for the weekend, and their father had prepared dinner. After they all sat around the table catching up for a while, the young woman was going to turn in for the night—maybe read a book, watch some TV—while her sister went to a party with her friends. Having already graduated from college and working full time, the woman was not exactly the weekend party animal; but, realizing that it was her only night to spend time with her sister, she decided to go along to the party too. She thought to herself, "Why not, there's a dumb party ten minutes from my house" (Baker, 2016). She would go, dance like a fool, and embarrass her younger sister. Knowing that she would be the oldest person at the party, she jokingly called herself "big mama," and her sister made fun of her for wearing a beige cardigan to a fraternity party like a librarian. The ladies drank some champagne and took a few shots of whiskey, and their mom dropped them off at the Stanford University campus. Once at the party, the young woman made silly faces, let her guard down, drank some beers, and took a few more shots—not realizing that her alcohol tolerance had significantly lowered since college.

The next thing she remembered, she woke up strapped to a gurney in a brightly lit hallway. There was dried blood and bandages on the backs of her hands and elbow. She thought that maybe she had fallen, and that she was in an administrative office on campus. It took a while for her to realize that she was in the hospital. A deputy told her that she had been assaulted. The woman was confused and assumed this officer had the wrong person. What was he talking about?

Once she was allowed to use the restroom, the woman realized that her underwear was missing, and that her hair was full of pine needles that were scratching the back of her neck. She didn't know where her underwear had gone, or where all the pine needles came from. Her clothes were confiscated, and she stood naked while two nurses held a ruler against various abrasions on her body and photographed them. She received needles, pills, and had multiple swabs inserted into her vagina and anus. She had a camera pointed between her legs, and had her vagina smeared with blue paint to check for abrasions. She was asked to sign papers that said "Rape Victim."

All the woman was told that morning was that she had been found behind a dumpster, that she was penetrated by a stranger, and that she should get retested for HIV in a few weeks' time. She was sent home and told that she should try to return to her normal life. For over a week after the incident, she didn't receive any calls or updates about that night or what had happened to her. She couldn't sleep, she couldn't eat, and she didn't feel like talking about what had happened with anyone. She wasn't ready to tell her long-term boyfriend or her parents that she may have been raped behind a dumpster, and that she didn't know who did it, when it happened, or how. She started to isolate herself and just tried (unsuccessfully) to pretend as if the whole thing wasn't real.

Then, one day at work, while scrolling through the news on her phone, she came across an article. In it, she learned for the first time about what had happened to her that night. Like the rest of the public, she read about how she was found unconscious by police—with her hair disheveled, her dress pulled up to her shoulders, her bra pulled out of her dress—naked all the way down to her boots, her underwear wadded up on the ground about half a foot away from her. She read about how she had been penetrated by the fingers of someone whom she did not recognize. Her breasts had been groped, pine needles and debris had been jabbed inside of her, and her bare skin and head had been rubbing against the ground behind a dumpster. She read that she was so intoxicated at the time of the incident that she didn't wake up for at least three hours afterward, and her blood-alcohol level was more than triple the legal driving limit.

She also learned that two men—Swedish graduate students—had been riding their bikes along a path near the fraternity party at around 1 a.m. They noticed a man and woman on the ground near a dumpster, seemingly having sex. At first, they thought it was a mutual interaction, but as they got closer, they realized that the woman looked to have passed out. She was not moving at all, her eyes were closed, and her head was tilted to the side. The man was on top of her, aggressively thrusting his hips into her. Horrified, the Swedes approached the man and asked what he was doing. The man got off her and immediately bolted from the scene. One of the Swedes ran after him and took him down, while the other checked to see if the woman was okay. She was completely non-responsive. The police were called, and the Swedes helped each other pin the man down on the ground until the police made an arrest. The police noted in their report that, when they were placing handcuffs on the man, they saw that his "crotch area" appeared "disheveled," and he had what appeared to be "a cylindrical bulge consistent with an erect penis underneath his pants" (Mei, 2016).

In the article, the woman also read about what the man, a freshman at Stanford, had told police about what happened. He said they had met at the fraternity party after he had already consumed about seven cans of beer and some whiskey. According to him, they drank beer together, danced, and started to kiss. He said that they decided to leave the party together, and they walked away from the house holding hands. She fell, and they ended up on the ground kissing. He took off her underwear and fondled her, he said, while she rubbed his back with both hands. He said that he consciously decided to engage in sexual activity with her and that "she also seemed to enjoy the activity" (Kadvany, 2015). He said he didn't know the woman, did not get her name, and that he wouldn't be able to describe her or recognize her if he saw her again. He stated that he never took off his pants and they did not have intercourse, and that his "intentions were not to try to rape a girl." He just wanted to "hook up." According to the article, the man was kicked out of Stanford and banned from campus, and charged with five felony counts of sexual assault.

The woman felt devastated to have to find all this out through the news. Weeks passed, and although she knew the man had been charged, she had not heard that he had been convicted. The woman thought, "There's no way this is going to trial: there were witnesses, there was dirt in my body, he ran but was caught. He's going to settle, formally apologize, and we will both move on" (Baker, 2016). Instead, she was told that he hired a powerful attorney and expert witnesses, and that the case was, in fact, going to trial. His legal team argued that the sexual assault was a misunderstanding, that he had simply been confused. His lawyer claimed that his client was not attempting rape, but was instead seeking "outercourse"–sexual contact while clothed–a version of "safe sex" (Kaplan, 2018). The man's father stated that his son should not do jail time for what he referred to as "the events" and "20 minutes of action." He said that his son suffered from depression and anxiety after being arrested and getting kicked out of Stanford, and that he no longer even wanted to eat "a big rib-eye steak" with his dad like he used to (Stack, 2016). He was a champion swimmer with a bright future. Drinking was the problem. It was the party culture, not him.

The woman was told that, because she couldn't remember the assault, technically she couldn't prove that it was unwanted. She was told to be prepared in case the prosecution didn't win the case. The defense argued that her testimony was weak, incomplete. During the trial she was pummeled with narrowed, pointed questions about her personal life, love life, past life, and family life (Baker, 2016). By the end of it all she felt broken, helpless, and drained. But, in the end, the jury decided to convict the man on three counts of felony sexual assault, which carried a 14-year maximum prison sentence.

Nevertheless, during sentencing, the judge noted that the man had no "significant" prior offenses, and that, because he was intoxicated at the time of the assault, there was "less moral culpability" involved (Stack, 2016). The judge also worried that "a prison sentence would have a severe impact on him" (Stack, 2016). Accordingly, on June 2, 2016, the man was sentenced to six months in county jail and three years' probation, and he was required to register as a lifetime sex offender. The man was released from jail after serving just three months.

This was the case of Brock Turner. It received international coverage and sparked anger from all sides. On the one side were advocates and survivors of sexual assault who felt that his sentence was too lenient, or that a white, college athlete was being let off the hook. On the other side were those who argued that the case was not clear-cut, who questioned whether someone could commit rape only with their fingers, while clothed, and who wondered if consent did perhaps happen (Miller, 2016). But, for the most part, the light sentence Turner received prompted widespread fury on social media.

After Turner's sentence was handed down, the impact statement read by the victim in court was published in full by *Buzz Feed*. It quickly went viral, drawing over ten million views within the first four days. All the major news outlets covered it. Ashley Banfield, the anchor of CNN's "Legal View," even read the entire 7,000-plus-word statement live on air. In response to the public's outrage, California Governor Jerry Brown signed two new bills into law in September 2016—one that imposed a mandatory minimum penalty for sexual offenses, and one that expanded the state's definition of rape beyond the use or threat of physical force. A public campaign was also launched on Change.org to recall the judge in the Brock Turner case, which drew over 1.3 million supporters. In June 2018, just under 60 percent of voters were in favor of removing the Judge from the Santa Clara County Superior Court. He was the first judge recalled in California in more than 80 years.

To be fair, the Brock Turner case is unique in a number of respects—especially in the amount of attention and media coverage it drew, as well as in the legislative responses that stemmed from it. Certainly not all rape cases attract this kind of attention, but it in other ways it is a typical case. Like many sexual assault cases, it challenges the conventional stereotypes about what "real rape" looks like and who a "genuine victim" is. Indeed, sexual intercourse did not happen, and the perpetrator did not exactly fit the "sex predator archetype" that society perpetuates (think: creepy guy with a mustache and coke-bottle glasses, who likes to hide in bushes and has a basement full of child pornography). In addition, as in many other cases, there was heavy drinking involved, and the two parties were possibly engaging in some form of consensual interaction prior to the assault. This is a far cry from the conventional view of rape—one that might involve a man lurking in a dark alley, who abducts a completely innocent, unsuspecting woman who happens to be passing by.

With these issues in mind, this chapter discusses violence against women—namely sexual assault and intimate partner violence. We will cover issues about the prevalence and predictors of violence against women, stereotypes and myths about these forms of violence, and also discuss ways to possibly intervene and address these forms of violence in society.

Scope of the problem

Violence against women is a major public health problem. Although women are usually found to be at lesser risk of victimization than men, global estimates published by the World Health Organization suggest that one in three women experience either intimate partner violence or non-partner sexual violence during their lifetime (World Health Organization, 2017). And while of course sexual abuse and intimate partner violence is also experienced by men, women are much more likely to experience these forms of violence repeatedly, and severely. Worldwide, 39 percent of all murders of women are committed by intimate partners or ex-partners, compared with 6 percent for male homicides (World Health Organization, 2017).

Recent estimates from the Crime Survey for England and Wales (2018) indicate that more than one in five women have experienced some type of sexual assault since the age of 16, and that more than 510,000 women—an estimated 3.1 percent of all women aged 16 to 59—experienced sexual assault in the past year. The 2018 survey also showed that women were five times more likely than men to have experienced sexual assault, including unwanted touching or indecent exposure, in the past 12 months. These statistics—while seemingly high—have changed little in England and Wales since 2005. The survey also showed that more than 80 percent of the victims of these incidents did not report their crimes to police (Crime Survey of England and Wales, 2018).

U.S. data from the NCVS show that, from 1995 to 2005, the estimated annual rate of female rape or sexual assault victimizations declined by 64 percent, from 5.0 victimizations per 1,000 females age 12 or older, to 1.8 per 1,000 females in 2005 (Planty et al., 2013). Since then, however, the rates have remained relatively stable. The NCVS also shows that, from 1994 to 2011, the rate of serious intimate partner violence (rape or sexual assault, robbery, and aggravated assault committed by the victim's current or former spouse, boyfriend, or girlfriend) against females declined by 72 percent, from 5.9 victimizations per 1,000 females aged 12 or older in 1994 to 1.6 per 1,000 in 2011 (Catalano, 2013). The majority of the decline occurred from 1994 to 2001, when the rate of serious intimate partner violence against females declined by 59 percent. So, while the rates of violence against women—like other forms of crime—were higher in the 1990s and have remained largely stable in recent years, they still represent significant social problems.

Sexual assault

Historically, we have not had an easy time defining sexual assault or rape. Well into the 1970s, the widely used definition of rape was this: *unlawful sexual intercourse committed by a man with a woman not his wife through force and against her will* (Doerner & Lab, 2017). Between 1927 and 2012, the definition of rape used in the UCR was this: *carnal knowledge by a male of a female, forcibly and against her will*. It goes without saying that these definitions were inherently problematic. Not only did they solely recognize females as victims and males as offenders, but the only act condemned here seemed to be forced penile penetration—or whatever "carnal knowledge" meant—something that husbands could apparently do to their wives legally. Although many states made changes to their own statutes over the years, the UCR continued to use their old definition for the purposes of recording rape statistics in the U.S.

In 2012, Attorney General Eric Holder announced revisions to the UCR's definition of rape, which he argued was needed for a more comprehensive statistical reporting of rape nationwide. The new definition was more inclusive, it better reflected state criminal codes, and it focused on the various forms of sexual penetration understood to be rape. The new definition was this: *The penetration, no matter how slight, of the vagina or anus with any body part or object, or oral penetration by a sex organ of another person, without the consent of the victim*. Note that this new definition includes any gender of victim or perpetrator, and encompasses instances where the victim may be incapable of giving consent (Holder, 2012). The new definition went into effect on January 1, 2013. A comparison between the rates of rape recorded in the UCR under the new definition and the old one (i.e., the "legacy definition") is shown in Table 9.1. Not surprisingly, the new definition captures more rape incidents.

Table 9.1 Rates of rape recorded in the UCR (2013–2016), per 100,000

Year	Rape (revised definition)	Rape (legacy definition)
2013	35.9	25.9
2014	37.0	26.6
2015	39.3	28.4
2016	40.4	29.6

Source: FBI Uniform Crime Reporting Program. *Crime in the United States, by volume and rate per 100,000 inhabitants, 1997-2016.*

Myths and realities about sexual assault

Attitudes toward rape began to change with the success of the women's movement in the 1970s and the creation of rape awareness programs throughout
the 1980s, particularly by framing rape as violent rather than sexual (Meyer,
2000). However, most people are still misinformed about the realities of sexual assault, and rape myths remain alive and well today. Rape myths may be
thought of as "prejudicial, stereotyped, or false beliefs about rape, rape victims
and rapists" (Burt, 1980: 217). They are considered to be "attitudes and beliefs
that are generally false but are widely and persistently held, and that serve to
deny and justify male sexual aggression against women" (Lonsway & Fitzgerald,
1994: 134). Rape myths are important to recognize, since they may be used
to discredit victims' allegations at various stages of criminal justice processing (Frohmann, 1991). They can influence police officers' decisions to make an
arrest (Tasca et al., 2013), and prosecutors' decisions to file charges (as we discussed in Chapter 7).

For example, rape myths generally suggest that sexual assaults are violent
encounters perpetrated by strangers. The reality, however, is that rape may
not involve physical force, and it is often committed by someone known to the
victim. As Ferro, Cermele, and Saltzman (2008: 765) state:

> Contrary to popular belief, rapists are not strangers lurking in dark alleys or
> hiding behind bushes looking for their next victims; rather, the majority of
> rapes involve a victim and an offender who had a prior relationship before
> the rape occurred.

Indeed, according to the NCVS, between 2005 and 2010, 78 percent of sexual
violence incidents involved an offender who was a family member, intimate
partner, friend, or acquaintance (Planty et al., 2013). And in the U.S. National
Violence Against Women Survey, 84 percent of reported rapes were committed
by an acquaintance or intimate partner (Tjaden & Thoennes, 2006).

Many rape myths play out in more covert attitudes about sexual assault, as
shown in Table 9.2. Each and every one of these beliefs is *categorically false*.
And while all of these attitudes loom large in the cultural imagination, perhaps
the ones which are most widely held are that women routinely lie about sexual abuse and file false accusations. There were, admittedly, some well-known
instances of this happening. In 2014, for example, *Rolling Stone* published (and
later retracted) the story of a student, identified as "Jackie," who said she
was brutally gang raped at a fraternity party at the University of Virginia in
2012, which later turned out to be false (Kennedy, 2016). And in 2006, widely
publicized false accusations were made against several innocent members of
the Duke University lacrosse team (Wilson & Glater, 2006). But putting these

Table 9.2 Selected rape myths

- If a girl is raped while she is drunk, she is at least somewhat responsible for letting things get out of control.
- When girls go to parties wearing slutty clothes, they are asking for trouble.
- If a girl goes to a room with a guy alone at a party, it is her own fault if she was raped.
- If a girl acts like a slut, eventually she is going to get into trouble.
- When girls are raped, it is often because the way they said "no" was unclear.
- If a girl initiates kissing or hooking up, she should not be surprised if a guy assumes she wants to have sex.
- If a girl does not physically resist sex—even if protesting verbally—it cannot be considered as rape.
- If a girl does not physically fight back, you cannot really say it was rape.
- A rape probably didn't happen if the girl has no bruises or marks.
- If the accused "rapist" does not have a weapon, you really cannot call it rape.
- If a girl does not say "no," she cannot claim rape.
- When guys rape, it is usually because of their strong desire for sex.
- Guys do not usually intend to force sex on a girl, but sometimes they get too sexually carried away.
- Rape happens when a guy's sex drive gets out of control.
- If a guy is drunk, he may rape someone unintentionally.
- It should not be considered rape if a guy is drunk and didn't realize what he was doing.
- If both people are drunk, it cannot be rape.
- A lot of times, girls who say they were raped agreed to have sex and then regret it.
- Rape accusations are often used as a way of getting back at guys.
- A lot of times, girls who say they were raped often led the guy on and then had regrets.
- A lot of times, girls who claim they were raped just have emotional problems.
- Girls who are caught cheating on their boyfriends sometimes claim that it was rape.

Source: McMahon, S. & Farmer, G.L. (2011). An updated measure for assessing subtle rape myths. *Social Work Research*, 35, 71-81.

well-known instances aside, research does not support the claim that sexual assault cases are falsely reported any more than other types of crimes. Let us be clear: false rape allegations are few and far between. The best available evidence suggests that the proportion of false reports ranges between 2 and 10 percent—no different than for other types of crimes (Lisak et al., 2010).

In general, the research shows that, relative to women, men demonstrate higher rape myth acceptance and attribute higher levels of blame to victims; that women who violate traditional gender roles are viewed as more responsible for their own victimization; and that women who consume alcohol prior to their attack are attributed more blame than those who are not intoxicated (Grubb & Turner, 2012). To be sure, the issue of alcohol in sexual assault is a complicated one. Although drinking and sexual assault frequently co-occur—with some studies suggesting that approximately 60 percent of sexual assaults involve alcohol consumption by the offender, the victim, or both (Abbey, McAuslan, & Ross, 1998)—it does not mean that alcohol *causes* sexual assault. As some scholars point out, "the causal direction could be the opposite; men may consciously or unconsciously drink alcohol prior to committing sexual assault to have an excuse for their behavior" (Abbey, 2002: 122). Alternatively, other factors may both simultaneously cause both alcohol consumption and sexual assault, such as peer group norms, low self-control (Franklin, 2011), and other cultural factors (Armstrong, Hamilton, & Sweeney, 2006).

Sexual assault in college

Females face the greatest risk of being sexually victimized during their late teens and early twenties—often spanning the years they are enrolled in college. Consequently, the college party culture is often looked at as a facilitator of sexual assault among young women. Statistics show that over half of incapacitated rapes and a quarter of forcible rapes take place at parties (Krebs et al., 2009), and existing research highlights that certain elements of the party culture—particularly at large universities—can increase sexual danger.

Some studies point to the role of college sports—such as football—in promoting a party culture that is dangerous to women. For example, in a recent study using NIBRS data, Lindo, Siminski, and Swensen (2018) found that on college football game days, reports of rape victimization among 17- to 24-year-old women increased by 28 percent. Home games were found to increase reports by 41 percent on the day of the game, and away games increased reports by 15 percent. These effects were found to be greater for Division 1 schools (i.e., the more prominent sports schools), and were largest for rapes in which offenders were unknown to the victim and were also college-aged.

In another study, Armstrong and colleagues (2006) focused on a large, Midwestern university—one that had the reputation of a "party school." Through interviews with students and observations of life in the dorms, the authors found that various processes at the individual, organizational, and interactional levels contributed to sexual assault. They found that party rape occurred at high rates in places that clustered young, single, party-oriented people together—such as

fraternity parties (Armstrong et al., 2006). Because only fraternities, not sorori-
ties, were allowed to have parties, the authors emphasized that men structured
these parties in ways that "controlled the appearance, movement, and behavior
of female guests" (Armstrong et al., 2006: 495). Party themes usually required
women to wear scanty, sexy clothing, and placed women in subordinate posi-
tions to men. Throughout the study period, women attended parties such as
"Pimps and Hos," "Victoria's Secret," and "Playboy Mansion" (Armstrong et al.,
2006: 489). During parties, men also controlled the distribution of alcohol,
which was highly policed and regulated elsewhere on campus. The gendered
expectation for women to be "nice" and to defer to men was only intensified
by men's position as hosts and women's as "grateful guests" at these parties,
which many men attended looking for casual sex (Armstrong et al., 2006: 495).
As one male student in the study described:

> Girls are continually fed drinks of alcohol. It's mainly to party but my room-
> ies are also aware of the inhibition-lowering effects. I've seen an old roomie
> block doors when girls want to leave his room; and other times I've driven
> women home who can't remember much of an evening yet sex did occur.
> Rarely if ever has a night of drinking for my roommate ended without sex.
> I know it isn't necessarily and assuredly sexual assault, but with the amount
> of liquor in the house I question the amount of consent a lot.
>
>   (Armstrong et al., 2006: 491).

These sorts of findings raise important questions about the role of party
culture in facilitating sexual assault, as well as the role universities can play in
reducing this problem. According to a recent U.S. poll, more than 77 percent of
U.S. college students agree that reducing drinking would be at least somewhat
effective in preventing sexual assault on their campus (*Washington Post*-Kaiser
Family Foundation, 2015). However, these policies are unlikely to be effective
unless they are also coupled with programs that serve to educate both men and
women about coercive behavior, rape myths, and the sources of victim-blaming
(Armstrong et al., 2006).

Intimate Partner Violence (IPV)

The other form of victimization that is overrepresented among women is intimate partner violence (IPV). Also known as "domestic violence," the term IPV
is an expansive one that includes violent acts perpetrated by current or former
spouses, boyfriends, or girlfriends. As with other forms of victimization, IPV took
center stage in policy and research in the late 1960s, along with the women's

rights movement. During that time, activists argued that IPV was a reflection of women's oppression, and they took issue with the fact that the criminal justice system seemingly did little to protect women. The traditional view of IPV was that it was a "domestic issue" or "private matter" rather than a criminal justice problem—and police were trained to treat it as such. But with the culmination of the women's rights and victim's rights movements, the first battered women's shelters opened in the early 1970s. These shelters sought to help women find the assistance they needed to get out of abusive relationships and stay safe.

Since that time, efforts to identify and prevent IPV have grown considerably. Recognition of the high prevalence of IPV in society has led to sweeping public health reforms, updated medical practices, and revised legal polices. Indeed, estimates from the Centers for Disease Control and Prevention suggest that 24.3 percent of women experience severe physical intimate partner violence during their lifetime (Black et al., 2011). Younger women are more likely to experience IPV than older women, and black women are approximately 2.5 times more likely to be victims of IPV than women of other races (Rand & Rennison, 2004). To best address the needs of these victims—particularly young women of color—it is recognized that responses to IPV need to be coordinated across multiple systems, including the justice system, the health care system, the education system, and social services (Shorey, Tirone, & Stuart, 2014).

Challenges of addressing IPV

Perhaps the biggest challenge these various agencies face in addressing IPV is that it is rarely disclosed. Many women choose not to report out of shame, fear of retaliation from perpetrators, fear of law enforcement involvement, feelings of disempowerment, fear of reporting policies, or their own denial of abuse (Rodriguez et al., 2001). Furthermore, in close and intimate relationships, it can sometimes be difficult for women to know whether they are being abused—especially if their partner gives them attention, supports them financially, and expresses love for them (Office on Women's Health, 2018). Moreover, many abusive behaviors fall short of outright violence, and relationships often become emotionally abusive well before they ever become physically abusive. Indeed, as Table 9.3 indicates, various non-violent behaviors can still characterize an abusive or unhealthy relationship.

Another challenge of addressing IPV is that it often operates in cycles. Walker's (1979) cycle of violence model characterizes this well, and recognizes that there are typically three distinct phases in abusive relationships. The first stage in the cycle is the *tension-building phase*. This is usually the longest phase, where tension escalates between the couple. The abuser might increase his use of threats and put-downs, make accusations of unfaithfulness, and start arguments.

Table 9.3 Am I Being Abused?

Does your partner ever:

- Monitor what you're doing all the time or ask where you are and who you are with every second of the day?
- Demand your passwords to your phone, social media, and email accounts?
- Demand that you reply right away to texts, emails, or calls?
- Prevent or discourage you from seeing friends or family?
- Prevent or discourage you from going to work or school?
- Act jealous, controlling, or angry?
- Act very jealous, including constantly accusing you of cheating?
- Have a quick temper, so you never know what you will do or say that may cause a problem?
- Control how you spend your money?
- Control your use of medicines or birth control?
- Make everyday decisions for you that you normally make for yourself, such as what to wear or eat?
- Demean you?
- Put you down, such as by insulting your appearance, intelligence, or activities?
- Humiliate you in front of others?
- Destroy your property or things that you care about?
- Blame you for his or her violent outbursts?
- Physically hurt or threaten to hurt you or loved ones?
- Threaten to hurt you, the children, or other people or pets in your household?
- Hurt you physically (such as by hitting, beating, pushing, shoving, punching, slapping, kicking, or biting you)?
- Use (or threaten to use) a weapon against you?
- Threaten to harm him- or herself when upset with you?
- Threaten to turn you over to the authorities for illegal activity if you report physical abuse?
- Guilt you into having sex when you don't want to?
- Force you to have sex or other intimate activity?

If you answered "yes" to any one of these questions, then you may be in an unhealthy or abusive relationship.

Source: Office on Women's Health. (2018). *Am I being abused?* Washington, DC: U.S. Department of Health and Human Services.

The second phase of the cycle of violence is the explosion of violence, which is called the *acute-battering phase*. This is when the abuser loses control both physically and emotionally. This can be in the form of verbal abuse and humiliation, extremely controlling behavior, or various forms of physical assault (e.g., slapping, punching, kicking, choking, throwing objects, or using weapons). After a battering episode, victims may deny the seriousness of their injuries and refuse to seek medical attention or call the police.

The third phase in Walker's (1979) cycle is the *honeymoon phase*, which is a period of calm, loving, and remorseful behavior on the part of the abuser. He may be genuinely sorry for the pain he caused and apologize profusely. He may attempt to make up for or justify his behavior, promise that it will not happen again, and maybe even promise to seek help. During this phase, the abuser will try to convince the victim that he can control himself, and the victim may feel hopeful and relieved, and agree to stay in the relationship. The victim, for her part, may also be made to feel at least partly responsible for causing the incident and for her partner's well-being. However, the honeymoon phase will not last forever, and eventually the tension-building phase of the cycle will start up again. Over time, the dynamic of the cycle is thought to change, with the reduction and eventual disappearance of the *honeymoon phase* and a shortening of the intervals between outbursts (Bensimon & Ronel, 2012).

Why women stay in abusive relationships

Walker's (1979) cycle of violence model can help shed light on the reasons why some women have a hard time leaving abusive relationships. To be sure, the ups and downs of being trapped in a cycle of abuse can be confusing emotionally. Often, when women do make a decision to leave, many subsequently return to their abusers. The National Domestic Violence Hotline (2018) even suggests that, on average, a woman will leave an abusive relationship seven times before she leaves for good. So why is walking away so difficult?

For one, many women are in love with or committed to the other person, despite the abuse. Some women may also be financially dependent on their partners, and feel that they will be unable to support themselves if they leave (Kim & Gray, 2008). Cultural or religious beliefs may forbid divorce, or women may be afraid of what will happen if they decide to leave. Research shows that the most dangerous point in an abusive relationship for women—that is, when their risk of homicide is highest—is when they move out or separate from their abusive partners (Campbell et al., 2003). Put simply, abused women's reasons for staying or leaving their partners are varied and complex—it is often not as simple as packing up and walking out of the door. A list of some additional reasons why women stay in abusive relationships is provided in Table 9.4.

Police responses to IPV

Over the past several decades many police responses to intimate partner violence have been proposed, studied, and adopted as policy. These responses range all the way from the police doing nothing, to providing counseling,

Table 9.4 Why do people stay in abusive relationships?

- *Love*: So often, victims feel love for their abusive partner. They may have children with them and want to maintain their family. Abusive people can often be charming, especially at the beginning of a relationship, and victims may hope that their partner will go back to being that person. They may only want the violence to stop, not for the relationship to end entirely.
- *Lack of money/resources*: Financial abuse is common, and victims may be financially dependent on their abusive partner. Without money, access to resources, or even a place to go, it can seem impossible for them to leave the relationship. This feeling of helplessness can be especially strong if the person lives with the abusive partner.
- *Fear*: Victims may be afraid of what will happen if they decide to leave the relationship. Abusers may threaten to commit suicide or kill their partners if they ever leave.
- *Embarrassment or shame*: It is often difficult for people to admit that they have been abused. They may feel that they have done something wrong by becoming involved with an abusive partner. They may also worry that their friends and family will judge them.
- *Believing abuse is normal*: Victims may not know what a healthy relationship looks like, perhaps from growing up in an environment where abuse was common, and they may not recognize that their relationship is unhealthy.
- *Low self-esteem*: When an abuser constantly blames their partner for the abuse, it can be easy for victims to believe those statements and think that the abuse is their fault.
- *Cultural/religious reasons*: Traditional gender roles supported by someone's culture or religion may influence them to stay rather than end the relationship for fear of bringing shame upon their family.
- *Language barriers/immigration status*: If victims are undocumented, they may fear that reporting the abuse will affect their immigration status. In addition, if their first language is not English, it can be difficult to express the depth of their situation to others.
- *Fear of being outed*: If someone is in an LGBTQ relationship and has not yet come out to everyone, his or her partner may threaten to reveal this secret.
- *Disability*: When victims are physically dependent on their abusive partner, they can feel that their well-being is connected to the relationship. This dependency could heavily influence the decision to stay in an abusive relationship.

Source: National Domestic Violence Hotline. (2018). *"Why don't they just leave?"* Austin, TX: National Domestic Violence Hotline. Retrieved from www.thehotline.org/is-this-abuse/why-do-people-stay-in-abusive-relationships.

separating the parties, issuing restraining orders, recommending professional treatment, and making an arrest. These policies have been based on theories of deterrence, rehabilitation, incapacitation, victim empowerment, officer safety, and a general concern for the efficacy of criminal law regarding intimate relationships (Maxwell, Garner, & Fagan, 2002). But perhaps the most widely adopted and preferred tactic of law enforcement agencies is arrest.

Mandatory arrest laws proliferated in the 1980s and 1990s following Sherman and Berk's (1984) influential Minneapolis Domestic Violence Experiment. The purpose of this experiment was to determine how effective various police responses were in preventing further domestic violence. The study used an experimental design whereby officers responding to misdemeanor domestic violence calls were randomly assigned one of the following responses: (1) arrest the perpetrator, (2) have one party leave for eight hours (i.e., a "cooling-off" period), or (3) provide some form of advice or informal mediation to the couple. Each responding officer in the field received a report pad, and this pad gave instructions about which option to invoke on a particular call. Offenders were tracked for six months following their police contact to determine whether more domestic violence occurred. The results based on official police records showed that only 10 percent of those who were arrested committed a subsequent offense, compared to 24 percent of those who were separated and 19 percent of those who were given advice or mediation. Victim interviews also supported a similar pattern. The findings were clear: arrest was the most effective way of responding to IPV.

Not long after these findings were released, states began revamping their laws to allow for the police to make mandatory arrests in IPV cases. The problem, however, is that the results of the Minneapolis Domestic Violence Experiment have not exactly been replicated. Specifically, replication studies conducted in Charlotte, Colorado Springs, Omaha, Milwaukee, and Miami-Dade County did not find the same thing. In only Miami-Dade was it found that arrest deterred future IPV, but this was only when the perpetrator was married. In Charlotte, Omaha, and Milwaukee it was found that arrest deterred offenders in the short term, but that it ended up causing an escalation of domestic violence over time (Garner, Fagan, & Maxwell, 1995).

Various criticisms have also been levied against Sherman and Berk's (1984) original study, such as that officers' responses may not have been totally random, that the six-month follow-up period was too short, and that Minneapolis was unique in that arrestees were kept overnight in jail. These issues aside, the research generally does not indicate that arrest alone deters IPV. Some studies suggest that just reporting IPV to the police carries deterrent effects which far outweigh that of arrest (Felson, Ackerman, & Gallagher, 2005). Yet, despite the lack of evidence supporting the notion that arrest deters domestic violence, many state laws and police agencies currently mandate or prefer arrest given probable cause. In the U.S. today, approximately 22 states have mandatory arrest policies in place (Xie, Lauritsen, & Heimer, 2012).

Gaps and challenges

Violence against women is gaining broader recognition as a pressing social problem on a global scale. Decades of mobilizing by civil society and women's movements have put ending gender-based violence high on national and international agendas. Today, most countries have laws against sexual assault and domestic violence, but many challenges still remain—both locally and abroad. For instance, in January 2017, Russia's Parliament voted 380 to 3 to decriminalize domestic violence in cases where it does not cause "substantial bodily harm" and does not occur "more than once a year" (Staglin, 2017). It would be difficult to view a policy like this as anything other than a significant step backward.

In addition, debates exist over whether violence against women requires its own distinct theoretical explanation from violence against men. While some research finds that the factors which predict violent victimization among males also predict violent victimization among females (Turanovic, Reisig, & Pratt, 2015), feminist critiques have questioned the generalizability of male-centered theories, arguing that such frameworks ignore the role of patriarchal power relations in society, which can differentially shape the involvement of males and females in both crime and victimization (Chesney-Lind & Pasko, 2004). Such challenges typically point out that women experience violence as a sanctioned response to oppressive social conditions associated with patriarchal norms, gendered inequality, and women's disempowerment (Rodríguez-Menés & Safranoff, 2012).

When it comes to violence against women, we must adopt an integrated, ecological framework to better understand its origins and to determine from the offender's perspective why it occurs (Heise, 1998). The vast majority of work in this area focuses on victims and not on offenders. Although we have learned a lot from the victim's perspective, unless we truly understand perpetrators, we will never fully understand the etiology of violence against women. Furthermore, in moving forward, we must ensure that the policies we adopt—whether they be mandatory arrest policies for IPV, or mandatory minimum sentences for sex offenders—are truly making victims safer, and that they can meaningfully reduce offenders' violent behaviors.

Key readings

Armstrong, E.A., Hamilton, L., & Sweeney, B. (2006). Sexual assault on campus: A multi-level, integrative approach to party rape. *Social Problems, 53,* 483-499.

Garner, J., Fagan, J., & Maxwell, C. (1995). Published findings from the spouse assault replication program: A critical review. *Journal of Quantitative Criminology, 11,* 3-28.

Grubb, A. & Turner, E. (2012). Attribution of blame in rape cases: A review of the impact of rape myth acceptance, gender role conformity and substance use on victim blaming. *Aggression and Violent Behavior, 17,* 443-452.

Sherman, L.W. & Berk, R.A. (1984). The specific deterrent effects of arrest for domestic assault. *American Sociological Review, 49,* 261-272.

Discussion questions

1. How does party culture relate to sexual violence?
2. Do you view Brock Turner as a rapist, even though he was under the influence, and he never had full-on sexual intercourse with the victim?
3. Why do women choose to stay in abusive relationships?
4. Why isn't arrest an effective strategy against reducing IPV?

References

Abbey, A. (2002). Alcohol-related sexual assault: A common problem among college students. *Journal of Studies on Alcohol and Drugs,* Supplement(s14), 118-128.

Abbey, A., McAuslan, P., & Ross, L.T. (1998). Sexual assault perpetration by college men: The role of alcohol, misperception of sexual intent, and sexual beliefs and experiences. *Journal of Social and Clinical Psychology, 17,* 167-195.

Armstrong, E.A., Hamilton, L., & Sweeney, B. (2006). Sexual assault on campus: A multi-level, integrative approach to party rape. *Social Problems, 53,* 483-499.

Baker, K.M. (2016). Here's the powerful letter the Stanford victim read to her attacker. *Buzz Feed,* June 3. Retrieved from www.buzzfeednews.com/article/katiejmbaker/heres-the-powerful-letter-the-stanford-victim-read-to-her-ra.

Bensimon, M. & Ronel, N. (2012). The flywheel effect of intimate partner violence: A victim–perpetrator interactive spin. *Aggression and Violent Behavior, 17*(5), 423-429.

Black, M.C., Basile, K.C., Breiding, M.J., Smith, S.G., Walters, M.L., Merrick, M.T., & Stevens, M.R. (2011). The national intimate partner and sexual violence survey: 2010 summary report. *Atlanta, GA: National Center for Injury Prevention and Control, Centers for Disease Control and Prevention, 19,* 39-40.

Burt, M.R. (1980). Cultural myths and supports for rape. *Journal of Personality and Social Psychology, 38,* 217-230.

Campbell, J.C., Webster, D., Koziol-McLain, J., Block, C., Campbell, D., Curry, M. A., & Sharps, P. (2003). Risk factors for femicide in abusive relationships: Results from a multisite case control study. *American Journal of Public Health, 93*(7), 1089-1097.

Catalano, S. (2013). *Intimate partner violence: Attributes of victimization, 1993-2011. Special report.* Washington, DC: U.S. Department of Justice, Bureau of Justice Statistics.

Chesney-Lind, M. & Pasko, L. (2004). *The female offender.* Thousand Oaks, CA: Sage.

Crime Survey of England and Wales. (2018). *Crime in England and Wales: Year ending March 2018.* Newport, South Wales: Office for National Statistics.

Doerner, W.G. & Lab, S.P. (2017). *Victimology* (8th edition). New York: Routledge.

Felson, R.B., Ackerman, J.M., & Gallagher, C.A. (2005). Police intervention and the repeat of domestic assault. *Criminology, 43*(3), 563–588.

Ferro, C., Cermele, J., & Saltzman, A. (2008). Current perceptions of marital rape: Some good and not-so-good news. *Journal of Interpersonal Violence, 23*(6), 764–779.

Franklin, C.A. (2011). An investigation of the relationship between self-control and alcohol-induced sexual assault victimization. *Criminal Justice and Behavior, 38*(3), 263–285.

Frohmann, L. (1991). Discrediting victims' allegations of sexual assault: Prosecutorial accounts of case rejections. *Social Problems, 38*, 213–226.

Garner, J., Fagan, J., & Maxwell, C. (1995). Published findings from the spouse assault replication program: A critical review. *Journal of Quantitative Criminology, 11*(1), 3–28.

Grubb, A. & Turner, E. (2012). Attribution of blame in rape cases: A review of the impact of rape myth acceptance, gender role conformity and substance use on victim blaming. *Aggression and Violent Behavior, 17*(5), 443–452.

Heise, L.L. (1998). Violence against women: An integrated, ecological framework. *Violence against Women, 4*, 262–290.

Holder, E. (2012). *Attorney General Eric Holder announces revisions to the Uniform Crime Report's definition of rape.* Washington, DC: U.S. Department of Justice.

Kadvany, E. (2015). Woman in Stanford sexual-assault case testifies. *Palo Alto Weekly*, October 5. Retrieved from www.paloaltoonline.com/news/2015/10/05/woman-in-stanford-sexual-assault-case-testifies.

Kaplan, T. (2018). Brock Turner wanted nothing more than "outercourse," not intercourse, lawyer argues. *East Bay Times*, July 24. Retrieved from www.eastbaytimes.com/2018/07/24/brock-turner-appeal-judges-hear-oral-arguments/.

Kennedy, M. (2016). Jury finds "Rolling Stone" reported liable for damages over rape allegation story. *NPR*, November 4. Retrieved from www.npr.org/sections/thetwo-way/2016/11/04/500701682/jury-finds-rolling-stone-reporter-liable-for-damages-over-rape-allegation-story.

Kim, J. & Gray, K.A. (2008). Leave or stay? Battered women's decision after intimate partner violence. *Journal of Interpersonal Violence, 23*(10), 1465–1482.

Krebs, C.P., Lindquist, C.H., Warner, T.D., Fisher, B.S., & Martin, S.L. (2009). College women's experiences with physically forced, alcohol- or other drug-enabled, and drug-facilitated sexual assault before and since entering college. *Journal of American College Health, 57*, 639–649.

Lindo, J.M., Siminski, P., & Swensen, I.D. (2018). College party culture and sexual assault. *American Economic Journal: Applied Economics, 10*(1), 236–265.

Lisak, D., Gardininer, L., Nicksa, S.C., & Cote, A.M. (2010). False allegations of sexual assault: An analysis of ten years of reported cases. *Violence against Women, 16*, 1318–1334.

Lonsway, K.A. & Fitzgerald, L.F. (1994). Rape myths. In review. *Psychology of Women Quarterly, 18*(2), 133–164.

Maxwell, C.D., Garner, J.H., & Fagan, J.A. (2002). The preventive effects of arrest on intimate partner violence: Research, policy and theory. *Criminology and Public Policy, 2*(1), 51–80.

McMahon, S. & Farmer, G.L. (2011). An updated measure for assessing subtle rape myths. *Social Work Research, 35*, 71–81.

Mei, G. (2016). This police report proves just how dishonest Brock Turner was during the Stanford Rape Trial. *Cosmopolitan*, June 9. Retrieved from www.cosmopolitan.com/lifestyle/news/a59705/police-report-brock-turner-stanford-rape-case/.

Meyer, J. (2000). History of sexual assault awareness and prevention efforts. Retrieved from /www.ncdsv.org/images/History_of_SAPE_Long_Version_2000.pdf.

Miller, M. (2016). All-American swimmer found guilty of sexually assaulting unconscious woman on Stanford campus. *Washington Post*. Retrieved from www.washingtonpost.com/news/morning-mix/wp/2016/03/31/all-american-swimmer-found-guilty-of-sexually-assaulting-unconscious-woman-on-stanford-campus/?utm_term=.30a98bb51d20.

National Domestic Violence Hotline. (2018). *"Why don't they just leave?"* Austin, TX: National Domestic Violence Hotline. Retrieved from www.thehotline.org/is-this-abuse/why-do-people-stay-in-abusive-relationships.

Office on Women's Health. (2018). *Am I being abused?* Washington, DC: U.S. Department of Health and Human Services. Retrieved from www.womenshealth.gov/relationships-and-safety/signs-abuse.

Planty, M., Langton, L., Krebs, C., Berzofsky, M., & Smiley-McDonald, H. (2013). *Female victims of sexual violence, 1994-2010. Special report.* Washington, DC: U.S. Department of Justice, Bureau of Justice Statistics.

Rand, M. & Rennison, C. (2004). How much violence against women is there? *Violence against Women and Family Violence: Developments in Research, Practice, and Policy*, 8.

Rodriguez, M.A., Sheldon, W.R., Bauer, H.M., & Pérez-Stable, E.J. (2001). The factors associated with disclosure of intimate partner abuse to clinicians. *Journal of Family Practice*, 50(4), 338-344.

Rodríguez-Menés, J. & Safranoff, A. (2012). Violence against women in intimate relations: A contrast of five theories. *European Journal of Criminology*, 9(6), 584-602.

Sherman, L.W. & Berk, R.A. (1984). The specific deterrent effects of arrest for domestic assault. *American Sociological Review*, 49, 261-272.

Shorey, R.C., Tirone, V., & Stuart, G.L. (2014). Coordinated community response components for victims of intimate partner violence: A review of the literature. *Aggression and Violent Behavior*, 19(4), 363-371.

Stack, L. (2016). Light sentence for Brock Turner in Stanford rape case draws outrage. *New York Times*, June 6. Retrieved from http://nyti.ms/1TS6gDq.

Staglin, D. (2017). Russia Parliament votes 380-3 to decriminalize domestic violence. *USA Today*. Retrieved from www.usatoday.com/story/news/2017/01/27/russian-parliament-decrimiinalizes-domestic-violence/97129912/.

Tasca, M., Rodriguez, N., Spohn, C., & Koss, M.P. (2013). Police decision making in sexual assault cases: Predictors of suspect identification and arrest. *Journal of Interpersonal Violence*, 28(6), 1157-1177.

Tjaden, P. & Thoennes, N. (2006). *Extent, nature, and consequences of rape victimization: Findings from the National Violence Against Women Survey.*

Turanovic, J.J., Reisig, M.D., & Pratt, T.C. (2015). Risky lifestyles, low self-control, and violent victimization across gendered pathways to crime. *Journal of Quantitative Criminology*, 31(2), 183-206.

Walker, L.E.A. (1979). *The battered woman.* New York: Harper and Row.

Washington Post-Kaiser Family Foundation. (2015). *Survey of current and recent college students on sexual assault.* Retrieved from http://files.kff.org/attachment/Survey%20Of%20Current%20And%20Recent%20College%20Students%20On%20Sexual%20Assault%20-%20Topline.

Wilson, D. & Glater, J.D. (2006). Files from Duke rape case give details but no answers. *New York Times*, August 25. Retrieved from www.nytimes.com/2006/08/25/us/25duke.html?mtrref=undefined.

World Health Organization. (2017). *Violence against women.* Retrieved from www.who.int/news-room/fact-sheets/detail/violence-against-women.

Xie, M., Lauritsen, J.L., & Heimer, K. (2012). Intimate partner violence in US Metropolitan areas: The contextual influences of police and social services. *Criminology*, 50(4), 961-992.

10 Victimization in prison

Norway is a really progressive country. Extremely rich in natural resources, Norway can lay claim to having one of the highest per capita GDP rates in the world, and a comprehensive welfare state that covers all citizens from birth to death. It should therefore come as no surprise that its prison system is equally progressive as well (Pratt, 2008). In one facility located about 75 kilometers south of Oslo, for example, a prison sits on Bastoy Island. Inmates take a small boat—one captained and manned by other fellow inmates—out to the prison complex. But the prison itself resembles more of a commune than a prison. Open spaces abound, inmates move about relatively freely, growing fresh vegetables, taking care of livestock, and taking part in a kind of self-reflection that prison administrators advocate. Indeed, the Norwegians believe very strongly in rehabilitation, so much so that life sentences do not exist—everyone is eligible to eventually return to society.

What is striking is how safe the prison is for the inmates who are housed there. This fact should be at least a little surprising given that it is not *actually* a commune. It is still a prison, one that houses people who have done bad things—including murder, rape, robbery, and assault—so there is no doubt that they have earned their way into incarceration. Even so, inmates at the facility have considerable autonomy to move about as they please and they experience far less direct supervision than is generally seen in the correctional systems of other nations (Sterbenz, 2017). They even have unfettered access to things like metal cutlery—forks, knives, and other pointy things—that they simply use for eating. The thought of using them as weapons against other inmates seems an unfathomable idea.

The Norway example stands in stark contrast to the state prison system in New York. There, in light of institutional problems and new legal requirements, the New York State Department of Corrections actually created an orientation film for incoming inmates on how to avoid being raped in prison, as discussed in Chapter 4. In the film—which was adapted into two versions to be gender-specific—inmates are advised about places in prison to either avoid or to be hyper-vigilant (e.g., areas of the prison that may be hidden from view), are cautioned about allowing other inmates to enter one's personal space (such as spotting someone while lifting weights), and are warned that inmates who offer unsolicited help or protection likely have ulterior motives and that becoming indebted to them is a bad idea.

The key here is that, where prison violence is seen as an aberration in Norway—so much so that potential weapons do not even need to be fashioned out of toothbrushes or razors because metal knives are already available to all—such violence is seen as an integral (perhaps even inevitable) part of prison life in New York. And with respect to sexual victimization in prison, it has become such a part of popular culture folklore that John Oliver recently dedicated a segment to it in his show *Last Week Tonight* which detailed the harm associated with how Americans tend to view sexual violence in prison as something to laugh at. But in comparing Norway to New York, the point is that, yes, violence and victimization in prison is always an ongoing concern. Nevertheless, there is considerable variation in violence and victimization from nation to nation and from prison to prison. There is also variation in terms of how we think about what causes prison violence and victimization, and how those differences in thinking influence how the problem is handled in different places.

Although incarceration rates vary considerably from nation to nation—with the United States leading the way—it is clear that the growth of incarceration is a global concern (Pratt, 2019). And as prison populations swell, there will inevitably be more and more prisoners who will eventually be released back into the community (Travis, 2005). Thus, this chapter presents an overview of the research regarding prison victimization in terms of overall levels of violence experienced, the sources and correlates of victimization in prison (e.g., individual, contextual, and institutional sources), the theoretical perspectives that have been developed in an effort to explain prison victimization, and the consequences of victimization in terms of the post-release behavior of those who were incarcerated. The broader purpose is to provide a better understanding of how these experiences may influence whether prisoners either will or will not successfully navigate their re-entry.

The nature and extent of victimization in prison

It should come as no shock to any reader that prisons can be violent places. And while instances of violent victimization may not be nearly as high as we might think—indeed, the vast majority of inmates will remain physically safe during their term of incarceration—rates of physical violence are typically higher inside of prisons and jails than they are outside of them. Wooldredge and Steiner's (2013) study of inmates in Ohio and Kentucky, for example, found that around one in ten had been violently victimized inside the facility in the past six months. That figure might strike some as comfortably low. After all, it means that nine in ten did not experience a violent victimization event. But when we compare that figure to victimization rates in American society at large—where the violent victimization rate in 2015 was 18.6 per 1,000 people—we see that the violent victimization rate in prison is more than five times that of the national average (Truman & Morgan, 2016).

Such violence can come in many forms and from many places inside of prison. Assaults, for example, can come from other inmates—both in a one-on-one context or collectively, often when tied to racial/ethnic identities or to gang affiliations (Scott & Maxson, 2016). They can also come from prison staff, where high-profile incidents of physical abuse have been reported across facilities for incarcerated males, females, and juveniles (Ross, Tewksbury, & Rolfe, 2016). But it certainly does not stop there. Interpersonal conflicts between inmates and between inmates and staff routinely result in verbal and physical aggression, group violence is not uncommon, large-scale riots are a constantly looming threat (Carrabine, 2005), weapons get fashioned and concealed for later use, and homicides occur with disturbing frequency (Reisig, 2002).

It is also important to highlight one form of victimization that tends to occupy a position of elevated importance in prison life: sexual victimization. Recent data show that, in the United States, an estimated 4 percent of state and federal prison inmates and 3.2 percent of jail inmates reported experiencing one or more incidents of sexual victimization by another inmate or by staff during the previous year (Beck et al., 2013). In addition, like other forms of victimization, some inmates (and facilities) are more vulnerable to this problem than others. For example, in The Oglala Sioux Tribal Offenders Facility in Pine Ridge, South Dakota, 10.8 percent of inmates reported sexual victimization by staff—the highest rate of any facility in the country (Beck et al., 2013).

This reality eventually led to the passage of the Prison Rape Elimination Act (PREA) in 2003, which set forth guidelines for reporting and handling sexual assaults in prison (Dumond, 2003). As part of the law, in 2009 the National Prison Rape Elimination Commission was established that proposed more concrete standards to prevent, monitor, and respond to the sexual abuse of those incarcerated (Jenness & Smyth, 2011)—standards that were eventually accepted by the U.S. Department of Justice in 2012. Either way, whatever form it comes in, institutional violence is apparently so ubiquitous that the entertainment industry has found a way to capitalize (literally) off of it with the development of hit television shows like *Lockup, Oz,* and *Orange is the New Black.*

Sources of prison violence and victimization

Just like victimization in the community—or what we might think of as "street victimization" (subjects covered in Chapters 3 to 5)—as well as more remote forms of victimization like fraud and cybervictimization (which will be covered in detail in Chapter 11), the sources of victimization in prison are complex. Indeed, as stated earlier, while prisons may certainly be dangerous places, and rates of victimization are often substantially higher than they are outside of prison walls, it is still the case that most inmates are able to successfully avoid being victimized, and that inmates (as well as prisons) who share certain characteristics are disproportionately more likely to experience higher levels of victimization. To that end, there are individual/demographic correlates of prison violence, as well as contextual and behavioral characteristics that make victimization more likely, and there are institutional factors that play an important role as well. We will cover these factors here so that we may be in a better position to evaluate how well existing theories of prison violence and victimization are able to explain why these sources exist and how they operate.

Individual/demographic sources of correlates

The individual-level/demographic correlates and sources of victimization in prison tend to mirror those found in the research on victimization in general. For example, research indicates that male inmates are much more likely to engage in violent behavior relative to their female counterparts (Levan, 2012), and are in turn more likely to be victimized as well (Wolff et al., 2007). These patterns hold true when "aggregated up" as well, where prisons for men in general experience higher rates of violence and victimization relative to institutions for women (Michalski, 2017). This is not to say that prison violence/victimization is somehow a uniquely "male problem"—far from it, particularly when it comes to sexual violence in prison, where females are generally at twice the risk of being sexually victimized relative to men (Sanchez & Wolff, 2016). Nevertheless, when it comes to overall levels of victimization in prison—particularly violent forms of victimization like assaults—male inmates are at an elevated risk (Jiang & Winfree, 2006).

In addition, similar to the well-established age-victimization curve (covered in Chapter 3), younger inmates are also more likely to be victimized in prisons when compared to older inmates (Lahm, 2015). This reality is even more pronounced for juvenile inmates who are being housed in adult facilities (Kuan-liang, Sorensen, & Cunningham, 2008). Not surprisingly, explanations for why these patterns exist vary. Some argue that younger inmates (like younger people in general) are more likely to behave in "risky" ways that put them into close proximity with potential offenders (Reid & Listwan, 2018). But prisons are, after all, full of offenders—and yet not everyone is victimized and not all inmates victimize others. So, given that reality, other scholars have argued that younger inmates simply make more vulnerable and attractive targets (e.g., due to size, stature, inexperience) to potential offenders (Connell, Farrington, & Ireland, 2016). Regardless of which explanation is ultimately more plausible (and recognizing full well that they are not necessarily mutually exclusive), the "aging-out" process, one that characterizes both offending and victimization generally, appears to hold true inside of prisons as well.

Finally, research shows that members of minority groups—particularly African-Americans—are more likely to engage in violence and to be victimized by others while incarcerated (Worrall & Morris, 2012; cf. Wooldredge & Steiner, 2012). And similar to the explanations associated with the age-victimization link, scholars disagree as to why such racial differences in victimization exist. Some have tied disproportionate rates of victimization to higher rates of violent behavior in prison among minority inmates (Harer & Steffensmeier, 1996), while others elevate rates of victimization among minorities as a reflection of institutional racism and discrimination (Noll, 2011). And while evidence exists in support of both perspectives (again, neither of which is mutually exclusive; see Bell, 2017; Schenk & Fremouw, 2012), the bottom line is that, with respect to racial/ethnic differences in the risk of victimization in prison, the patterns observed outside of the prison walls tend to hold on the inside as well.

Contextual and behavioral sources and correlates

In addition to individual and demographic factors associated with victimization in prison, research has also revealed that certain contextual and behavioral factors, particularly those related to how inmates spend their time, may also put them at an elevated risk of being victimized. Such factors are important in no small part because inmates tend to have a lot of time on their hands and not everyone spends that time in the same way (there is even a body of literature on "inmate boredom" that dates back a few decades; see Sabath & Cowles, 1990). So it should come as little surprise, then, that some of the ways in which inmates choose to pass their days are riskier than others when it comes to the odds of being victimized.

Research has revealed, for example, that inmates who spend more of their time in "unstructured routines"—those that typically occur with other inmates and with little to no structure or supervision—are more likely to be victimized (Wooldredge & Steiner, 2013). This finding is consistent with the broader criminological literature on "unstructured socializing" and how youth who spend more time with peers with no real agenda and no adult supervision, are more likely to get into trouble (Hoeben et al., 2016). This does not mean, however, that participating in structured activities is an easy fix for the problem of prison violence. To be sure, the evidence on that front is relatively mixed, where some studies find that engaging in prison programming (e.g., education, rehabilitation, employment, or religious programming) reduces one's risk of being victimized (Teasdale et al., 2016), where others find the opposite to be true (Listwan et al., 2014).

But what is not mixed are the findings concerning engaging in misbehavior while incarcerated. Indeed, the empirical record on this is quite clear, where inmates who experience adjustment problems—particularly those that amount to official misconduct (e.g., breaking rules of various kinds such as possessing contraband and participating in the illicit institutional economy; see Reyns et al., 2016)—are more likely to be victimized (see, e.g., Lahm's (2015) study of female inmates). Even more problematic is engaging in violent behavior, where research results consistently reveal that such conduct significantly elevates the risk of violent victimization in studies conducted in the United States (Wooldredge & Steiner, 2013) and among Korean inmates (Reyns et al., 2016). Thus, the well-established "victim-offender overlap" that exists in the criminological literature appears to reproduce itself in the prison context again. And more broadly, once again we see that, similar to the likelihood of experiencing victimization in the community, engaging in "risky routines" while incarcerated elevates the odds of being victimized in prison.

Institutional sources and correlates

When it comes to victimization in prison, institutional context is critically important. Some prisons are fairly safe places, while for others violence is a part of daily life. What, then, do violent prisons look like relative to those that are comparatively much safer? One factor that becomes immediately important is security level—yet the relationship between prison security level and institutional violence/victimization may not be as straightforward as one might think. In particular, it may be tempting to think that it is maximum security prisons—those that tend to house a more violent inmate population—that experience the most violence and victimization. And while select facilities can be plucked out to illustrate that very thing, the reality is that inmates housed in such places typically have most of their movements tightly controlled by the prison administration (Wooldredge & Steiner, 2013). Alternatively, it is often medium or even minimum security facilities—those where inmates have much more freedom to move about in unstructured ways and to interact with other inmates in an unsupervised context—that experience higher rates of violence and victimization (Wooldredge & Steiner, 2015).

Since the opportunity for inmates to rub shoulders with one another is undoubtedly a key factor in understanding prison violence and victimization, a second factor that immediately comes to mind is prison overcrowding. Most prisons in the United States, for example, are operating well above their rated capacity for housing inmates, and prison overcrowding is common (Bastow, 2013). The problem is that the literature on the relationship between prison overcrowding and a wide array of institutional problems (e.g., misconduct, violence, victimization) is mixed. Some studies find evidence of "crowding effects" while others do not (e.g., Wooldredge & Steiner, 2009), and broader assessments of this literature have found that crowding—in and of itself—is only moderately predictive of prison-related problems (Franklin, Franklin, & Pratt, 2006).

There is, however, evidence that the overcrowding/violence/victimization link may simply be more complex in that some inmates are more vulnerable to overcrowding effects than others. Specifically, research has shown that younger inmates tend to have a tougher time adjusting to prison life when housed in overcrowded facilities, which in turn elevates their odds of engaging in and experiencing negative events during their term of incarceration (Wooldredge, Griffin, & Pratt, 2001). Thus, it is possible that, with respect to prison violence and victimization, overcrowding matters most through how it may condition the influence of other individual-level factors.

Finally, an easily overlooked prison-level source of institutional violence and victimization—one that is difficult to measure directly using large, publicly available datasets in institutional corrections—is the incentive structure for inmates' behavior put in place by the prison administration. In one particularly vivid example, Mark Colvin's (1992) analysis of the 1980 prison riot at the Penitentiary of New Mexico—one that left 33 inmates dead and more than 200 injured in the most violent riot in American prison history—showed rather clearly how changes in the incentives extended to inmates can seriously affect how a facility functions. In particular, long-standing rewards for good behavior on the part of prisoners (e.g., access to employment, trade school/college courses, and other amenities) were taken away when a new administrative regime took over. The rational system of rewards and punishments was replaced with incentives from staff for inmates to inform on one another (a practice referred to as "snitch jackets"), which created an environment ripe for retaliation and collective violence. And while other lax control mechanisms certainly contributed to the breakdown of control over the inmates and ultimately the riot itself (e.g., unlocked doors to other housing units, blowtorches and other tools that could be weaponized if left unattended), the change in the incentives intended to guide prisoners' behavior bred considerable anger and resentment that added fuel to the riot.

Theoretical perspectives on prison violence and victimization

Given the sources and correlates of prison and violence and victimization reviewed above, it is now useful to take a close look at the major theories associated with how prisons function and operate to see how well they are able to explain *why* such incidents occur. To that end, while some early efforts were made at understanding how prisons function (Clemmer, 1940; Polanski, 1942), it was Gresham Sykes' (1958) *The Society of Captives* that really established prisons as an important social institution which should become the focus of academic research (Reisig, 2001). In this work, Sykes drew upon his experience observing inmate life in the New Jersey State Maximum Security Prison system—one that encompassed three facilities, employed over 300 staff, and housed more than 1,200 inmates. His central thesis was that there are certain "pains of imprisonment"—those associated with being deprived of freedom, autonomy, heterosexual contact, and even personal safety. Thus, as a result of having to cope with these "deprivations," prisoners will adopt certain behavioral strategies and identities in an effort to manage their lives during their term of incarceration.

These identities—which Sykes (1958: 84) referred to as "argot roles"—included those that govern relationships with staff (*rats* and *center men*), those connected to participation in and control of the illicit prison economy (*gorillas* and *merchants*), those that dealt with sexual behavior in various ways (*wolves*, *punks*, and *fags*), and those oriented around either perpetrating violence or avoiding it (*ball busters* and *real men*). But regardless of the role any given inmate adopts, the important thing to remember is that, according to Sykes (1958), all of these roles are a response to the prison environment itself. To be sure, in what became known as the "deprivation model" of prison organization, the prison environment was viewed as inherently harsh and even fundamentally inhumane by scholars who followed Sykes's work (see, e.g., Haney, Banks, & Zimbardo, 1973), even to the point of turning otherwise "good" people into those who would gladly victimize others (Zimbardo, 2007).

Through the 1960s and into the 1970s, however, scholarly thinking about how prisons operate began to change. Concerns over structural inequality in society at large—particularly the ways in which such inequalities systematically disadvantaged members of racial/ethnic minority groups (Clark,

1965)–translated into discussions of how prisons and other public institutions functioned as well (Rothman, 1971). During this time, scholars became less focused on the deprivations imposed by prisons and instead became more concerned with how social and structural problems outside of prisons–for instance, racial strife and economic inequality–found their way inside the prison walls. Even more explicitly, scholars began to see the "argot roles" that Sykes discussed not as responses to the deprivations associated with being incarcerated, but rather as extensions of inmates' pre-prison lives.

The most influential work in what would become known as the "importation model" theoretical tradition is arguably *Stateville* by James Jacobs (1977). In his analysis of the Illinois State Penitentiary, Jacobs was quick to note that violence in prison was becoming increasingly interracial. Just as important, he noted that instances of collective violence–including the infamous prison riot in Attica, New York–bore a close resemblance to instances of collective violence outside of the prison walls (e.g., race-related riots in Harlem, New York in 1964; Philadelphia in 1964; Watts in Los Angeles in 1965; the 1967 riots in Newark, New Jersey; and the 1968 riots in Chicago, Washington, DC, and Baltimore). Thus, the fundamental argument being made here is that one cannot really understand prison violence and victimization without understanding inmates' pre-prison experiences with violence and victimization.

But this new way of thinking about prisons–and in particular prison violence and victimization–did not replace the idea that prisons themselves can be a breeding ground for violence. Instead, it inspired a decade's worth of empirical studies (Gaes & McGuire, 1985; Poole & Regoli, 1983)–a line of work that continues today (Kigerl & Hamilton, 2016; Tewksbury, Connor, & Denney, 2014)–that pitted deprivation "versus" importation factors as potentially competing explanations of prison violence. In the process, researchers went to considerable lengths to assess whether "imported" factors like race, age, or pre-prison gang affiliation would predict violence and/or victimization above and beyond "deprivation" factors like prison crowding and overall levels of institutional violence, and vice versa (Morris & Worrall, 2014; Steiner, Butler, & Ellison, 2014).

Things stayed this way for a while in the prison violence (and, more broadly, prison organization) literature. Things changed when Dilulio's (1987) *Governing prisons* was published–a work that began with a rather simple observation: not all prisons are the same. Some are violent places, where both staff and inmates alike victimize each other and engage in all manner of problematic behavior. Other prisons, however, are well-run and relatively safe places–a comparison wholly consistent with the examples that led off this very chapter. So what Dilulio (1987) argued was that an overlooked variable–prison management–could help explain why rates of violence and victimization (as well as other institutional problems) vary from prison to prison. Good management, he stated—where rules are clear and fairly enforced, where services and amenities are available and used as incentives for good behavior among inmates, and where order is maintained via consistent standards—can mitigate against the potential pains of imprisonment that Sykes (1958) discussed, and can successfully soften the potential problematic imported characteristics that inmates bring with them to the institution.

Subsequent research has provided considerable support for this perspective. Studies have shown, for example, that prisons which are more effectively managed experience lower rates of misconduct, violence, and even lethal violence (Reisig, 1998, 2002). Alternatively, studies have also shown that management failures can result in increased violence and victimization, and can even be the source of riots and other forms of collective violence (Colvin, 1992; Useem & Reisig, 1999). Yet what is interesting to note is that this body of work has developed its own vocabulary (e.g., importation, and deprivation factors) separate from the study of violence and victimization in general. This is understandable, at least in part, because scholars who study prison violence and victimization rarely also study violence and victimization in the community setting. But the problem is that insights from the victimization literature at large—for example, those coming from theoretical traditions like routine activity, risky lifestyles, and self-control perspectives—which have proven to be of considerable intellectual value have long been absent from the literature on prison violence and victimization.

More contemporary criminological work has, however, begun to take up the task of importing more traditional, mainstream criminological theories into the study of prison violence and victimization. Some of this new work draws upon an integrated self-control and risky lifestyles perspective (see, e.g., Reyns et al., 2016), where inmates who lack self-control are more likely to behave in problematic ways (e.g., breaking institutional rules, engaging in violent behavior) that, in turn, place them at an elevated risk of being victimized themselves. More common, however, are recent studies that draw upon the general strain theoretical tradition (see Agnew, 2006). This new line of work focuses on how negative experiences while incarcerated—victimization being chief among them—can create pressure for inmates to engage in coping behaviors (Zweig et al., 2015). Some of these behaviors may be prosocial (e.g., seeking treatment or administrative protection), while others are more maladaptive, such as engaging in retaliatory violence (Leban et al., 2016). Either way, the general takeaway from this new generation of work is that traditional perspectives in mainstream criminology—those that attempt to understand why people offend and are victimized generally—represent a promising avenue for understanding violence and victimization in prison.

Consequences of victimization in prison

In Part III (Chapters 6 to 8) we covered in detail the consequences of victimization in general. These included personal consequences like psycho-emotional distress and behavioral problems like substance abuse and offending (Turanovic & Pratt, 2013); legal consequences like the barriers some victims face in getting access to legal assistance, and how experiencing the legal process can amount to a form of "dual victimization" (Cross, 2013); and social and political consequences like how victimization can result in elevated levels of fear of crime, which in turn can be a source of community change (e.g., residents withdrawing from community life or moving to a different community; see Xie & McDowall, 2008). And, when it comes to violence in prison, we can now add another potential consequence of victimization: compromised public safety.

In the United States alone, over 600,000 offenders are released from prison back into the community each year (Travis, 2005). It therefore makes sense that we would want to take the re-entry process seriously, and to do as much as we can for inmates while they are incarcerated to reduce the risk that they will continue to offend and victimize others upon their release. The problem, however, is that estimates of recidivism among released prisoners remain relatively high—with some studies placing the figure of released inmates returning to prison at around 50 percent, and even the most conservative estimates placing the rate at around 33 percent (Rhodes et al., 2016). Part of the problem can be traced to prison conditions themselves, where facilities can still be unsafe and unhealthy places, and where few services often exist to assist inmates in adjusting to community life when they are released (Burch, 2017).

Prison violence and victimization also play a role in contributing to higher recidivism rates and therefore compromised public safety. Such a statement does, however, fly in the face of a relatively common form of political rhetoric that has long surrounded the relationship between prison conditions and recidivism. In particular, policy makers have found that political capital can be gained by claiming that the worse prisons are, the more likely that inmates will "think twice" about misbehaving again because they will not want to return to such a dismal environment (Bierie, 2012). After all, these are convicted criminals—not law-abiding citizens—so why should we make an effort to make their lives at all pleasant during their stint of incarceration? This assumption was given the veneer of scholarly credibility with a study by Katz, Levitt (of "Freakonomics" fame), and Shusterovich (2003). Their analysis of state-level data—one which failed to control for valid indicators of either economic deprivation or structured inequality—found that the death rate among prisoners (the measure they thought best captured poor prison conditions) was correlated with lower crime rates.

Nevertheless, this single (and methodologically problematic) study aside, a large body of literature clearly shows that experiencing harsh prison conditions actually increases the odds of recidivism among released inmates (Cullen, Jonson, & Nagin, 2011). More specifically, there is a growing roster of studies which show that experiencing victimization while incarcerated is associated with an elevated risk of reoffending upon release. Research has shown, for example, that experiencing victimization while imprisoned is associated with higher recidivism rates generally, and that the "victimization effect" is most pronounced among inmates convicted of serious and violent offenses (Taylor, 2015). The victimization effect is also not confined to direct forms of victimization either. To be sure, research reveals that even witnessing victimization while incarcerated is associated with an elevated risk of various forms of problematic post-release behavior, including parole violations and re-arrest (Daquin, Daigle, & Listwan, 2016). Thus, the bottom line is that, regardless of how one may feel about what inmates do or do not deserve, experiencing victimization is harmful to inmates and undermines public safety.

Gaps and challenges

Prison violence and victimization have been studied by scholars for over half a century. In that time we have definitely learned a great deal—we have attempted to demonstrate just that with this chapter. Nevertheless, most of what we "know" about prison violence and victimization is tied to research on adult male inmates (Celinska & Sung, 2014). Accordingly, there are still certain key substantive areas with respect to victimization in prison where we know far less than we would like. One of those areas has to do with understudied portions of the inmate population.

Female inmates and institutions, for example, are still on the periphery of scholars' attention. For years female inmates had been largely overlooked—at least implicitly—because they represented such a small proportion of the overall inmate population (Clear & Frost, 2014). But in recent decades the rate of incarceration for women has risen considerably. According to a recent analysis (see McCarthy, 2014), we have now reached a point where one-third of all of the women incarcerated worldwide now have one thing in common: they are in the United States. Yet, despite this growth, understanding the nature of victimization in prison for women lags behind the production of new knowledge concerning violence among male inmates (Butcher, Park, & Piehl, 2017).

And since one form of violent victimization experienced disproportionately by female inmates—sexual violence—remains notoriously difficult to study (Kubiak et al., 2017), we still have a lot of work in front of us if we truly want to understand women inmates' experiences with violence and victimization while incarcerated.

There is also an important change to the demographic landscape with respect to trends in incarceration, at least in the United States. Patterns of immigration—particularly among Hispanics since the 1980s—have meant that the Latino population in the United States has risen substantially (Light & Ulmer, 2016). This increase in the overall Hispanic population in the U.S. has translated into an increase in the Hispanic inmate population as well, with recent data showing that Hispanic rates of incarceration are three times that of Whites (National Research Council, 2014). Yet we still know comparatively little about how this growth has affected the Hispanic inmate population with respect to prison violence, victimization, and their consequences.

The same could also be said of violence and victimization among the juvenile offenders who are currently locked up in over 2,500 secure juvenile facilities in the United States (Hockenberry, Sickmund, & Sladky, 2015). In 1996 this population of incarcerated youth peaked at just over 116,000, which is approximately the size of the combined *adult* prison population of inmates collectively housed in the states of Colorado, Indiana, Kentucky, Maine, Massachusetts, Minnesota, New Mexico, and Oregon (Carson, 2015). And although rates of juvenile incarceration have leveled off in recent years and are even showing signs of declining, this is still an extremely vulnerable proportion of the inmate population (Mears, Pickett, & Mancini, 2015), and a systematic attempt among scholars to understand the nature of violence and victimization among youthful offenders has never really come to fruition. This is unfortunate, since one of the things we do know is that getting tough with juvenile offenders in general tends to be a bad idea—one that rarely translates into an increase in public safety (Ogle & Turanovic, 2016). So to the extent that being victimized is particularly harmful for youthful offenders—something that is entirely likely given the developmental literature on the consequences of adolescent victimization (Turanovic & Pratt, 2015)—then understanding the nature of violence and victimization in correctional facilities for juveniles is extremely important.

Finally, there is still considerable room for theoretical development in the study of prison violence and victimization. The first generation of this work—that which relied primarily on comparing deprivation versus importation factors—was useful when it began. But at this point that approach has outlived its usefulness, particularly since the typical conclusion from studies that assess these groups of variables comparatively will inevitably conclude that "they both matter." Instead, what would be most welcome is for the current trend of bringing traditional criminological theories–such as general strain and lifestyle/routine activity perspectives–into the study of violence in prison and its consequences. There is still much to be learned here, particularly with respect to how these more well-traveled criminological consequences–factors such as self-control, deviant peers, and antisocial attitudes (see, e.g., Pratt & Cullen, 2000; Pratt et al., 2010)–translate into understanding victimization in a structural context where the autonomy of both offenders and victims is limited.

Key readings

Cullen, F.T., Jonson, C.L., & Nagin, D.S. (2011). Prisons do not reduce recidivism: The high cost of ignoring science. *The Prison Journal, 91*, 48S-65S.

DiIulio, J.J. (1987). *Governing prisons: A comparative study of correctional management.* New York: Free Press.

Jacobs, J.B. (1977). *Stateville: The penitentiary in mass society.* Chicago, IL: University of Chicago Press.

Leban, L., Cardwell, S.M., Copes, H., & Brezina, T. (2016). Adapting to prison life: A qualitative examination of the coping process among incarcerated offenders. *Justice Quarterly, 33*, 943-969.

Sykes, G.M. (1958). *The society of captives: A study of a maximum security prison.* Princeton, NJ: Princeton University Press.

Discussion questions

1. How common is violence/victimization in prison? Do these incidents happen more or less often than you may have previously thought?
2. What are some of the key individual/demographic, behavioral, and institutional sources and correlates of victimization in prison?
3. How do the importation, deprivation, and management models differ with respect to how they explain prison violence and victimization?
4. Why might it be useful to incorporate traditional criminological explanations into the study of victimization in prison?
5. What is the relationship between experiencing violence/victimization in prison and successful re-entry into society upon release?

References

Agnew, R. (2006). *Pressured into crime: An overview of general strain theory.* Los Angeles, CA: Roxbury.

Bastow, S. (2013). *Governance, performance, and capacity stress: The chronic case of prison crowding.* New York: Palgrave MacMillan.

Beck, A.J., Berzofsky, M., Caspar, R., & Krebs, C. (2013). *Sexual victimization in prisons and jails reported by inmates, 2011-12.* Washington, DC: Bureau of Justice Statistics.

Bell, K.E. (2017). Prison violence and the intersectionality of race/ethnicity and gender. *Criminology, Criminal Justice, Law and Society, 18*, 106-121.

Bierie, D.M. (2012). Is tougher better? The impact of physical prison conditions on inmate violence. *International Journal of Offender Therapy and Comparative Criminology, 56,* 338–355.

Burch, M. (2017). (Re)entry from the bottom up: Case study of a critical approach to assisting women coming home from prison. *Critical Criminology, 25,* 357–374.

Butcher, K.F., Park, K.H., & Piehl, A.M. (2017). Comparing apples to oranges: Differences in women's and men's incarceration and sentencing outcomes. *Journal of Labor Economics, 35,* S201–S234.

Carrabine, E. (2005). Prison riots, social order and the problem of legitimacy. *British Journal of Criminology, 45,* 896–913.

Carson, E.A. (2015). *Prisoners in 2014.* Washington, DC: Bureau of Justice Statistics Bulletin.

Celinska, K. & Sung, H.E. (2014). Gender differences in the determinants of prison rule violations. *The Prison Journal, 94,* 220–241.

Clark, K.B. (1965). *Dark ghetto: Dilemmas of social power.* New York: Harper & Row.

Clear, T.R. & Frost, N.A. (2014). *The punishment imperative.* New York: New York University Press.

Clemmer, D. (1940). *The prison community.* Boston, MA: The Christopher Publishing House.

Colvin, M. (1992). *The penitentiary in crisis: From accommodation to riot in New Mexico.* Albany: State University of New York Press.

Connell, A., Farrington, D.P., & Ireland, J.L. (2016). Characteristics of bullies and victims among male young offenders. *Journal of Aggression, Conflict and Peace Research, 8,* 114–123.

Cross, A.L. (2013). Slipping through the cracks: The dual victimization of human-trafficking survivors. *McGeorge Law Review, 44,* 395–422.

Cullen, F.T., Jonson, C.L., & Nagin, D.S. (2011). Prisons do not reduce recidivism: The high cost of ignoring science. *The Prison Journal, 91,* 48S–65S.

Daquin, J.C., Daigle, L.E., & Listwan, S.J. (2016). Vicarious victimization in prison: Examining the effects of witnessing victimization while incarcerated on offender reentry. *Criminal Justice and Behavior, 43,* 1018–1033.

Dilulio, J.J. (1987). *Governing prisons: A comparative study of correctional management.* New York: Free Press.

Dumond, R.W. (2003). Confronting America's most ignored crime problem: The Prison Rape Elimination Act of 2003. *Journal of the American Academy of Psychiatry and Law, 31,* 354–360.

Franklin, T.W., Franklin, C.A., & Pratt, T.C. (2006). Examining the empirical relationship between prison crowding and inmate misconduct: A meta-analysis of conflicting research results. *Journal of Criminal Justice, 34,* 401–412.

Gaes, G.G. & McGuire, W.J. (1985). Prison violence: The contribution of crowding versus other determinants of prison assault rates. *Journal of Research in Crime and Delinquency, 22,* 41–65.

Haney, C., Banks, C., & Zimbardo, P. (1973). Interpersonal dynamics in a simulated prison. *International Journal of Criminology and Penology, 1,* 69–97.

Harer, M.D. & Steffensmeier, D.J. (1996). Race and prison violence. *Criminology, 34,* 323–355.

Hockenberry, S., Sickmund, M., & Sladky, A. (2015). *Juvenile residential facility census, 2012: Selected findings.* Washington, DC: Office of Juvenile Justice and Delinquency Prevention.

Hoeben, E.M., Meldrum, R.C., Walker, D., & Young, J.T.N. (2016). The role of peer delinquency and unstructured socializing in explaining delinquency and substance abuse: A state-of-the-art review. *Journal of Criminal Justice, 47,* 108–122.

Jacobs, J.B. (1977). *Stateville: The penitentiary in mass society.* Chicago, IL: University of Chicago Press.

Jenness, V. & Smyth, M. (2011). The passage and implementation of the Prison Rape Elimination Act: Legal endogeneity and the uncertain road from symbolic law to instrumental effects. *Stanford Law and Policy Review, 22,* 489–528.

Jiang, S. & Winfree, L.T. (2006). Social support, gender, and inmate adjustment to prison
life: Insights from a national sample. *The Prison Journal, 86,* 32–55.

Katz, L., Levitt, S.D., & Shusterovich, E. (2003). Prison conditions, capital punishment, and
deterrence. *American Law and Economics Review, 5,* 318–343.

Kigerl, A. & Hamilton, Z. (2016). The impact of transfers between prisons on inmate misconduct: Testing importation, deprivation, and transfer theory models. *The Prison
Journal, 96,* 232–257.

Kuanliang, A., Sorensen, J.R., & Cunningham, M.D. (2008). Juvenile inmates in an adult
prison system: Rates of disciplinary misconduct and violence. *Criminal Justice and
Behavior, 35,* 1186–1201.

Kubiak, S.P., Brenner, H.J., Bybee, D., Campbell, R., Cummings, C.E., & Darcy, K.M. (2017).
Sexual misconduct in prison: What factors affect whether incarcerated women will
report abuses committed by prison staff? *Law and Human Behavior, 41,* 361–374.

Lahm, K.F. (2015). Predictors of violent and nonviolent victimization behind bars: An
exploration of women inmates. *Women and Criminal Justice, 25,* 273–291.

Leban, L., Cardwell, S.M., Copes, H., & Brezina, T. (2016). Adapting to prison life: A qualitative examination of the coping process among incarcerated offenders. *Justice Quarterly, 33,* 943–969.

Levan, K. (2012). *Prison violence: Causes, consequences and solutions.* London: Routledge.

Light, M.T. & Ulmer, J.T. (2016). Examining the gaps in white, black, and Hispanic violence
since 1990: Accounting for immigration, incarceration, and inequality. *American Sociological Review, 81,* 290–315.

Listwan, S.J., Daigle, L.E., Hartman, J.L., & Guastaferro, W.P. (2014). Poly-victimization risk
in prison: The influence of individual and institutional factors. *Journal of Interpersonal
Violence, 29,* 2458–2481.

McCarthy, N. (2014). Nearly a third of all female prisoners worldwide are incarcerated in
the United States. *Forbes,* September 23.

Mears, D.P., Pickett, J.T., & Mancini, C. (2015). Support for balanced juvenile justice:
Assessing views about youth, rehabilitation, and punishment. *Journal of Quantitative
Criminology, 31,* 459–479.

Michalski, J.H. (2017). Status hierarchies and hegemonic masculinity: A general theory of
prison violence. *British Journal of Criminology, 57,* 40–60.

Morris, R.G. & Worrall, J.L. (2014). Prison architecture and inmate misconduct: A multilevel
assessment. *Crime and Delinquency, 60,* 1083–1109.

National Research Council. (2014). *The growth of incarceration in the United States:
Exploring causes and consequences of high rates of incarceration,* ed. J. Travis, B.
Western, & S. Redburn. Washington, DC: National Academic Press.

Noll, D. (2011). Building a new identity: Race, gangs, and violence in California prisons.
University of Miami Law Review, 66, 847–877.

Ogle, M.R. & Turanovic, J.J. (2016). Is getting tough with low-risk kids a good idea? The
effect of failure to appear detention stays on juvenile recidivism. *Criminal Justice
Policy Review.* doi: 10.1177/0887403416682299.

Polanski, N.A. (1942). The prison as an autocracy. *Journal of Criminal Law and Criminology, 33,* 16–22.

Poole, E.D., & Regoli, R.M. (1983). Violence in juvenile institutions: A comparative study.
Criminology, 21, 213–232.

Pratt, J. (2008). Scandinavian exceptionalism in an era of penal excess: Part I: The nature
and roots of Scandinavian exceptionalism. *British Journal of Criminology, 48,* 119–137.

Pratt, T.C. (forthcoming). *Addicted to incarceration: Corrections policy and the politics of
misinformation in the United States* (2nd edition). Thousand Oaks, CA: Sage.

Pratt, T.C. & Cullen, F.T. (2000). The empirical status of Gottfredson and Hirschi's general theory of crime: A meta-analysis. *Criminology, 38,* 931–964.

Pratt, T.C., Cullen, F.T., Sellers, C.S., Winfree, L.T., Madensen, T.D., Daigle, L.E., Fearn, N.E., & Gau, J.M. (2010). The empirical status of social learning theory: A meta-analysis. *Justice Quarterly, 27,* 765–802.

Reid, S.E. & Listwan, S.J. (2018). Managing the threat of violence: Coping strategies among juvenile inmates. *Journal of Interpersonal Violence, 33,* 1306–1326.

Reisig, M.D. (1998). Rates of disorder in higher-custody state prisons: A comparative analysis of managerial practices. *Crime and Delinquency, 44,* 229–244.

Reisig, M.D. (2001). The champion, contender, and challenger: Top-ranked books in prison studies. *The Prison Journal, 81,* 389–407.

Reisig, M.D. (2002). Administrative control and inmate homicide. *Homicide Studies, 6,* 84–103.

Reyns, B.W., Woo, Y., Lee, H.D., & Yoon, O.K. (2018). Vulnerability versus opportunity: Dissecting the role of low self-control and risky lifestyles in violent victimization risk among Korean inmates. *Crime and Delinquency, 64,* 423–447.

Rhodes, W., Gaes, G., Luallen, J., King, R., Rich, T., & Shively, M. (2016). Following incarceration, most released offenders never return to prison. *Crime and Delinquency, 62,* 1003–1025.

Ross, J.I., Tewksbury, R., & Rolfe, S.M., (2016). Inmate responses to correctional officer deviance: A model of its dynamic nature. *Corrections: Policy, Practice and Research, 1,* 139–153.

Rothman, D. (1971). *The discovery of the asylum: Social order and disorder in the republic.* Boston, MA: Little, Brown.

Sabath, M.J. & Cowles, E.L. (1990). Using multiple perspectives to develop strategies for managing long-term inmates. *The Prison Journal, 70,* 58–72.

Sanchez, F.C. & Wolff, N. (2016). Self-report rates of physical and sexual violence among Spanish inmates by mental illness and gender. *Journal of Forensic Psychiatry and Psychology, 27,* 443–458.

Schenk, A.M. & Fremouw, W.J. (2012). Individual characteristics related to prison violence: A critical review of the literature. *Aggression and Violent Behavior, 17,* 430–442.

Scott, D.W. & Maxson, C.L. (2016). Gang organization and violence in youth correctional facilities. *Journal of Criminological Research, Policy and Practice, 2,* 81–94.

Steiner, B., Butler, H.D., & Ellison, J.M. (2014). Causes and correlates of prison inmate misconduct: A systematic review of the evidence. *Journal of Criminal Justice, 42,* 462–470.

Sterbenz, C. (2017). Why Norway's prison system is so successful. *Business Insider,* November 16.

Sykes, G.M. (1958). *The society of captives: A study of a maximum security prison.* Princeton, NJ: Princeton University Press.

Taylor, C.J. (2015). Recent victimization and recidivism: The potential moderating effects of family support. *Violence and Victims, 30,* 342–360.

Teasdale, B., Daigle, L.E., Hawk, S.R., & Daquin, J.C. (2016). Violent victimization in the prison context: An examination of the gendered contexts of prison. *International Journal of Offender Therapy and Comparative Criminology, 60,* 995–1015.

Tewksbury, R., Connor, D.P., & Denney, A.S. (2014). Disciplinary infractions behind bars: An exploration of importation and deprivation theories. *Criminal Justice Review, 39,* 201–218.

Thompson, A., Nored, L.S., & Dial, K.C. (2008). The Prison Rape Elimination Act (PREA): An evaluation of policy compliance with illustrative excerpts. *Criminal Justice Policy Review, 19,* 414–437.

Travis, J. (2005). *But they all come back: Facing the challenges of prisoner reentry.* Washington, DC: The Urban Institute Press.

Truman, J.L. & Morgan, R.E. (2016). *Criminal victimization, 2015.* Washington, DC: Bureau of Justice Statistics.

Turanovic, J.J. & Pratt, T.C. (2013). The consequences of maladaptive coping: Integrating general strain and self-control theories to specify a causal pathway between victimization and offending. *Journal of Quantitative Criminology, 29,* 321-345.

Turanovic, J.J. & Pratt, T.C. (2015). Longitudinal effects of violent victimization during adolescence on adverse outcomes in adulthood: A focus on prosocial attachments. *The Journal of Pediatrics, 166,* 1062-1069.

Useem, B. & Reisig, M.D. (1999). Collective action in prisons: Protests, disturbances, and riots. *Criminology, 37,* 735-760.

Wolff, N., Blitz, C.L., Shi, J., Siegel, J., & Bachman, R. (2007). Physical violence inside prisons: Rates of victimization. *Criminal Justice and Behavior, 34,* 588-599.

Wooldredge, J. & Steiner, B. (2009). Comparing methods for examining relationships between prison crowding and inmate violence. *Justice Quarterly, 26,* 795-826.

Wooldredge, J. & Steiner, B. (2012). Race group differences in prison victimization experiences. *Journal of Criminal Justice, 40,* 358-369.

Wooldredge, J. & Steiner, B. (2013). Violent victimization among state prison inmates. *Violence and Victims, 28,* 531-551.

Wooldredge, J. & Steiner, B. (2015). A macro-level perspective on prison inmate deviance. *Punishment and Society, 17,* 230-257.

Wooldredge, J., Griffin, T., & Pratt, T.C. (2001). Considering hierarchical models for research on inmate behavior: Predicting misconduct with multilevel data. *Justice Quarterly, 18,* 203-231.

Worrall, J.L. & Morris, R.G. (2012). Prison gang integration and inmate violence. *Journal of Criminal Justice, 40,* 425-432.

Xie, M. & McDowall, D. (2008). Escaping crime: The effects of direct and indirect victimization on moving. *Criminology, 46,* 809-840.

Zimbardo, P. (2007). *The Lucifer effect: Understanding how good people turn evil.* New York: Random House.

Zweig, J.M., Yahner, J., Visher, C.A., & Lattimore, P.K. (2015). Using general strain theory to explore the effects of prison victimization experiences on later offending and substance abuse. *The Prison Journal, 95,* 84-113.

11 Cybervictimization

Cybercrime and cybervictimization occur in all manner of different ways. It is generally defined as a crime where a computer and/or electronic network is used in the commission of a crime or is treated as the target of the offense (Steinmetz & Nobles, 2018). These include crimes like: fraud and other forms of financial crime (Roberts, Indermaur, & Spiranovic, 2013); the use of computers to facilitate gang activity or other forms of violence (Pyrooz, Decker, & Moule, 2015); the use of computers to harass, stalk, or otherwise engage in illegal sexual activity (Reyns, Henson, & Fisher, 2011); and even using computers and networks to aid in drug trafficking (Martin, 2014). It is important to note that these kinds of crime/victimization events run the full spectrum from the global and complex to the local and embarrassingly simple. Two concrete examples will help to illustrate this point.

First, in 2013 the American retailer Target experienced a mass hacking event during the November/December holiday season. In it, the personal (names, addresses, and phone numbers) and financial information (credit and ATM card numbers) of upward of 110 million people was compromised by malware that infected Target's payment system, along with the same systems of several other retailers (Abrams, 2017). The theft, which resulted in multiple class-action lawsuits and a full federal investigation, also resulted in the enhanced ability of the hackers to impersonate victims or to lure them into providing additional sensitive information that could be used for the commission of additional crimes (Yang & Jayakumar, 2014). The security firm IntelCrawler identified the malware as being written by a 17-year-old Russian computer whiz, along with another unidentified Ukranian accomplice, as the culprits (Gumuchian & Goldman, 2014). Clearly, this was a well-planned and well-executed cyber-attack that had a clear target and objective, and that took considerable expertise to pull off in a way that required no participation—active or otherwise—on the part of the 110 million victims.

As a second example, consider the following incident. Our colleague's mother—let us call her Jacquelyn (to protect her anonymity)—received an email from someone whom she thought was her good friend Denise. The email contained a message to Jacquelyn which let her know that there was a great opportunity to get a free pair of Ray-Ban sunglasses. The email also included a link to click on to take advantage of the deal; after all, who wouldn't want a sweet pair of Ray-Bans—and for free! So Jacquelyn quickly clicked on the link, and in the process another app on her phone which just happened to also be open at the time—her Facebook page—now immediately posted as her status the ad (and link) to the website to get the free sunglasses. As you may have guessed, the email from her friend Denise was not from her at all, and was instead a scam. Jacquelyn had been hacked. To make matters worse, one of her friends promptly posted on her Facebook page the comment: "Thank you for sharing this awesome deal! I'm going to look into it right away!" Now Jacquelyn's friends had also been hacked.

The above example of the mass-hacking event is the kind that tends to attract a lot of attention, but is also incredibly rare (Steinmetz & Nobles, 2018). The second example tends to attract very little attention but is also incredibly common. The result is that we have a distorted picture in our heads of what victimization looks like when cybertechnology is involved (Pratt & Turanovic, 2018). High-level computer-based theft makes for good storytelling, but much more common is the teen who uses her unwitting parents' credit card to buy video games on Amazon, or the Idaho resident who uses text messaging on his phone to organize getting legal marijuana from the neighboring state of Washington back to his Idaho home (assuming, of course, that society is the victim); or the high school boy who uses social media to bully a disabled classmate.

Therefore, the purpose of this chapter is to provide an accurate view of what that picture really looks like. To do so, we first discuss the nature and extent of cybervictimization in terms of the myths and realities that surround it. This chapter then goes on to review the cybervictimization research from the standpoint of both the victim (e.g., what factors place people at risk to be victimized) as well as the offender (e.g., how offenders target victims and complete their crimes). The key here will be to discuss how various forms of cybervictimization are either essentially "unique," or instead resemble other forms of personal victimization in terms of their causes and consequences.

Myths and realities of cybervictimization

The rise of new technologies—from cell phones to the internet to social media—tends to produce new forms of victimization (Felson & Boba, 2010). The case of cybervictimization is no different, and as these forms of victimization have become more common, two key myths have emerged that need to be dispelled right from the start.

The genius myth

There is no shortage of high-profile cases of cybervictimization where incredibly intelligent people have used technology to play a major part in the commission of a crime, from stealing millions of credit card numbers from major retailers' databases, to hacking an email server belonging to the Democratic National Committee during the 2016 U.S. Presidential election, to the theft of scores of classified documents from the National Security Agency by Edward Snowden. And because such crimes tend to blow up into a public spectacle, there is a temptation to view cybervictimization through the lens of the genius, mastermind criminal who preys on the helpless, law-abiding victims at their mercy.

Yet that really is not the case at all. Such celebrated crimes notwithstanding, the reality is that most cybercrime/victimization events entail mundane, low-level, easy-to-commit offenses that require little in the way of planning or expertise to pull off (Donner, Jennings, & Banfield, 2015). To be sure, much of what constitutes cybercrime and cybervictimization involves what we have referred to as "low hanging fruit" (Pratt & Turanovic, 2018). And most of the offenders who engage in cybercrime tend to target victims who, through either their own careless negligence, their own misbehavior, or even unwittingly through no fault of their own, have put themselves at risk of being victimized (Pratt et al., 2014).

Nevertheless, it is important to acknowledge that high-tech cybercrimes like major hacking and security breaches do happen. When they do, they tend to be done by highly disciplined, focused people who have considerable drive and motivation (Taylor, Fritsch, & Liederbach, 2014). But they are the minority. Most cybercrimes are incredibly mundane—such as the guy who finds someone's credit card in an apartment building's laundry unit and uses it to do some online shopping; the middle school girl who stumbles across a former friend's social media password and uses it to hack the account and to send harassing messages to a bunch of her classmates; and the high school delinquent who cruises social media to stalk a love interest who has no interest in him. None of these cybercrimes is terribly sophisticated, but they are far more common than the high-tech ones that actually require some form of expertise.

The myth of the tech-savvy teen and the clueless senior citizen

In addition to the "genius myth" surrounding cybercrime and cybervictimization, a second myth has also emerged: that of the tech-savvy teen and the clueless senior citizen. The working assumption is that young people are more technologically literate and are therefore better able to protect themselves from a wide array of forms of cybervictimization relative to older adults— particularly those in the later stages of the life course who may not even be aware of their victimization risk (James, Boyle, & Bennett, 2014). The truth, however, is just the opposite: young people (particularly teenagers) are much more likely to become cybervictims and older people are far less likely to suffer the same fate (see, e.g., Pratt, 2018).

Of course, the old person who has trouble with technology is easy to make fun of. *Saturday Night Live* recently got in on the joke with a sketch about how senior citizens cannot even navigate voice-activated internet browsers. The sketch featured a device that was "super-loud" and would answer to any name that sounded even close (or not so close) to the name "Alexa," Amazon's virtual assistant. So it has become commonplace to portray the bumbling senior as someone who cannot even do basic things like change their email password (they would need a savvy younger person to do that for them), which can leave them vulnerable to a wide range of cybercrimes like hacking, phishing, and identity theft (Grimes et al., 2010).

Along those lines, there is evidence that older citizens are disproportion- ately the victims of particular cybercrimes like financial fraud (Reisig & Holt- freter, 2013). This makes sense because, compared to teenagers, older people usually have more money and therefore make more desirable targets for those doing the scamming (Holtfreter et al., 2014). As a result, considerable resources are devoted each year to advertising campaigns and educational materials aimed at promoting cyber-based protective behaviors for older citizens to help them avoid being victimized. These efforts run the spectrum from implement- ing curricula designed to teach seniors how to protect themselves by changing electronic passwords regularly, avoiding providing credit card or banking infor- mation on websites not vetted for quality, and being mindful of who to interact with on social media (see Mears et al., 2016). The AARP's (American Association of Retired People) website even offers tips to the children of senior citizens so that they might help keep their parents protected from being victimized (e.g., "Here's how to talk to mom and dad about steering clear of fraudsters"). And it has now become an area ripe for profit, where companies like LifeLock, Radial, and Experian all market themselves heavily to older citizens with assurances that they can keep them safe from online scams and frauds. All of this, it is believed, will help older citizens avoid being hacked, having their identities sto- len or hijacked, or being stalked or harassed online.

The working assumption associated with these efforts is that older people— not young ones—are most vulnerable to being targeted for these kinds of offenses and are therefore the ones who are most at risk of being victimized (see, e.g., Stamatel & Mastrocinque, 2011). But such an assumption flies in the face of some well-established "criminological facts," the first of which we have already covered in Chapter 3: that criminal behavior tends to follow a clear "age-crime curve" and that rates of victimization over the life course tend to follow closely the very same age-graded curve.

So why would things be any different when it comes to cybervictimization? Well, as it turns out, for the most part they are not. Indeed, when it comes to cybervictimization, it is still being experienced disproportionately by the young. Younger people are more likely to be the victims of online harassment (Lindsay et al., 2016), to be stalked online by a current or former (or even spurned) romantic partner (Marcum, Higgins, & Ricketts, 2014), and to have their identities co-opted by a third party in an attempt to commit some other cyber-based crime (Marcum et al., 2015). This is not to say that these kinds of victimization events (and others like them) do not happen to older people—they certainly do (Holtfreter et al., 2015). It is, however, to say that patterns of cybervictimization tend to mirror the more general age-crime-victimization curve over the life course.

There is good reason for this. Older people, for example, do not spend a great deal of time on social media (Correa, Hinsley, & de Zuniga, 2010). And, when they do, the nature of their time spent is qualitatively different than it is for their younger counterparts. Older people are less likely, for instance, to post either aggressive or belittling comments online about their peers that might invite retaliation later on (Gardner et al., 2016); they are less likely to stalk someone via social media platforms and to harass them upon doing so (DreBring et al., 2014); and they are less likely to impersonate someone else online in order to bully a peer (Marcum et al., 2015). These are, of course, just a few examples, but they illustrate how, when it comes to the use of technology, the young and the old really do run in different circles, which contributes to the relative safety of older people when it comes to many forms of cybervictimization.

Yet, even so, cybervictimization is still alarmingly common overall. Research indicates, for example, that nearly 30 percent of adults have been targeted for fraud (Holtfreter, Reisig, & Pratt, 2008), over 40 percent of college students have been stalked online (with women being significantly more likely to be stalked than men; see Reyns, Henson, & Fisher, 2012), and upward of 56 percent of youth have been the victims of online bullying or harassment (Modecki et al., 2014). So our next step is to try to understand these victimization events from both the offender's and the victim's point of view.

The offender's point of view

It is worth being reminded at this point of some of the material covered in Chapter 5—victimization from the offender's point of view. You will recall in that chapter that a clear picture of the offender emerged: one where offenders were noted to be rather impulsive and are generally not all that prone to thinking very far into the future (Pratt, 2016); one where offenders are not all that good at making plans and managing tasks—whether it be their crimes or their lives in general (Pratt et al., 2016); and one where offenders tend to seek out easy targets as victims so that they do not have to work all that hard to accomplish their crimes (Gottfredson & Hirschi, 1990). So when a person makes the decision to victimize someone in an online context, it is the same general set of offender characteristics that still come into play.

Thus, when it comes to the research on cybercrime, much of it emerges from the self-control and social learning theoretical traditions (see, e.g., Runions, 2013; Vazsonyi et al., 2012). With respect to self-control, for example, the assumption is that criminal opportunities exist online all over the place. Such opportunities rarely require the potential offender to have things well planned or thought out, and even if thought out a little, they are not all that hard to take advantage of. It takes little particular expertise, for instance, to write a fake Craigslist ad claiming to be selling a motorcycle when you are just trying to get someone to give you their banking information; it requires little to no technical skill to be able to harass someone on social media; and it requires little specialized training to send a threatening email to a peer or co-worker. The key here is that, from the offender's standpoint, committing a cybercrime is not all that difficult, which fits relatively well within the self-control theoretical perspective. Not surprisingly, there is a large body of empirical evidence demonstrating that those who lack self-control are much more likely to commit a wide array of offenses in the online environment (Bae, 2017).

The same goes for research rooted in the social learning theoretical perspective. A key component of social learning theory is the role peers play in one's deviant and illegal behavior (Akers, 1998). But the reason why peers might matter has been the subject of much theoretical debate. Some argue that peers provide a certain measure of "normative influence," where they communicate attitudes and justifications for crime and deviance that can then be adopted (e.g., a peer who says "pirating software isn't really wrong"; or "don't worry about illegally downloading a movie, everyone does it"). Harboring such attitudes can make engaging in misbehavior a lot less psychologically stressful (McGloin & Thomas, 2016). An alternative explanation for the importance of peers is that they can help facilitate crime and deviance (e.g., the peer who teaches another how to pull an email scam). Viewed in this way, peers can open up opportunities for engaging in illegal activity that a person by themselves may not be able to take advantage of (Osgood et al., 1996). While some view these explanations as competitors, they share the property of making crime easier to commit—again, something that is typically attractive to offenders. And to that

end, there is a growing body of empirical literature demonstrating the importance of peer influences—regardless of which mechanism may be at work (e.g.,
normative influence or opportunity)—on cyberoffending (Bastiaensens et al.,
2016; Li et al., 2016).

The key in all of this is to recognize that cybercrime is not necessarily a
unique form of criminal behavior. It does not necessarily require a unique
explanation of unique causes. For the most part, the "generality of deviance"
still holds—people who are willing to commit one kind of crime are also usually
willing to commit others (Hirschi & Gottfredson, 1994); indeed, few offenders
specialize in any particular form of criminal activity (see, e.g., the discussion
by Sullivan et al., 2006). And when it comes to offending in the virtual world, it
is generally safe to say that if you misbehave on the streets, you probably also
misbehave online.

The victim's point of view

As is the case with much of the victimization research in general, most of the
research on cybervictimization is based on some version of a combined lifestyle/
routine activity theoretical model. Nevertheless, as we discussed in Chapter 3,
combining these perspectives in the context of cybervictimization may not be
a good idea. In particular, the routine activity perspective focuses on how the
mundane, daily activities of life (e.g., driving to work, shopping for groceries,
or going to a movie) can place people at risk of being victimized because they
expose potential victims to potential offenders in time and space (Cohen & Felson, 1979). The lifestyle perspective, on the other hand, is quite explicit that
some behaviors are a lot riskier than others when it comes to being victimized
(Hindelang, Gottfredson, & Garofalo, 1978). It is reasonable to assume, for example, that walking home at midnight drunk—by yourself—carries a greater risk of
victimization than buying clothes in a shopping mall.

The same general principle also holds when it comes to cybervictimization:
not all online behaviors are created equal. Some behaviors—like giving your
address to someone on a dating app or visiting "fringe" websites—place people
at far greater risk of being victimized than reading the New York Times online
or googling your own name (Zerach, 2016). This does not mean that you have to
engage in such risky behaviors to be victimized—it can certainly happen even to
people who are behaving themselves online (Felson & Boba, 2010). But it needs
to be recognized that the nature of online behavior matters when it comes
to the likelihood of cybervictimization (Pratt & Turanovic, 2016). And, just like
offending, the role of self-control needs to be considered here. In particular, it
tends to be those who lack self-control who are most likely to engage in risky

online behaviors and who are therefore more likely to be victimized themselves (Bossler & Holt, 2010; Reyns, Fisher, & Randa, 2018). So, once again consistent with the "generality of deviance" thesis, the bottom line appears to be that if you engage in risky behavior on the streets you also tend to engage in risky behavior online, where cybervictimization becomes more likely.

There is, however, a notable exception to this pattern. Specifically, one form of cybervictimization is arguably the most common, especially among young people, and that is being the victim of online bullying (Hinduja & Patchin, 2017). Bullying in general is defined as:

> Any unwanted aggressive behavior(s) by another youth or group of youths who are not siblings or current dating partners that involves an observed or perceived power imbalance and is repeated multiple times or is highly likely to be repeated.
>
> (Gladden et al., 2014: 7)

Whether it occurs online or offline, one consistent finding in the literature is that such forms of victimization often have less to do with engaging in traditionally "risky" behaviors (like engaging in various forms of delinquent behavior), but instead have more to do with other aspects of their lives that make them "vulnerable." Such vulnerability may be tied to things like having a physical or mental disability, being small in stature, or being a member of a sexual minority group (Kulig et al., 2017). Added to this risk is the consistent finding in the developmental psychology literature that adolescents will often pick on their peers and victimize them in various ways as a method of elevating their own social status (Turanovic & Young, 2016). Youths therefore face multiple challenges when it comes to victimization in general, and to cybervictimization as well.

Gaps and challenges

The large and rapidly growing body of criminological research on cybervictimization has taught us a great deal, not the least of which are the lessons that, for the most part, the causal structure underlying offending in the online environment is largely the same as that in the "real world"—namely that if you are an offender on the street you are also probably an offender when you open up a computer. The same may also be said of cybervictimization, where there are certain "risky" routines that people engage in which elevate their odds of being victimized online. Yet, despite this growth in knowledge, there are still two key substantive areas where we still know far less than we would like.

First, studies that employ theoretically relevant measures of risky online routines are still relatively rare. What is instead most common are studies that employ quite broad measures of time spent online or vague indicators that are assumed to be proxies of how that time is spent (e.g., whether someone has a Facebook or other social media account; whether they have shopped online). On the one hand, this is understandable, since these measures are often contained in large, publicly available datasets, but they tell us very little about how people actually behave online. What is instead needed are studies that examine the specific risky behaviors that may be linked to specific forms of cybervictimization. For example, are the behaviors that lead to cyberstalking victimization the same or different from those that lead to financial fraud? In addition, what are the online behaviors which "signal" to offenders that someone is potentially vulnerable to be victimized in some way? Research that addresses these questions would be particularly useful because it would help us develop a set of both general and domain-specific measures of risky behaviors online.

Second, we know very little about the kinds of changes people make to their behavior as a result of cybervictimization, or why some people make changes and others do not. When it comes to violent victimization, we have a much more well-developed knowledge base on these issues. This literature indicates that people who lack self-control are the least likely to make changes to potentially risky behaviors (e.g., committing crimes and hanging out with other offenders) after being violently victimized (Turanovic & Pratt, 2014), and that those who reside in community contexts characterized by "structural constraints" imposed by economic deprivation are also less likely to change their behavior after being the victim of violence (Turanovic, Pratt, & Piquero, 2018). There is also evidence that people who lack self-control are more likely to respond to being victimized in negative ways, such as engaging in substance abuse (Turanovic & Pratt, 2013). The problem, however, is that we know little about how these processes and constraints may—or may not—translate into the online environment. Hopefully researchers will take up that task in the future.

Key readings

Mears, D.P., Reisig, M.D., Scaggs, S., & Holtfreter K. (2016). Efforts to reduce consumer fraud victimization among the elderly. *Crime and Delinquency, 62,* 1235-1259.

Modecki, K.L., Minchin, J., Harbaugh, A.G., Guerra, N.G., & Runions, K.C. (2014). Bullying prevalence across contexts: A meta-analysis measuring cyber and traditional bullying. *Journal of Adolescent Health, 55,* 602-611.

Pratt, T.C., Turanovic, J.J., Fox, K.A., & Wright, K.A. (2014). Self-control and victimization: A meta-analysis. *Criminology, 52,* 87-116.

Reyns, B.W, Henson, B., & Fisher, B.S. (2012). Stalking in the twilight zone: Extent of cyberstalking victimization and offending among college students. *Deviant Behavior, 33,* 1-25.

Steinmetz, K.F. & Nobles, M.R. (2018). *Technocrime and criminological theory.* New York: Routledge, Taylor & Francis.

Discussion questions

1. What is the "genius myth" with respect to committing cybercrimes?
2. What does the "age-victimization curve" in general look like when it comes to cyber-victimization?
3. Does the link between self-control and victimization look any different when it comes to various forms of cybervictimization?
4. Why is it useful to make a distinction between "risky" and "routine" online activities when it comes to cybervictimization?

References

Abrams, R. (2017). Target to pay $18.5 million to 47 states in security breach settlement. *The New York Times,* May 23.

Akers, R.L. (1998). *Social learning and social structure: A general theory of crime and deviance.* New Brunswick, NJ: Transaction.

Bae, S.M. (2017). The influence of strain factors, social control factors, and self-control and computer use on adolescent cyber delinquency: Korean National Panel Study. *Children and Youth Services Review, 78,* 74-80.

Bastiaensens, S., Pabian, S., Vandebosch, H., Poels, K., Van Cleemput, K., DeSmet, A., & De Bourdeaudhuji, I. (2016). From normative influence to social pressure: How relevant others affect whether bystanders join in cyberbullying. *Social Development, 25,* 193-211.

Bossler, A.M. & Holt, T.J. (2010). The effect of self-control on victimization in the cyeberworld. *Journal of Criminal Justice, 38,* 227-236.

Cohen, L.E. & Felson, M. (1979). Social change and crime rate trends: A routine activity approach. *American Sociological Review, 44,* 588-608.

Correa, T., Hinsley, A.W., & de Zuniga, H.G. (2010. Who interacts on the web? The intersection of users' personality and social media use. *Computers and Human Behavior, 26,* 247-253.

Donner, C.M., Jennings, W.G., & Banfield, J. (2015). The general nature of online and offline offending among college students. *Social Science Computer Review, 33,* 663-679.

DreBring, H., Bailer, J., Anders, A., Wagner, H., & Gallas, C. (2014). Cyberstalking in a large sample of social network users: Prevalence, characteristics, and impact upon victims. *Cyberpsychology, Behavior, and Social Networking, 17,* 61-67.

Felson, M. & Boba, R. (2010). *Crime and everyday life* (4th edition). Thousand Oaks, CA: Sage.

Gardner, D., O'Driscoll, M., Cooper-Thomas H.D., Roche, M., Bentley, T., Catley, B., Teo, S.T.T., & Trenberth, L. (2016). Predictors of workplace bullying and cyber-bullying in New Zealand. *International Journal of Environmental Research and Public Health, 13,* e448.

Gladden, R.M., Vivolo-Kantor, A.M., Hamburger, M.E., & Lumpkin, C.D. (2014). *Bullying surveillance among youth: Uniform definitions for public health and recommended data elements, version 1.0.* Atlanta, GA: National Center for Injury Prevention and Control, Centers for Disease Control and Prevention and U.S. Department of Education.

Gottfredson, M.R. & Hirschi, T. (1990). *A general theory of crime.* Palo Alto, CA: Stanford University Press.

Grimes, G.A., Hough, M.G., Mazur, E., & Signorella, M.L. (2010). Older adults' knowledge of internet hazards. *Educational Gerontology, 36,* 173-192.

Gumuchian, M.L. & Goldman, D. (2014). Security firm traces Target malware to Russia. *CNN.com,* January 21.

Hindelang, M.J., Gottfredson, M.R., & Garofalo, J. (1978). *Victims of personal crime: An empirical foundation for a theory of personal victimization.* Cambridge, MA: Ballinger.

Hinduja, S. & Patchin, J.W. (2017). Cultivating youth resilience to prevent bullying and cyberbullying victimization. *Child Abuse and Neglect, 73,* 51-62.

Hirschi, T. & Gottfredson, M.R. (1994). *The generality of deviance.* New Brunswick, NJ: Transaction.

Holtfreter, K., Reisig, M.D., & Pratt, T.C. (2008). Low self-control, routine activities, and fraud victimization. *Criminology, 46,* 189-220.

Holtfreter, K., Reisig, M.D., Mears, D.P., & Wolfe, S.E. (2014). *Financial exploitation of the elderly in a consumer context.* Washington, DC: National Institute of Justice.

Holtfreter, K., Reisig, M.D., Pratt, T.C., & Holtfreter, R.E. (2015). Risky remote purchasing and identity theft victimization among older internet users. *Psychology, Crime and Law, 21,* 681-698.

James, B.D., Boyle, P.A., & Bennett, D.A. (2014). Correlates of susceptibility to scams in older adults without dementia. *Journal of Elder Abuse and Neglect, 26,* 107-122.

Kulig, T.C., Pratt, T.C., Cullen, F.T., Chouhy, C., & Unnever, J.D. (2017). Explaining bullying victimization: Assessing the generality of the low self-control/risky lifestyle model. *Victims and Offenders, 12,* 891-912.

Li, C.K.W., Holt, T.J., Bossler, A.M., & May, D.C. (2016). Examining the mediating effects of social learning on the low self-control-cyberbullying relationship in a youth sample. *Deviant Behavior, 37,* 126-138.

Lindsay, M., Booth, J.M., Messing, J.T., & Thaller, J. (2016). Experiences of online harassment among emerging adults: Emotional reactions and the mediating role of fear. *Journal of Interpersonal Violence, 31,* 3174-3195.

Marcum, C.D., Higgins, G.E., & Ricketts, M.L. (2014). Juveniles and cyber stalking in the United States: An analysis of theoretical predictors of patterns of online perpetration. *International Journal of Cyber Criminology, 8,* 47-56.

Marcum, C.D., Higgins, G.E., Ricketts, M.L., & Wolfe, S.E. (2015). Becoming someone new: Identity theft behaviors by high school students. *Journal of Financial Crime, 22,* 318-328.

Martin, J. (2014). Lost on the silk road: Online drug distribution and the "cryptomarket." *Criminology and Criminal Justice, 14,* 351-367.

McGloin, J.M. & Thomas, K.J. (2016). Considering the elements that inform perceived peer deviance. *Journal of Research in Crime and Delinquency, 53,* 597-627.

Mears, D.P., Reisig, M.D., Scaggs, S., & Holtfreter K. (2016). Efforts to reduce consumer fraud victimization among the elderly. *Crime and Delinquency, 62,* 1235-1259.

Modecki, K.L., Minchin, J., Harbaugh, A.G., Guerra, N.G., & Runions, K.C. (2014). Bullying prevalence across contexts: A meta-analysis measuring cyber and traditional bullying. *Journal of Adolescent Health, 55,* 602-611.

Osgood, D.W., Wilson, J.K., O'Malley, P.M., Bachman, J.G., & Johnston, L.D., (1996). Routine activities and individual deviant behavior. *American Sociological Review, 61,* 635-655.

Pratt, T.C. (2016). A self-control/life-course theory of criminal behavior. *European Journal of Criminology, 13,* 129-146.

Pratt, T.C. (2018). The myth of the tech-savvy teen and the clueless senior citizen: Revisiting technology-based victimization over the life course. *Criminal Justice Review, 43,* 360-369.

Pratt, T.C. & Turanovic, J.J. (2016). Lifestyle and routine activity theories revisited: The importance of "risk" to the study of victimization. *Victims and Offenders, 11,* 335-354.

Pratt, T.C. & Turanovic, J.J. (2018). Low hanging fruit: Rethinking technology, offending, and victimization. In K.F. Steinmetz & M.R. Nobles (Eds.), *Technocrime and criminological theory* (pp. 147-158). New York: Routledge, Taylor & Francis.

Pratt, T.C., Barnes, J.C., Cullen, F.T., & Turanovic, J.J. (2016). "I suck at everything": Crime, arrest, and the generality of failure. *Deviant Behavior, 37,* 837-851.

Pratt, T.C., Turanovic, J.J., Fox, K.A., & Wright, K.A. (2014). Self-control and victimization: A meta-analysis. *Criminology, 52,* 87-116.

Pyrooz, D.C., Decker, S.H., & Moule, R.K. (2015). Criminal and routine activities in online settings: Gangs, offenders, and the internet. *Justice Quarterly, 32,* 471–499.

Reisig, M.D. & Holtfreter, K. (2013). Shopping fraud victimization among the elderly. *Journal of Financial Crime, 20,* 324–337.

Reyns, B.W., Fisher, B.S., & Randa, R. (2018). Explaining cyberstalking victimization of college women using a multitheoretical approach: Self-control, opportunity, and control balance. *Crime and Delinquency, 64,* 1742–1764.

Reyns, B.W., Henson, B., & Fisher, B.S. (2011). Being pursued online: Applying cyberlifestyle-routine activities theory to cyberstalking victimization. *Criminal Justice and Behavior, 38,* 1149–1169.

Reyns, B.W, Henson, B., & Fisher, B.S. (2012). Stalking in the twilight zone: Extent of cyberstalking victimization and offending among college students. *Deviant Behavior, 33,* 1–25.

Roberts, L.D., Indermaur, D., & Spiranovic. (2013). Fear of cyber-identity theft and related fraudulent activity. *Psychiatry, Psychology and Law, 20,* 315–328.

Runions, K.C. (2013). Toward a conceptual model of motive and self-control in cyber-aggression: Rage, revenge, reward, and recreation. *Journal of Youth and Adolescence, 42,* 751–771.

Stamatel, J.P. & Mastrocinque, J.M. (2011). Using national incident-based reporting system (NIBRS) data to understand financial exploitation of the elderly: A research note. *Victims and Offenders, 6,* 117–136.

Steinmetz, K.F. & Nobles, M.R. (2018). *Technocrime and criminological theory.* New York: Routledge, Taylor & Francis.

Sullivan, C.J., McGloin, J.M., Pratt, T.C., & Piquero, A.R. (2006). Rethinking the "norm" of offender generality: Investigating specialization in the short-term. *Criminology, 44,* 199–233.

Taylor, R.W., Fritsch, E.J., & Liederbach, J. (2014). *Digital crime and digital terrorism.* Upper Saddle River, NJ: Prentice-Hall.

Turanovic, J.J. & Pratt, T.C. (2013). The consequences of maladaptive coping: Integrating general strain and self-control theories to specify a causal pathway between victimization and offending. *Journal of Quantitative Criminology, 29,* 321–345.

Turanovic, J.J. & Pratt, T.C. (2014). "Can't stop, won't stop": Self-control, risky lifestyles, and repeat victimization. *Journal of Quantitative Criminology, 30,* 29–56.

Turanovic, J.J., Pratt, T.C., & Piquero, A.R. (2018). Structural constraints, risky lifestyles, and repeat victimization. *Journal of Quantitative Criminology, 34,* 251–274.

Vazsonyi, A.T., Machackova, H., Sevcickova, A., Smahel, D., & Cerna A. (2012). Cyberbullying in context: Direct and indirect effects by low self-control across 25 European countries. *European Journal of Developmental Psychology, 9,* 210–227.

Yang, J. & Jayakumar, A. (2014). Target says up to 70 million more customers were hit by December data breach. *The Washington Post,* January 10.

Zerach, G. (2016). Pathological narcissism, cyberbullying victimization and offending among homosexual and heterosexual participants in online dating websites. *Computers in Human Behavior, 57,* 292–299.

12 Wrapping it up: emerging issues in victimization

On the morning of July 18, 2006, Charles Kinsey—a 47-year-old African-American man—left his home to head off to his job as a behavioral therapist at the Miami Achievement Center for the Developmentally Disabled. A father of five and a member of a positive community action group called the "Circle of Brotherhood," he had been working at the facility for a little over a year as a counselor for developmentally disabled adults. At around 5 p.m., it was brought to his attention that one of the clients in his care—a severely autistic 23-year-old named Arnaldo Rios, a young man who needed around-the-clock supervision—had wandered away from the home. But he didn't go very far; he had sat down in the middle of a nearby street with a little silver tanker truck toy he had taken with him.

So Kinsey went outside to persuade Rios to return to the facility, not knowing that someone had seen Rios and had called 911 on the whole situation. As Kinsey was sitting down talking to Mr. Rios, he was more than a little surprised to see several law enforcement officers show up on the scene with their weapons drawn both at himself and at the confused adult under his care. Already sitting down, Kinsey immediately put both of his hands up in the air and pleaded with the officers not to shoot, saying, "Sir, there is no need for firearms. I'm unarmed, he's an autistic guy. He got a toy truck in his hand" (Silva, 2017). As with many police shooting incidents in recent years, much of this encounter was caught on video by a nearby spectator with a phone.

Kinsey's pleas went unheeded by 30-year-old Officer Jonathan Aledda who, in his fourth year as a police officer, was a current member of the Special Weapons and Tactics (SWAT) unit. Aledda, who was about 120 feet away from Kinsey and Rios and holding a rifle (two other officers were closer, at around 20 feet), fired three shots at the two men seated on the ground. Two of the shots missed both men, but one of the shots hit Kinsey in the leg. After being hit, Kinsey—who thought the shot was a mosquito bite at first—said, "I still got my hands in the air!" Still lying down in the street, he then went on to ask Officer Aledda, "why did you shoot me?" Aledda's answer was "I don't know." When interviewed later, Kinsey said, "As long as I've got my hands up, they're not gonna shoot me, that's what I'm thinking . . . wow, I was wrong" (Berlinger, 2016).

This incident may be perceived in a number of different ways, depending upon which classroom one happens to be sitting in. In a course on policing, for example, it could be used as a discussion point to talk about how officers go about making decisions—particularly in light of incomplete or even inaccurate information—or even about the conditions under which police officers can and should exercise deadly force (or at least attempt to do so). In a class on race and the criminal justice system, on the other hand, the incident might be used to discuss issues of race and class inequalities, and how such inequities might get translated into how members of racial minority groups are treated by state agents. In yet another example, in a course about the intersection of criminal justice and mental health, the incident could illustrate to students the intimate relationships that tend to surround criminal behavior, mental illness, and the treatment of such illness. And there is no doubt that all of these discussions would be instructive.

We can, however, also view this incident through the lens of victimization, but in a way that we might not immediately see. In particular, it could be viewed that Mr. Kinsey was *victimized* by an agent of the state. To be sure, Officer Aledda was eventually charged with attempted manslaughter (as well as culpable negligence, a first-degree misdemeanor; see Chappell, 2017). Legally speaking, this incident was thus considered a crime and Kinsey is considered a victim of violence.

So, in wrapping up this book, that is the purpose of this chapter: to point out that there are a few forms of victimization which we often view from a different intellectual standpoint. Victimization is an exciting area of theory and research and is growing rapidly, so in this chapter we take stock of what we see as important emerging issues in victimization theory, research, and policy. These topics will include victimization by legal authorities (e.g., police violence), state-sponsored violence/terrorism (i.e., those that result in widespread deaths and displacement of citizens), and the role that public concern about victimization plays in discussions regarding immigration policy both in the U.S. and Europe. Each of these issues will most certainly fill volumes all on their own in the future. Yet it is possible that new insights into each might be reached—even now—if we were also to look at these issues through a victimization lens.

Victimization by legal authorities

In February 2018, seven correctional officers who worked at the Lackawanna County Prison in Scranton, Pennsylvania were charged with sexually abusing several female inmates—some for more than a decade (Haag, 2018). Court documents indicate that the officers used their position of power and authority over the women—as well as offering them cigarettes, commissary goods, and additional telephone time—to force or coerce them into sexual acts. During several of the assaults, the offending officers even worked out a system with each other as "lookouts," where if one officer was assaulting an inmate in her cell, another would "click" the cell lock to alert the guard that someone was approaching. Apparently, the assaults were widely known among the inmate population, and the prison administration did little to meaningfully address it, even going so far as to respond to an inmate's complaint by sending guards into her cell to destroy any potential evidence (Rubinkam, 2018).

Such abuses occur far more often in prison than we might care to admit, and along with the case of Charles Kinsey (and so many like it), they point to a different way of viewing the actions of people like correctional officers and the police; that is, *victimization* at the hands of legal authorities. With respect to violence at the hands of correctional staff, for example, research indicates that up to one in four inmates will experience a serious physical assault at the hands of prison staff (e.g., being hit, kicked, choked, and/or threatened with a weapon; see Wolff & Shi, 2009). This should come as no real surprise, since scholars have long noted that the use of physical force is a core part of the job of being a correctional officer (Liebling, 2011). Marquart's (1986) classic study of correctional officers' use of physical coercion as a mechanism for prisoner control, for example, is littered with all manner of methods at their disposal, from the "severe beating" (reserved for the more egregious forms of inmate misbehavior), to "tune ups" (minor slaps/punches to the head to attract an insolent inmate's attention), to a "tap dance" (standing on the head of a disobedient prisoner). Of course, whether the inmates deserved such treatment or otherwise "had it coming" is certainly debatable, but the broader point is that it is possible to look at such instances as examples of institutionalized citizens being victimized by agents of the state.

While the research with respect to violence and victimization on the part of correctional staff is still a little sparse, the research on the extent and nature of police violence is more extensive. On the one hand, the research findings vary somewhat with respect to how many police shootings occur in the U.S. each year depending on the data sources used (e.g., the FBI's Supplementary Homicide Reports versus the Centers for Disease Control's National Vital Statistics System; see Maskaly & Donner, 2015). But recent evidence suggests that estimates will generally converge on the figure of nearly 1,000 police shootings per year (at least with respect to the past few years). In addition, data from the newly formed U.S. Police-Shooting Database, however, indicates significant bias with respect to the killing of unarmed black Americans relative to unarmed white Americans. In particular, the odds of being unarmed and shot for black Americans is nearly four times that for whites, with the odds approaching 20 to 1 in certain U.S. counties (Ross, 2015).

On the other hand, it should be noted that, at least with respect to Western industrialized nations, violence at the hands of the police appears to be a uniquely American problem. Indeed, *The Economist* compiled some comparative data with respect to the U.S. versus a handful of other industrialized nations. While the data they collected were on an admittedly small sample of countries, the comparisons they presented were quite stark: where the U.S. experienced 458 deaths from police shootings in 2016, Germany only had 8, and both Japan and Great Britain had zero (Lopez, 2018a). Such severe nation-level differences naturally give rise to questions concerning what it is about the U.S. that results in such high levels of police shootings, but the opposite may also be just as useful: what is it about other nations that tends to insulate their citizens from this particular form of state-based victimization?

This question is important since, when it comes to victimization at the hands of agents of the state, there is also a risk that the state may begin to lose its "legitimacy" in the eyes of those being governed–particularly when there are racial disparities with respect to the use of force by police (Nix et al., 2017). This is not a small problem, as research over the past two decades has clearly shown that when people view law enforcement personnel (in whatever capacity they may be serving) as "legitimate"–that is, the perception that law enforcement officers are fair in their dealings with citizens and that they exercise their authority in a just and equitable manner– they are more likely to comply with the law (Hamm, Trinker, & Carr, 2017; McLean, Wolfe, & Pratt, 2018). The perception that the police make such decisions in a potentially arbitrary way–particularly when it comes to their interactions with minority citizens–can potentially threaten their ability to enforce the law and to gain compliance among citizens (Nix, 2017). This form of state-based victimization–a form that could be perpetrated by all manner of criminal justice practitioners (e.g., from probation officers to border patrol agents to correctional treatment providers)–therefore may have consequences that extend well beyond the victims themselves.

State-sponsored violence and terrorism

It is one thing when agents of the state victimize citizens in the course of doing their job poorly, whether they are or are not held accountable for such actions. While there are instances of correctional officers, police officers, prosecutors, and even judges being criminally prosecuted for illegal behavior, such instances are for the most part relatively rare (Stinson & Liederbach, 2013; Murphy, 2017).

Either way, it is quite another thing when violence and victimization are actively encouraged and sponsored by the state itself.

In but one recent example of the state being responsible for violence, on April 7, 2018, just outside of Douma, Syria (a city that lies just east of Damascus), a government helicopter flew in and dropped several exploding barrels full of an unknown chemical substance into a residential neighborhood. On the heels of a seven-year civil war in Syria, this action—ordered by Syrian President Bashar al-Assad and backed by the governments of both Russia and Iran—killed over 40 Syrian citizens and injured dozens more (Hubbard, 2018). This is not the first chemical attack that the Syrian government has waged against its own citizens—they were also gassed in 2013—and it points to another form of violence that is rarely examined through the lens of victimization: state-sponsored violence and terrorism.

This type of violence and victimization—one perpetrated by the state itself—is not new. Indeed, the caustic mix of religion and politics that produces what we think of as "terrorism" goes back at least to the *hashashin* of the Middle Ages (Ezeldin, 1989). But in terms of more contemporary examples, such victimization is typically viewed as a specific kind of political violence; one that comes with legal and military elements as well (LaFree & Dugan, 2007). In that vein, there is a wide variety of forms such violence can take, including political assassinations, guerrilla warfare, and terror-supported states (Combs, 2018). There is also an equally wide variety of purported causes of such violence, most of which focus on how religious and ethnic conflict can create vulnerable populations within a nation—populations that become the target of the state (Hoffman, 2006; Kegley, 2003).

What this means is that we cannot effectively understand this form of victimization very well if we rely on the same theoretical perspectives that dominate most victimization research (e.g., those discussed in detail in Chapters 3 to 5 that cover the individual, situational, and contextual sources of victimization). Such violence stands in stark contrast to the forms of personal victimization that lend themselves well to explanations couched in the routine activity or risky lifestyles theoretical frameworks. To be sure, when it comes to state-sponsored violence, it is not engaging in street crime or staying out too late drinking in public places or being interpersonally belligerent that puts someone at an elevated risk of becoming a victim of crime (see, e.g., Pratt & Turanovic, 2016). What instead puts people at risk of being victimized can merely be living in a particular place or identifying with a particular religious or ethnic group (Wright, 2006). It is therefore important that, as this work moves forward empirically, it does so with additional theoretical development as well.

Immigration and violence

Closely related to the problems associated with state-sponsored violence and terrorism is an issue that has taken on increasing importance in the United States and Western Europe: the potential relationship between immigration and violence. In particular, armed conflicts in the Middle East have resulted in the widespread migration of citizens into several Western European nations, including France, Germany, and the United Kingdom—places where significant anti-immigrant sentiment is taking hold (The Economist, 2018). In the United States, President Donald J. Trump was elected in 2016 in no small part due to his anti-immigration political stance—one that targeted primarily immigrants from Central and South America (although similar anti-immigrant sentiments would also later be directed toward those from Muslim nations by the Trump Administration; see Jackson, 2018). Embedded in nearly all of the anti-immigrant rhetoric is the notion that immigrants are responsible for a disproportionate share of crime and violence, which puts "native" citizens at a heightened risk of being victimized (Lopez, 2018b).

It turns out, however, that the rhetoric surrounding immigration and violence is just that: rhetoric. The reality is very different, and there is actually quite a large body of empirical research that has examined the link between immigration and crime. The bulk of this research comes out of the United States, and much of it is focused on Hispanic immigrants, but the findings generally translate to other immigrant groups as well. A consistent finding in this literature is that immigrants actually commit crimes at a lower rate than do American citizens who were born in the United States. To be sure, Ousey and Kubrin (2018) conducted a meta-analysis of 51 studies published between 1994 and 2014, and found that, on average, communities with a higher concentration of immigrants experienced significantly lower crime rates, and that these findings were "general" across a wide variety of crime types (e.g., violent, property, even homicide). Such findings are attributed to the notion that immigrant communities are characterized by stronger social ties among families and community members, and higher levels of collective efficacy and the ability to both support and control the behavior of community members (Kubrin, Hipp, & Kim, 2018).

However, these findings are clearly at odds with the research on public opinion about immigration and crime. Recent polling data, for example, show that in 2017, only 9 percent of U.S. respondents believed that immigration was making the "crime situation" better, with 45 percent thinking that it was making it worse (Gallup, 2018). This disconnect between perception and reality points to the political power associated with tapping into the fear of victimization. Recall the discussion from Chapter 8 about the social and political consequences of victimization, where fear of victimization—even if such fear is not rooted in one's actual risk of being victimized—can still be exploited by elected leaders for political gain, especially if citizens can be convinced that their fear should be linked to the perceived "lenience" of policies (Pratt, 2019). Yet the reality is that such high levels of citizens' fear over the potential link between immigration and victimization is not warranted empirically and, to the extent that citizens' fears are rooted in their own victimization experiences, they likely had little to do with immigration at all.

Gaps and challenges

Victimization is a fascinating topic—one that is complicated theoretically, legally, and empirically. There are rarely simple answers to complex problems, and the study of victimization is no different. That is why we have ended each of the chapters in this book with "gaps and challenges" so that readers will be aware, with respect to each of the topics we cover, about the important work that has yet to be done. And so in this chapter we do the same, although with an eye toward the larger issues facing victimization research. In particular, we are facing a time when there will be new theoretical developments, new studies, and new ways of thinking about the nature, sources, and consequences of victimization. As the field moves forward, gaining access to good data will always be a challenge—something we have got better at but still have a long way to go.

Yet even with good data, solid information will always have to fight it out with ideology. The unfortunate truth is that data are often no match for emotion—something that permeates each of the issues covered in this book. That emotion would play such an integral role in discussions about victimization should not be surprising given its intensely personal nature. But this does not mean that data do not matter—all of us need to make sure that valid and reliable information stays in the conversation about how to most effectively combat sources and address the consequences of victimization. In the process, the broader challenge facing us is to keep our own biases in check, and to be willing to entertain new ways of thinking if the old ones fail to hold up in the face of new and compelling evidence. Doing so is not easy—we tend to want to hold onto our cherished beliefs even in the face of strong evidence to the contrary. But when it comes to an issue as important as victimization, all of us should be constantly trying to do better—doing so will be necessary if we are to impact victims' lives and communities in a meaningful way.

Key readings

Combs, C.C. (2018). *Terrorism in the twenty-first century* (8th edition). New York: Routledge.

Marquart, J.W. (1986). Prison guards and the use of physical coercion as a mechanism of prisoner control. *Criminology, 24*, 347-366.

McLean, K., Wolfe, S.E., & Pratt, T.C. (2018). Legitimacy and the life course: An age-graded examination of changes in legitimacy attitudes over time. *Journal of Research in Crime and Delinquency, 56*, 42-83.

Ousey, G.C. & Kubrin, C.E. (2018). Immigration and crime: Assessing a contentious issue. *Annual Review of Criminology, 1*, 63-84.

Ross, C. (2015). A multi-level Bayesian analysis of racial bias in police shootings at the county-level in the United States, 2011-2014. *PLoS One, 10(11)*, e0141854.

Discussion questions

1. Why might it be useful to examine violence committed by agents of the state—such as by police officers or by correctional officers—through the lens of victimization?
2. How does state-sponsored violence challenge the "traditional" theories of victimization (e.g., routine activity and risky lifestyle perspectives) that dominate victimization research?
3. Is the risk of victimization higher in communities with a larger population of immigrants?

References

Berlinger, J. (2016). Miami shooting: Man shot by cops was lying down with hands up, lawyer says. *CNN.com*, July 21.

Chappell, B. (2017). North Miami officer is arrested over shooting of therapist during standoff. *NPR*, April 12.

Combs, C.C. (2018). *Terrorism in the twenty-first century* (8th edition). New York: Routledge.

Economist, The (2018). Confusion over immigration and crime is roiling European politics. *The Economist*, June 30.

Ezeldin, A.G. (1989). Terrorism in the 1990's: New strategies and the nuclear threat. *International Journal of Comparative and Applied Criminal Justice, 13*, 7-16.

Gallup. (2018). *Immigration*. News.gallup.com.

Haag, M. (2018). 7 prison guards in Pennsylvania charged with sexually abusing inmates. *New York Times*, February 16.

Hamm, J.A., Trinker, R., & Carr, J.D. (2017). Fair process, trust, and cooperation: Moving toward an integrated framework of police legitimacy. *Criminal Justice and Behavior, 44*, 1183-1212.

Hoffman, B. (2006). *Inside terrorism*. New York: Columbia University Press.

Hubbard, B. (2018). Dozens suffocate in Syria as government is accused of chemical attack. *New York Times*, April 8.

Jackson, D. (2018). Trump says he likes the immigration issue in this election. *USAToday.com*, June 23.

Kegley, C.W. (2003). *The new global terrorism: Characteristics, causes, controls*. Upper Saddle River, NJ: Prentice Hall.

Kubrin, C.E., Hipp, J.R., & Kim, Y.A. (2018). Different than the sum of its parts: Examining the impacts of immigrant groups on neighborhood crime rates. *Journal of Quantitative Criminology, 34*, 1-36.

LaFree, G. & Dugan, L. (2007). Introducing the global terrorism database. *Terrorism and Political Violence, 19*, 181-204.

Liebling, A. (2011). Distinctions and distinctiveness in the work of prison officers: Legitimacy and authority revisited. *European Journal of Criminology, 8*, 484-499.

Lopez, D. (2018a). Police shootings are also part of America's gun problem. *Vox*, April 9.

Lopez, G. (2018b). Trump: After Mollie Tibbetts's murder, "we need the wall." *Vox*, August 23.

Marquart, J.W. (1986). Prison guards and the use of physical coercion as a mechanism of prisoner control. *Criminology, 24*, 347-366.

Maskaly, J. & Donner, C.M. (2015). A theoretical integration of social learning theory with terror management theory: Towards an explanation of police shootings of unarmed suspects. *American Journal of Criminal Justice, 40*, 205-224.

McLean, K., Wolfe, S.E., & Pratt, T.C. (2018). Legitimacy and the life course: An age-graded examination of changes in legitimacy attitudes over time. *Journal of Research in Crime and Delinquency, 56*, 42-83.

Murphy, T.R. (2017). Federal habeas corpus and systemic official misconduct: Why form trumps constitutional rights. *Kansas Law Review, 66*, 1-38.

Nix, J. (2017). Do the police believe that legitimacy promotes cooperation from the public? *Crime and Delinquency, 63*, 951-975.

Nix, J., Pickett, J.T., Wolfe, S.E., & Campbell, B.A. (2017). Demeanor, race, and police perceptions of procedural justice: Evidence from two randomized experiments. *Justice Quarterly, 34*, 1154-1183.

Ousey, G.C. & Kubrin, C.E. (2018). Immigration and crime: Assessing a contentious issue. *Annual Review of Criminology, 1*, 63-84.

Pratt, T.C. (2019). *Addicted to incarceration: Corrections policy and the politics of misinformation in the United States* (2nd edition). Thousand Oaks, CA: Sage.

Pratt, T.C. & Turanovic, J.J. (2016). Lifestyle and routine activity theories revisited: The importance of "risk" to the study of victimization. *Victims and Offenders, 11*, 335-354.

Ross, C. (2015). A multi-level Bayesian analysis of racial bias in police shootings at the county-level in the United States, 2011-2014. *PLoS One, 10(11)*, e0141854.

Rubinkam, M. (2018). 7 prison guards accused of sexually abusing female inmates in PA. *USAToday.com*, February 15.

Silva, D. (2017). Florida cop charged with attempted manslaughter in shooting of autistic man's unarmed therapist. *Nbcnews.com*, April 12.

Stinson, P.M. & Liederbach, J. (2013). Fox in the henhouse: A study of police officers arrested for crimes associated with domestic and/or family violence. *Criminal Justice Policy Review, 24*, 601-625.

Wolff, N. & Shi, J. (2009). Contextualization of physical and sexual assault in male prisons: Incidents and their aftermath. *Journal of Correctional Health Care, 15*, 58-82.

Wright, L. (2006). *The looming tower: Al-Qaeda and the road to 9/11*. New York: Random House.

INDEX

Note: Information in figures and tables is indicated by page numbers in *italics* and **bold**, respectively.

Made in the USA
Coppell, TX
22 August 2022

81825227R00122